Culinary Herbs

Grow. Preserve. Cook!

Yvonne Tremblay

whitecap

Published in Canada by Whitecap Books, 314 West Cordova Street, Suite 209, Vancouver, BC V6B 1E8
Published in the United States by Whitecap Books. 311 Washington Street, Brighton, MA 02135

Whitecap Books acknowledges with thanks the financial support of the Government of Canada through the Canada Book Fund (CBF) and the Province of British Columbia through the Book Publishing Tax Credit.

Library and Archives Canada Cataloguing in Publication

Title: Culinary Herbs : Grow Preserve Cook / Yvonne Tremblay.
Names: Tremblay, Yvonne, author.
Description: Includes index. | Originally published: Toronto : Prentice Hall Canada, 2002.
Identifiers: Canadiana 20200215043 | ISBN 9781770503359 (softcover)
Subjects: LCSH: Cooking (Herbs) | LCSH: Herb gardening. | LCGFT: Cookbooks.
Classification: LCC TX819.H4 T74 2020 | DDC 641.6/57—dc23

Cover and interior design by Peggy & Co. Design
Recipe photos by Mike McColl
Food styling by Maria Bachmaier
Herb Directory photos by Bryn Gladding
Stock photos (recipes and herbs) from Shutterstock
Proofread by Holly Doll
Printed in Hong Kong by Sheck Wah Tong Printing

Dedication

This book is dedicated in memory of
Carol King Ferguson, mentor and friend

CONTENTS

ACKNOWLEDGMENTS

The late Carol Ferguson, who I have dedicated this book to, was the ultimate foodie before anyone was called such a thing. She was the Food Editor for *Canadian Living* magazine, and created many special occasion issues of their magazine. She co-authored the *Canadian Living Cookbook* and *A Century of Canadian Home Cooking* cookbooks. She was also Food Editor for *Homemakers* magazine and taught food writing at a local college. She was the consummate editor for all things food - proper recipe writing style and concise, descriptive copy to accompany recipes for a story.

We first met each other when I was developing recipes for one of the *Canadian Living* magazine contributors/cookbook authors. We were reacquainted years later when I was teaching herb cooking classes in her neighbourhood. She offered me the position of Associate Food Editor to work with her at *Homemakers*, and gave me the opportunity to write regular food and recipe articles, the first called Pesto Pizzazz. A few years later she asked me to contribute a number of my recipes to her cookbook *New Canadian Basics*. Her Scottish grandmother's delicious scone recipe is in my jam books and you will find it here also in the Preserves chapter. Carol was a top-notch food editor and I learned so much from her. She was warm and encouraging in many ways in my career and personal life. This is just a small way to say thank you.

Thank you to publisher Holly Doll, at Whitecap Books, for adding cooking with fresh herbs to their exquisite cookbook collection and for her helpful editing. Thank you to Peggy Issenman, of Peggy and Co. Design, for her beautiful design work of the inside content and for the cover. Thanks to photographer Mike McColl, food stylist Mia Bachmaier and assistant Lori Quinn for many of the colorful and appetizing looking recipe photos in this book.

Thank you to publisher Robert Rose Inc. for allowing me to use some of my jam and jelly recipes with herbs, from *250 Home Preserving Favorites*.

I am grateful for my long-time friends Sandra, Sonja, Ruth, Pat and Wendi (all great cooks) for their ideas and feedback on recipes. To them and to Luisa, Celia and Micki as well, thank you for your loving support. Additional thanks especially to Wendi Hiebert, a professional recipe developer and chocolate aficionado, who created Lavender Honey Dark Chocolate Truffles, and Lavender, Cherry and Pistachio White Chocolate Bark recipes, and for her fine-tuning edits. My gratitude to Patricia Moynihan, also a professional recipe developer and cooking instructor, for her recipes for Braised Lamb Shanks with Rosemary and Buttery Rosemary Buns and to my friend Sandra for her Tuscan Tomato and Bread Soup recipe. Thank you also to Dana McCauley, food writer and food trend tracker, for her Tangy Thai Coleslaw recipe, Carol Ferguson for Cream Tea Scones, and Tomatoes and Bocconcini with Basil and Balsamic, and to my late mom Beti Tremblay for her Vegetable Tempura.

INTRODUCTION

It is late summer as I am writing this. My herb garden looks incredible after a summer that was low in rain, sunny and warm – perfect conditions for abundant production of flavourful leaves.

Cooking with fresh herbs got its start in the places they grew naturally, primarily the temperate regions of the world. Nowadays, many types of herbs can be found in every grocery store year round and at local markets in the summer. You don't even have to grow your own and some herbs you may not have enough space for. Some you may *want* to grow herbs though, because they are not as readily available to buy (i.e. lavender, lemon verbena, chervil, marjoram) and it is so handy to have them out in your garden for quick access. In this book, I have covered everything you need to know to grow your own herb garden, with tips to get a good yield, when best to harvest, etc. It's really quite easy and herbs can be grown in pots as well as in the ground, even indoors, with enough light.

As a recipe developer, I have a keen sense of taste and suggest that you follow the recipes first as they are, then if you like more or less of an herb, adjust to your own taste. Don't just add all the herb you have because it is chopped. Use measures, chop herbs finely and level the top. Too much can overpower.

When you have an excess of some herbs, whether from growing, or what you purchase, use them up by drying, freezing, infusing into oil, vinegar, honey and syrups, or adding to butter, mustard, salt or sugar. Your dried herbs will be fresher and a nice green colour. Information on how to prepare them starts on page 18.

At one time herbs were an ingredient only used by chefs. You can easily learn how to use them to enhance your cooking. Fresh herbs have the ability to change the taste of foods with their unique flavours, and by their very colour, add life to dishes by sprinkling with fresh herbs before serving or as pretty and edible garnishes. Even herb flowers are edible!

Enjoy the recipes in this book and have fun growing herbs too. I always say, It's aroma therapy for the cook!

WHAT ARE HERBS?

Herbs are plants found primarily in the temperate climates of the northern hemisphere. Specifically, herbs are the leaves of soft green plants and low bushy shrubs, as well as leaves of the bay laurel tree. Botanically, true herbs also include plants that yield dried seeds (i.e., anise, cumin, coriander, dill, fennel, parsley, etc.).

Spices come mainly from tropical regions and are the barks, flower buds, fruit or root bulbs of trees. They are seldom used without first being dried.

In this book I will focus on the most common *culinary* herbs, leaving the medicinal uses of herb plants to other sources.

USING HERBS

FRESH VS. DRIED
It is the aromatic (volatile) oils that give fresh herbs their unique flavor. These are concentrated when the herb is dried. The rule of thumb for substituting fresh herbs for dried in recipes is 3 to 1. Use 1 tbsp chopped fresh herbs for every 1 tsp dried herbs.

Exceptions
*   Rosemary – Substitute fresh for dried in equal amounts, as it does not diminish in size when dried and has a strong flavor when fresh.
*   Tarragon – Use half the amount of fresh as dried, as its flavor is more intense when fresh than dried.

HOW TO MEASURE FRESH HERBS
Fresh herbs are usually chopped before measuring, except when used whole or in pesto. Finely chopped means cut into small pieces; minced means *very* small pieces; snipped means cut with kitchen scissors (e.g., chives are snipped into 1/2-inch lengths.) See also the "Terms" on page 3.

Always pack herbs loosely into measuring spoons and cups (unless instructed otherwise). They should be level, not packed. You can always add more to a dish after tasting. Some herbs can be overpowering if used with a heavy hand.

HERB MIXTURES
The following terms are commonly referred to in recipes.

Bouquet Garni
French term used to describe a small bunch of fresh herbs. It consists of one bay leaf, a sprig of thyme and several sprigs of parsley, complete with long stalks. The parsley is usually wrapped on the outside of the bunch to prevent the thyme leaves from being knocked off during cooking. The bunch is tied with a piece of kitchen string, with a long strand that is draped over the edge of the pot so it can be easily removed after flavor has been imparted to the food. It is used in stews, ragouts and meat casseroles.

Herbes de Provence

Originating in Provence, France, this is a blend of usually dried herbs (but can be made fresh) that includes thyme, marjoram, rosemary and bay leaves. It occasionally includes summer savory, sage or lavender, and sometimes basil. It has a multitude of uses: as a marinade for grilled chicken, sprinkled on pizza before cooking, in potato soup, with chèvre cheese, roast lamb or pork, with fish, in breads, in honey, etc. Purchase commercially in kitchen stores or try this recipe to make your own. Best if made from fresh dried herbs (see Drying Herbs, page 20).

1 tbsp	dried thyme leaves
1 tbsp	dried marjoram or oregano leaves
1 tbsp	dried rosemary leaves
1 tbsp	dried summer savory leaves
2	dried bay leaves, finely crushed
1 tsp	dried lavender flowers (optional)

1. In a small bowl combine thyme, marjoram, rosemary and savory leaves. Lightly crumble with your fingers. Stir in crushed bay leaves. Add lavender, if using.

2. Store in a covered glass jar in a cool, dark place. Keeps up to a year.

Fines Herbes

French term meaning "finely chopped herbs," it refers to "sweet herbs" consisting of chervil, chives, parsley and tarragon used together in equal amounts. It can also include basil or marjoram. Fines herbes are best with egg dishes, and with food that requires no cooking or light cooking. Delicious in sandwich fillings, cream cheese and green salads such as mesclun mix.

Persillade

Persil is the French word for parsley. Add to soups, stews and casseroles preferably at the end of cooking. Add to olive oil and brush over potatoes for roasting, or stir into crumbs for breading meats or fish.

See also Gremolata (page 137) with grated lemon rind added.

MAKES ABOUT 1/4 CUP

1/4 cup	finely chopped fresh parsley
1	large clove garlic, minced

1. Mix together parsley and garlic in a small bowl.

TERMS

Chiffonade

When leaves of herbs such as basil, mint or sage are stacked on top of each other, rolled lengthwise into a "cigar" then finely sliced into strips or ribbons. Chiffon ribbons are sprinkled over food.

Infuse

To steep herbs in a liquid – such as vinegar, oil, water, juice, cream, tea, etc. – to extract the flavor; the result is called an infusion.

Za'atar (fresh or dried)

This is a uniquely flavored herb and sesame seed mixture of Middle Eastern origin. It contains sumac which gives it a unique lemony taste. You will find sumac at bulk or specialty food stores. It can be used on fish or meats, in marinades, on vegetables (such as carrots, sweet potato, potatoes, cauliflower, beets, butternut squash) for roasting (rub with oil then mixture), a topping for hummus, in yogurt dips or to finish toasted pita bread that is dipped in olive oil.

3 tbsp	finely chopped fresh thyme or lemon thyme (or 2 tbsp dried)
2 tbsp	finely chopped fresh oregano or marjoram (or 2 tsp dried)
2 tbsp	toasted sesame seeds
1 tbsp	ground sumac (see below)
1/2 tsp	kosher or coarse salt

1. Combine ingredients in a small bowl. Stir to combine well. Cover and store fresh herb mixture in the refrigerator up to a week. Dried mixture keeps in a jar in a cool, dry place up to a month.

   NOTE: Sumac is ground from the dried, tart berries of the sumac bush.

TIPS FOR COOKING WITH HERBS

The distinctive flavor of any herb should not be allowed to become too prominent, but should remain tantalizingly in the background. The secret is to know when a little is enough. You can always add a little more if needed.

- Do not use herbs in every dish or course in a meal.

- Do not season more than one dish in the same meal with the same herb.

- Do not fry herbs along with meat or fish, as they end up as bitter, black specks. Herbs for flavoring fried foods should be served in an accompanying sauce or be finely chopped and sprinkled over the dish at the time of serving.

- In general, fresh herbs don't stand up to long cooking, so add right before the dish is done.

- Herbs for casseroles and stews should be added after the liquid has been added to the pre-browned meat.

- Herb salad dressings and cold sauces should be made well ahead of time so that flavors have time to blend thoroughly.

- Chop fresh herbs well to bring out all their flavor and aroma. When using dried herbs, crush them first by rolling them between your hands, or crush with a mortar and pestle. This will release their essential oils.

- Herbs that are "ground" or "powdered" will lose their character more quickly than whole leaves.

- Replace dried herbs as soon as they lose their scent and color, turning pale and grayish, as they will have lost most of their flavor too. If they do not have their own distinctive smell, they are useless in food and may as well be discarded. If you don't know how long you have had your herbs, throw them out and get new ones.

- Store dried herbs away from the light in a cool, dry place to prevent loss of color and flavor. The worst place to store herbs is above the stove. A spice rack or turntable inside a cupboard is a good choice.

- When buying dried herbs, do not buy the cheapest brands in tin containers or from bulk bins. The more expensive brands are often the best in the long run. Always store dried herbs in glass jars with airtight lids.

HERB DIRECTORY

BASIL
ALSO CALLED SWEET BASIL

GROWING: An annual; grow in full sun; vulnerable to frost

FLAVOR PROFILE: Spicy, sweet, anise (licorice) and clove-like; flavor changes when dried. Purple basil (opal, ruffled) has a more delicate flavor that is clove-like. Other varieties include cinnamon basil, lemon basil, Thai basil and globe basil (small leaves, great for drying).

USES: Salads, soups, dips and sauces, stews, rice dishes; as part of fines herbes mixture; frequent addition to Italian tomato dishes; excellent in red lentil soup, gazpacho, and ratatouille. Good in omelettes, egg salad, cottage cheese; main ingredient of pesto (see page 162); great with tomatoes, eggplant, zucchini. Purple basil makes a beautiful red vinegar. (See page 22 for herb vinegars)

NOTE: Leaves are very delicate; handle gently; wash and chop just before using.

BAY LEAVES
ALSO CALLED LAUREL LEAF

GROWING: A perennial evergreen tree; grow in full sun to partial shade

FLAVOR PROFILE: Slightly bitter, savory

USES: Soups and chowders; add to water for cooking vegetables (i.e., potatoes) or pasta; spaghetti sauce, casseroles, stews; meat, especially beef dishes, chicken and turkey; fish (when poaching shrimp or cooking shellfish); in marinades; part of bouquet garni; in milk to flavor rice pudding. Almost indispensable in cooking.

NOTE: Seldom used fresh, as dried bay leaves have a better, sweeter flavor than fresh; flavor intensifies the longer it cooks. Remove at end of cooking.

CHERVIL

GROWING: An annual; grow in partial shade; sow from seeds; goes to seed easily, especially if dry; plant every two weeks for steady supply

FLAVOR PROFILE: Mild anise-pepper, parsley; delicate fern-like leaves. Two main types: plain and curly

USES: Poultry and fish dishes (oysters); egg dishes; soups (vichyssoise); with tomatoes, in tartar sauce, as a garnish; part of fines herbes mixture (see page 3). Goes well with any new vegetables, such as new peas, potatoes, baby carrots, and asparagus.

NOTE: This herb is a staple of French cooking, so is often called French parsley. Add at end of cooking to preserve its delicate flavor.

CHIVES

GROWING: A perennial; grow in full sun to partial shade; flowers in June; remove flower stalks as soon as they appear to prevent loss of flavor

FLAVOR PROFILE: Onion chives – thin, hollow leaves, mild onion flavor; garlic chives – flat leaves like blades of grass, mild onion/garlic flavor

USES: Omelettes, quiche, cheese spreads and dips, tuna salad; sprinkled over broiled tomatoes, green salad, potato salad, potato soup, baked potatoes and other vegetables; to garnish soups. The purple flowers of onion chives are edible (soups, salads), have an oniony flavor and make a beautiful pink-purple vinegar. Separate flower balls into smaller florets to use for cooking and garnishes. Use whole for vinegar.

NOTE: Use kitchen scissors to snip chives, rather than cutting or chopping them.

CILANTRO

ALSO CALLED FRESH CORIANDER, CHINESE PARSLEY

GROWING: An annual; grow in full sun to partial shade; goes to seed easily; plant every two weeks for steady supply

FLAVOR PROFILE: Citrus and sage

USES: Chicken, fish, lamb and rice, pasta or vegetable dishes. Also good in salsa, taco fillings, black bean and corn salad, lentil or black bean soups; in butters for vegetables or fish. Distinctive flavor found in Caribbean, Indian, Thai, Chinese, Mexican and Latin American dishes. Seems to go well with most "hot" cuisines. Seeds (coriander) also used, can be collected and ground.

NOTE: Leaves do not retain flavor well when dried.

DILL
ALSO CALLED
FRESH DILL
OR DILLWEED

GROWING: An annual; grow in full sun, look for Fern Leaf dill; goes to seed easily

FLAVOR PROFILE: Parsley, anise and celery, subtle lemon. Feathery leaves are used.

USES: Lentil, bean or pea soups; in all egg dishes, with cheese and most fish; lamb, chicken. Add to dressing for sliced cucumbers or with beets. Delicious in potato, tuna, egg or pasta salads, with cabbage, seafood cocktail, salad dressings; dips, sauces for fish. Seeds, which have a stronger flavor, used in breads, salads, pickling.

NOTE: Name derives from Norse *dilla*, meaning "to lull," as it was used to induce sleep.

LAVENDER

GROWING: An evergreen shrub, perennial in some climates, especially if protected from winter elements; grow in full sun

FLAVOR PROFILE: Sweet, sharp, pungent; look for English lavender

USES: In desserts, sugars, syrups, preserves, vinegars, with fruit such as peaches, raspberries, strawberries, apples

NOTE: Use only organically grown (without herbicide and pesticides) flowers.

LEMON BALM
ALSO CALLED
SWEET MELISSA

GROWING: A perennial; grow in full sun to partial shade

FLAVOR PROFILE: Lemon with hint of mint

USES: Poultry dishes (or stuffing) and with pork chops; with shrimp, lobster and mussels; with vegetables; in green or fruit salads; to make vinegars. Dried leaves make a pleasant tea or addition to black tea. Add leaves to white wine.

MARJORAM
ALSO CALLED SWEET
MARJORAM

GROWING: A perennial, but treat like an annual where winter temperatures go below freezing; grow in full sun; distinctive knot-like flower buds

FLAVOR PROFILE: Perfumy, subtle lemon with hint of balsam, more delicate than oregano

USES: Pasta sauces; with veal and pork roasts; with ground beef (meatloaf, shepherd's pie); in scrambled eggs and omelettes; with bread cubes for stuffing; in chicken liver pâté; with green beans, mushrooms, carrots; in lentil, pea, bean, potato soups; when grilling or baking fish. Ideal for lamb; in stews, marinades, herb butters. Common in French, Italian and Portuguese cooking.

MINT

GROWING: A perennial; grow in full sun to partial shade; will overtake (plant in pots to contain)

FLAVOR PROFILE: Sweet-flavored, cool and refreshing; flavor varies from the heat of peppermint and coolness of spearmint to the fruitiness of apple mint, pineapple mint and orange mint; even chocolate mint

USES: New potatoes, green beans, tabbouleh salad or with tomatoes as a change from basil; mint sauce or jelly for lamb. Sprinkle chopped fresh mint on top of green pea soup. Put a sprig in the water when boiling green peas or potatoes. Adds a refreshing taste to fruit salads, iced tea and lemonade. Stir into cream cheese spreads; garnish for desserts.

OREGANO
ALSO CALLED WILD MARJORAM

GROWING: A perennial; grow in full sun; look for Greek oregano for best flavor

FLAVOR PROFILE: Earthy and intense with hints of clove and balsam

USES: In almost any tomato dish; pasta sauces, pizza, chili con carne, barbecue sauce. Excellent in egg and cheese dishes; meat or poultry stuffings; on pork, lamb, chicken and fish. Essential ingredient of chili powder. Common in Italian, Greek and Mexican dishes.

NOTE: This herb is best used dried.

PARSLEY

GROWING: A biennial; grow in full sun to partial shade

FLAVOR PROFILE: Mild, savory flavor, slightly peppery; curly or Italian (flat leaf) parsley most common types – Italian has a stronger flavor

USES: In pasta dishes, sauces, scrambled eggs, soups, mashed or boiled potatoes, vegetable dishes (carrots, cabbage, tomatoes, turnip, beets); with poultry or fish. When making soup or stew, add the whole frond and remove before serving. Blends well with other herbs. Part of bouquet garni and fines herbes. Great deep-fried or in tempura batter. Use for garnish, especially sprinkled chopped over stews, pasta dishes and casseroles that need a bit of color.

NOTE: Dried parsley is a poor substitute for fresh. A quick way to chop parsley leaves is in a glass measuring cup using kitchen scissors. For large quantities, chop in a food processor.

ROSEMARY

GROWING: A perennial in some areas; grow in full sun to partial shade

FLAVOR PROFILE: Piney, resinous with hint of lemon; works well with basil or thyme

USES: Beef, lamb, veal, pork, rabbit, goose, duck and poultry; for roasts, make slits with a knife and insert garlic slivers and rosemary leaves. Rosemary is particularly good with lamb. Use when cooking eggplant, squash and in sauce for lasagna; in vinegars, oils and marinades; with thyme for frying or roasting potatoes, focaccia, marinated olives. In baking cookies, breads, cornbread, biscuits, etc.

NOTE: When using individual fresh leaves (vs. sprigs), always chop finely, as leaves are tough. Dries well.

SAGE

GROWING: A perennial; grow in full sun

FLAVOR PROFILE: Earthy, musty mint, camphor-like with hint of lemon. English pineapple sage, purple sage and variegated sage are most popular varieties. Combines well with rosemary, thyme or marjoram.

USES: Stuffings for poultry, fish, game and other meats; in sauces, soups and chowders, meat pies; in marinades; in barbecue sauces with rosemary and thyme. Use sparingly. For roast pork: with a sharp knife, make slits in the skin 1/4 inch apart; brush with olive oil to which a handful of fresh crushed leaves has been added. Excellent deep-fried as an appetizer or garnish, in Saltimbocca (see page 110); in herbal oil to brush over meats, yeast breads. Good with onions, cabbage, carrots, corn, eggplant, squash, tomatoes and other vegetables.

NOTE: Used in commercial sausage (so-sage!).

SAVORY

GROWING: An annual (summer savory) or perennial (winter savory); grow in full sun

FLAVOR PROFILE: Summer savory – aromatic, peppery, more readily found and more subtle in flavor than winter savory; resembles thyme and marjoram. Winter savory – stronger with a more piney flavor.

USES: With any kind of beans or legumes; with Brussels sprouts, cabbage, corn. Add a sprig to the water when cooking green or wax beans, lima beans or green peas; flavor dressings for bean or potato salad; add a pinch to split-pea soup, lentils. Sprinkle chopped on grilled tomatoes, on sliced cucumbers. Include in stuffings for chicken, turkey or pork. Good with ground lamb; in meatloaf, chicken or beef soups. Mix chopped savory and grated lemon rind with breadcrumbs for a coating for veal or fish. Winter savory is especially good in pâtés and with game meats.

NOTE: Leaves dry very well and retain flavor, which is less lemony and more musty than fresh.

TARRAGON

GROWING: A perennial, but may not overwinter in cold areas; grow in full sun to partial shade; difficult to grow from seed, but available as small plants from nurseries in early spring

FLAVOR PROFILE: Sweet, anise-like (licorice); look for French tarragon for best flavor

USES: In soups, fish/shellfish and egg dishes; green salads, French salad dressing. Add tarragon vinegar to tartar sauces served with poached salmon, or to make mayonnaise. Mix with butter and lemon to serve with most grilled fish. Also good with chicken, port, beef, lamb, game; distinctive flavor in Béarnaise sauce. Good with green beans, asparagus, peas or carrots. Used widely in French cooking, part of fines herbes mixture.

THYME

GROWING: A perennial; grow in full sun to partial shade

FLAVOR PROFILE: Slightly pungent, spicy, savory, clove-like. Lemon thyme – a bit milder, with a lemony flavor. Blends well with other herbs, especially rosemary.

USES: All meats, vegetables, casseroles, soups, stuffings, meatloaf, marinades and pâtés. Excellent for herb bread and flavored butters. Good with mushrooms, fried potatoes, carrots (and other vegetables) and in omelettes. Commonly used in clam chowder and gumbo; used in French, Creole and Cajun cooking. Lemon thyme is excellent with fish and chicken.

NOTE: Has a strong flavor, so only a little is needed. Dries well.

LEMONY HERBS

This group of herbs all have a hint of lemon, some in addition to their traditional herb flavor. Lemon herbs go well with any food that is enjoyed with a bit of lemon such as vegetables, fish and seafood, chicken, and in drinks and desserts. Here I will focus on herbs where the leafy green part of the plant is used. Lemon Grass is not included as it is mainly the white bulb that is used. Lemon flavored herbs can be added to blended herb vinegars and herb oils, and in herb butters.

LEMON BALM

This perennial herb of the mint family tends to spread even more than mint does. However, while mints spread via their roots, lemon balm spreads from its rhizomes and its seeds. To prevent it from getting all over, remove flower heads. Leaves are mint-like, rounded with serrations. Add with a light hand to fish, root vegetables such as beets and carrots, in fruit or vegetable salads and iced tea or lemonade (place leaves in glass along with the ice cubes), add to custards and fruit salads, lemon balm and tarragon vinegar. Younger leaves are best for culinary uses as older leaves can taste a bit soapy. Doesn't mind a bit of shade.

LEMON BASIL

The flavor here is subtle, with more citrus than lemon and has a milder basil flavor. Use with fish and seafood, try it in pesto and salads. Excellent in drinks such as a Bloody Mary or Caesar (Virgin or spiked!), Mojitos, Gimlets, Margaritas, etc. Or fruity iced teas such as blackberry. Stir some, chopped, into fresh sliced strawberries. Likes sun. Water midday.

LEMON-SCENTED GERANIUM

The leaves of geranium are somewhat thick, so its usage is either as an infusion where it is then discarded, or to line a cake pan, which then allows for transfer to your baked good i.e. cake or loaf. Comes in several varieties.

LEMON MINT

Spreads easily like most mints do. Best planted in a pot. Its flavor which is similar to earthy thyme/oregano is more suited to savory dishes than desserts or drinks. Add to salads or brew as a tea/tisane. Use for mint sauce or jelly, in stuffing and soups. Doesn't mind a bit of shade.

LEMON THYME

The most popular variety is golden lemon thyme with its variegated little leaves. It has a lovely flavor and makes a beautiful garnish. Substitute for regular thyme in recipes. Chop just before adding to dishes for best taste. Does not keep flavor well when dried. Great in soups and stews, good with fish and vegetables. Likes sun.

LEMON VERBENA

Perhaps the queen of lemon herbs with its very apparent lemon taste. It is certainly one of my favourites. It grows in to a pretty shrub, two to three feet high as well as wide, with long pointed leaves. Pick up a bedding plant in the spring to add to your garden. As you take leaves, the branches will split and grow more branches. It is a tender perennial. In cold climates plant may not survive winter. Plant in a large pot, prune back and take indoors but give it lots of sun or use grow lights. Harvest and dry older leaves for teas/tisanes. Steep fresh leaves or add a few leaves to your favorite pot of tea. Also combines well with equal parts mint leaves. Chop young leaves and add to fruit salads and marinades for poultry, pork and fish, or add to vegetables or soups. For desserts such as cakes, infused into a simple syrup, or infused in cream for custards, panna cotta, ice cream or whipped cream (to top fruit desserts). Layer leaves with sugar and leave for a few weeks; use to sweeten tea, fruit or in baking. Likes sun.

MARVELOUS MINTS

The mint family has many members with widely differing flavors but most are refreshing. Mints have a cooling effect and are excellent with meats and in savory grain and vegetable or fruit salads. Some classics are mint jelly and mint sauce (see index for recipe pages). They even flavor chocolate (see mint fondue and chocolate mint sauce). Perfect in cool drinks as a garnish and a main component of the popular Mojito, Mint Julep and Mint Mimosa. Here are several interesting ones, part of a much longer list. Many newer mints were developed by phenomenal late American mint breeder Jim Westerfield, including his patented one named after then First Lady, Hillary Clinton.

APPLE MINT
Grey-green rounded leaves with an apple-menthol fragrance.

CHOCOLATE MINT
When I first saw this mint at an herb fair many years ago, I wondered how they got the chocolate flavor into it! Tastes a bit like a peppermint patty.

GINGER MINT
Gold-flecked leaves and a fruity flavor with a hint of ginger.

LEMON MINT
Look for one called Hillary's Sweet Lemon Mint (named after Hillary Clinton) which is a cross developed between apple and lime mints and has a mild mint flavor with a touch of lemon.

LIME MINT
Look for one called Margarita Mint which has a bold lime-scent. Its grooved green leaves at times has a hint of bronze.

MOJITO MINT
The scent and flavor is mild and warm, not overly pungent, perfect for Mojitos. (See page 257).

ORANGE MINT
Truly one of my favorite mints, it has a milder mint flavor. The leaves are rounded and variegated. Infuse in milk or cream for delicious desserts, or add to fruit mixtures.

PEPPERMINT
Peppery and sharp it is a widely used mint in confections.

SPEARMINT
This mint is the most common one you will find in grocery stores and markets.

WINTERGREEN MINT
Hundreds of mints were crossed to come up with this mint, with its remarkable aroma and flavor similar to a wintergreen candy.

GROWING YOUR OWN HERBS

Growing your own herb garden can be a rewarding experience. You will always have your favorite herbs on hand and you can cut as much as you need. They will always be fresher than store-bought, too. This is especially beneficial when you are drying them or preserving them in oils, vinegars, butters, etc. You get to pick the best leaves, at their freshest. You have access to the flowers, too, which are not usually included in store-bought herbs (which are picked just before flowering). Some herbs are not readily available in grocery stores such as purple basil, chervil, garlic chives, lemon thyme and lemon verbena, chocolate mint, etc.

Herbs can be grown outdoors in the summer, or indoors in the winter on a windowsill or under fluorescent lights. You can bring some of your outdoor plants indoors for the winter, but be sure to allow a transition period; dig up the plant and place it in a pot with plenty of its own soil and good drainage. Then leave it outside for two weeks until it has adjusted to the potting. For indoor growing, keep soil damp and maintain drainage. Use top-quality potting soil that drains well and is pH balanced. Provide sunlight and fresh air, but avoid drafty areas.

Plant herbs in a small herb bed, tucked in among your flowers or in boxes or pots on a balcony. Most herbs – basil, tarragon, marjoram, rosemary, savory and thyme – thrive in hot sun. Chervil and most mints require shade in summer; parsley and sage do better in partial shade, though they survive strong sun. Anise, coriander, cumin, caraway and dill require sun for ripening the seed.

GROWING HERBS IN POTS

For growing in pots, terra cotta is best for drainage and air. The size of the pot will determine the size of the herb plant you end up with. Larger pots will result in larger plants with more leaves for harvesting. If the plant is too small, you will have to wait a while for the leaves to grow back before cutting again. A 10-inch diameter pot is a good size.

Plant one variety per pot. Mixed pots of herbs are not recommended, unless they all thrive on the same amount of sun and moisture. Otherwise, half of them are likely not to be happy. Some herbs grow faster and larger than others and may take over the pot. If you have a large window box or container that gives them each plenty of room, they may do well.

SOIL

The soil should be free-draining, sandy loam. Avoid soil that is nitrogen rich, as the herb's flavor will not be as strong. Obtain soil from a nursery or mix up your own using equal amounts of soil, river sand (not salty sand) and leaf mold. *Herbs do not like wet feet!* If there is no drainage hole in your container, provide a thickly pebbled drainage bed and regulate watering carefully. Do not use weed killers or pesticides around your herbs.

OUTDOOR GROWING TIPS

- Full sun produces the best herbs.
- Fertilizer produces large plants with lush foliage and strong roots. Use time-released synthetic fertilizer or organic fish fertilizer every two to three weeks. Fertilize bedding plants after planting in the ground to help them get established.
- Watering: *Wet Herbs* (basil, chives, dill, lemon balm, mint and parsley) like lots of water. Plant separately from others. *Dry Herbs* (marjoram, oregano, rosemary, sage, thyme) like to dry between waterings. (If they are wilting, then they are too dry!) Feel about 1 inch into the soil; if dry at that level, they need watering.
- Regular pruning is the best way to get lush, bushy plants and the new growth often has the best flavor. Trim just above the leaf node (where the leaf emerges from the stem) by pinching the stem with your fingers. Or prune with garden shears about one-third of the way down the stem. Remove any yellowed or damaged leaves.
- Once the plant flowers, the leaves will have less flavor. Regular trims will delay blossom formation. Pinch off developing flower buds (heads) to postpone maturation. I like to let some go to flower at the end of the season. Flower blossoms are edible and taste like the herb they come from, only milder; use in salads or butters, and to decorate herb vinegars.

- Herbs of the *umbellifer* family (coriander, dill, etc.) have a tendency to go to seed more quickly than other herbs. You may wish to let them go to seed to use in cooking (see Herb Seeds, page 40). You can do successive plantings to ensure a steady supply through the summer.
- Mulching around your plants helps to retain moisture, to keep the soil from getting too hot and to keep soil from splashing up on the lower leaves during rains and watering. Mulching also helps keep insects and disease from moving from the soil up into the plant. Use organic material such as wood chips, fine grass cuttings, straw (if you have a large garden), etc.

GROWING HERBS INDOORS

You can grow herbs indoors when it is too cold to grow them outside. Yields are usually smaller than from herbs grown outdoors, but you can still get decent results if you provide adequate light and moisture. Perennials, such as chives, oregano, mint and tarragon, seem to weather well and return in the spring with no problem. Other perennials, such as rosemary, thyme and parsley, may not. Herbs that are near a building or in a sheltered area have a better chance of survival where winters are harsh. Herbs such as lemon verbena must be dug up and stored indoors where temperatures go below freezing (they will lose their leaves), but may be returned to the garden the following season.

Herbs that do well indoors include basil, bay leaves, chives, dill, marjoram, mint, oregano, parsley, rosemary and sage.

LIGHT

Choose a south- or west-facing window where plants will get at least five hours of direct sunlight per day. It can be difficult for plants to get sufficient light when days are short or overcast. If herbs start to look lanky, supplement light with two or more fluorescent grow lights above, perhaps attached under upper cupboards, or use an incandescent reflector grow lamp. Look for grow lights in your local nursery or plant store.

TEMPERATURE

Keep the temperature at 72°F to 78°F (22°C to 26°C) during the day; 65°F to 68°F (18°C to 20°C) during the night. Guard against cold drafts from windows. Pull curtains between windows and plants.

MOISTURE

Mist plants regularly; keep a minimum of 30 percent relative humidity (measure with hydrometer near plants). In winter use a room humidifier; kitchen steam from cooking and dishes is sometimes enough.

WATERING

Herbs indoors need more frequent water than outdoor herbs. Don't let pots dry out completely – water when top 1 inch of soil is dry to the touch. Herbs in clay pots need to be watered more often. Make sure the soil is wet to the bottom of the pot but not water-logged; don't let herbs sit in water.

SOIL

Combine equal parts sterilized potting soil, peat moss and perlite or sand with 1 tbsp composted, sterilized manure per 5-inch pot.

Or combine equal parts garden loam, builder's or silica sand and peat moss or leaf mold with 1 tbsp sterilized manure per 5-inch pot.

INSECTS

Misting regularly and rinsing weekly under the tap helps control bugs. Also good are Safer's Insecticidal Soap and Trounce (contains soap and pyrethrum – made from a plant of the daisy family); both are safe. Spray plants right after bringing indoors and keep away from other plants for the first few weeks.

TIPS FOR RE-POTTING HERBS TO BRING INDOORS

- Minimize disturbance of the roots.
- Unglazed clay pots are best because they allow air to get to the roots.
- Re-pot herbs in late summer and let them remain outside for a few weeks to get used to the new pot.
- Bring herbs in for increasing lengths of time each day so they can get accustomed to lower levels of light.
- Cut leaves back so the amount of leaves is the same as the amount of roots (this will depend on the size of the pot).
- Water well, allowing good drainage; discard excess drained water.

HOW AND WHEN TO HARVEST HERBS

It is the aromatic (volatile) oils that give herbs their flavor, so we try to maximize and preserve the oils in harvesting. The best time to cut herbs is around mid-morning on a warm, dry day. The leaves must be clear of dew but the sun must be not so far advanced that the sun's heat has liberated the aromatic oils.

When cutting early in the season, do not take more than one-third of the plant. By mid-summer you can take about two-thirds without adversely affecting the growth. Use kitchen scissors and cut one-third of the way down the stem. This way of removing leaves encourages new growth.

Look at the plants carefully to see where the new growth is coming from. Leave small leaves to mature, taking larger leaves from further up the stem (towards the tip) and all around the plant. Harvest chives and parsley from the outside as their new growth comes from the center.

Avoid taking too much from perennials (see Herb Directory, page 6) in their first season; allow them to get used to their surroundings and establish good roots.

Flavor is most potent if leaves are harvested just before flowering starts. Pluck flower buds/heads to prevent plants from going to seed.

HOW TO STORE AND HANDLE HERBS

Herb leaves retain more flavor if left on stems until needed. (Do rinse off any dirt.) Store loosely in a plastic bag with stems wrapped in a damp paper towel; leave a little air in the bag. This will provide a moist environment for the herbs and prevent them from being crushed. Refrigerate.

Hearty herbs – ones with woody stems, such as rosemary and thyme – will store longer than soft leaf herbs – basil, cilantro, dill, etc. Some will keep up to two weeks. But try to use them as quickly as possible for maximum flavor.

When ready to use, rinse herbs well under running water or by swishing them in a bowl of water (or the bowl of a salad spinner). Some herbs such as cilantro and dill (particularly store-bought ones) can have quite a bit of sand on them. Take great care to ensure that all grit is removed or it will ruin any dish you add the herbs to. I rinse several times, until all traces of sand are gone (feel the bottom of the bowl; rinse the bowl in between).

I find the best way to dry herbs is with a salad spinner. It not only saves a lot of paper towel, it prevents over-handling and crushing of delicate leaves. The leaves will have a little water clinging to them; that is okay.

Once the herbs are fairly dry, place them in a length of good quality paper towel about three sections long. Fold the paper towel over to completely enclose the herbs; do this fairly loosely but snugly enough so they do not fall out. (There should be just a bit of dampness to the paper towel.) Place wrapped herbs inside a plastic bag and seal, leaving a bit of air inside the bag. Most herbs will keep like this, refrigerated, for a considerable time. Re-wrap herbs after opening. Check occasionally and remove any yellowed or wilted leaves and mist (or spray) the paper towel lightly to moisten if it becomes dry.

FREEZING AND DRYING HERBS FOR LATER USE

You can preserve the exquisite flavors from your summer herb garden, or deal with that excessive bunch of herbs from the grocery store quite easily. Some herbs lend themselves better to freezing, others are better dried; some are good both ways. The method you choose may depend on the intended use. My approach is that if herbs dry well (meaning that they retain a good flavor when dried), I dry them; if they don't, I freeze them. Flavor may be lost or changed with either method.

FREEZING HERBS

Herbs that freeze well: basil, chives, cilantro, dill, mint, oregano, parsley, rosemary, sage, savory, tarragon, thyme.

When thawed they will be wilted but will retain most of their fresh flavor. Use good quality plastic freezer bags and plastic freezer storage containers to prevent flavor loss, freezer burn and transfer of odors from other foods. Frozen herbs will keep for four to six months.

Parsley

Remove clusters of parsley from their stems. Place in plastic freezer bag or plastic freezer container; freeze. To use, simply remove, chop and add to your dishes. (The result will not be good for garnishes.)

For large quantities, chop very dry parsley leaves in food processor and store in plastic freezer containers.

Chives

Snip chives at their base using scissors. Lay chives flat, in a single row on a large piece of plastic wrap. Roll up, leaving 2 inches to seal at end. Place in freezer bag for extra protection; freeze. (Cut chives to fit in freezer bags without bending.) To use, simply unroll and remove desired number of chives. These whole chives are perfect for tying appetizer bundles or wrapping around bunches of green beans or carrot sticks. Their limpness when thawed makes them like string.

Or snip chives using kitchen scissors into 1/2-inch lengths; place in plastic freezer container.

Basil

Remove leaves from stems, discarding any that are damaged. Pack leaves into plastic freezer bag or plastic freezer storage container; freeze. Also see Herb Pastes, page 20.

Dill, Cilantro, Oregano, Rosemary, Tarragon

Remove smaller clusters of leaves from their stalks. Finely chop, then place 2 to 3 tsp in each section of an ice cube tray. Pour water over herbs to cover. Freeze, then transfer cubes to a freezer bag; label bag. To use, blocks may be dropped straight into soups and casseroles. To thaw, place on a piece of paper towel in the microwave oven for a few seconds, or leave at room temperature to thaw, then add to sauces or use as you would the fresh herb.

HERB PASTES

Another method for freezing is to purée the prepared leaves in a food processor with enough oil or olive oil to make a smooth paste. Use 2 cups herbs to 1/2 cup oil plus 1/2 tsp salt. Transfer to small containers, cover with thin layer of oil. Freeze.

See also Basil Pesto, page 162.

DRYING HERBS

Herbs that dry well include basil, dill, lemon verbena, marjoram, mint, oregano, rosemary, sage, savory, tarragon, thyme.

Drying concentrates the flavor of most herbs. As an herb is dried it loses volume, which is why you use only about one-third the amount of a dried herb in a recipe calling for fresh. The flavor of some herbs such as oregano actually improves with drying. Sage is also commonly used dried, although I have included recipes where it is used fresh. Some herbs lose their distinctive flavor when dried. I avoid using dried chives, cilantro and parsley, as their flavor is poor quality and does not resemble the fresh herb.

Paper Bag Drying

Gather the opening of a paper bag (approximately 10 × 6 inches) around several stems held in one hand; fasten tightly around stems with elastic band or string. Poke a few holes in the bag for ventilation. Write the name of the herb and the date on the bag. Place the bag in a dry area or cupboard. (Do not store in the kitchen, which will have steam from cooking.) The amount of time herbs take to dry depends on the air dryness and quantity of herbs. (Do not overstuff bags, as air needs to circulate.)

In a week or two, the leaves should be completely dry. Test by crumbling some leaves; they should be crispy. Remove leaves from stems, leaving them whole. (Keep stems to throw on briquettes when barbecuing.)

See How to Store Dried Herbs, see page 21.

Microwave Drying

This is a very quick method that produces excellent results. Leaves may be slightly damp from washing. Arrange leaves in a single layer between double thicknesses of good quality, plain paper towels. If drying a lot of herbs, use three pieces of paper towel on the bottom.

Microwave on high for one to two minutes. Remove from microwave, uncover and check to determine crispness. Move some herbs from center to the edges and edges to the center. The process will vary with the wattage of your microwave and if you have a turntable. If you do not have a turntable, turn paper towel 90 degrees when placing back into microwave.

Holding at the sides, flip the paper towel over. The damp paper towel from the bottom will now be on the top. Microwave on high for another minute or until leaves are dry and very crisp. Remove all crisp leaves; microwave any semi-crisp leaves until crisp. Try 15- to 30-second intervals. Do not microwave any longer than necessary, as flavor and color will be lost. Let rest until cooled.

Remove leaves from stems. (Keep stems to throw on briquettes when barbecuing.)

See below for How to Store.

HOW TO STORE DRIED HERBS

1   Place completely dry herbs in a glass jar. Use airtight containers. Cover and label with the name of the herb and the date. Use jars sized so there is not a lot of excess air space.

2   Store in a cool, dry place, away from heat and light, such as inside a cupboard on a rack or small turntable.

3   Stored properly, dried herbs will take you through to the next season. To determine whether your herbs are still fresh enough, crumble a bit between your fingers. When you smell them, they should have a strong, recognizable fragrance. If they do not have their distinctive herb smell, they will not be very tasty; best to discard them. This freshness test goes for dried herbs that you purchase as well.

USEFUL TIPS FOR USING FRESH HERBS

- Here's a quick way to chop fresh parsley. Place bunches in a 1-cup glass measure and chop with kitchen scissors, especially the spring-loaded kind. When done, jiggle the container to level the chopped herb and check measurement. Easy clean-up too!

- Use a food processor to chop large quantities of parsley.

- Create a chiffonade (translates literally as "made of rags") of herbs for sprinkling over salads, soups, etc. (See page 3).

- Use kitchen scissors to snip fresh chives into 1/2-inch lengths; store about 1/2 cup of them in a small covered bowl or plastic container. They will keep in the refrigerator several days. Use to sprinkle on vegetables, salads and omelettes.

HERB VINEGARS

Making herb vinegars is an extremely easy way to capture the flavor of herbs. These fragrant vinegars are sprinkled over hot vegetables, spritzed on fish in place of lemon juice, added to soups and stews; they are used in marinades, to make salad dressings, mayonnaise and sauces; in place of lemon or lime juice in drinks and salsas; in pickles and chutneys.

Recycle and re-use glass bottles from liquor and commercial sauces. Ask friends or local bars to save bottles for you (some brands of scotch and imported beers come in beautiful bottles). Some kitchen stores carry decorative glass bottles with corks. I have also purchased small wine bottles from make-your-own wine stores. I prefer bottles with broad bases instead of tall, narrow ones, which can tip over. Clear glass is best for pretty colored vinegars, such as chive flower or purple basil, and to show off herb sprigs in vinegars made with lighter-colored vinegars. Ones made with red wine vinegar or many combined herbs can come out an unattractive brownish color and are better in dark brown or green bottles.

For gift-giving, you can find rubber stamps with herbs to make pretty labels. The tops of the corks can be sealed with wax or with the plastic seals used to top wine bottles (from make-your-own wine stores). These small plastic covers go loosely onto the bottle top then are heated with a heat gun or boiling kettle to shrink on tightly. Use raffia to tie a small label to the neck with usage ideas or a recipe. Place the bottle in a fancy liquor store gift bag with tissue or put in a basket with a bottle of herb oil.

MAKING HERB VINEGARS

VINEGAR

A good quality white wine vinegar will do for any herb. Delicate herbs (dill, chervil, and cilantro) are better with lighter vinegars, such as rice wine or white wine vinegar. The more pungent herbs (sage, savory, rosemary, and thyme) suit stronger-flavored vinegars (red wine, apple cider). Vinegar should be a minimum 5 percent acetic acid by volume (this information is usually written on the label).

Clear distilled (white) vinegar is ideal for making vinegars from flowers of chives, nasturtiums, violets, roses and carnations, as well as purple basil, where a clean color is desired. Remove the bitter green base from the flowers. (See Edible Flowers, page 38.)

Herbs

Do not use dried herbs to make herb vinegars.

I like to make single herb vinegars, then blend them when cooking for a unique taste. For instance, if a dressing recipe calls for 3 tbsp vinegar, I may use 1 tbsp of purple basil vinegar and 2 tbsp of chive flower vinegar. One of my other standard vinegars is tarragon.

I steep the vinegar first, then strain and discard the spent herbs. I add fresh herbs for decorative purposes when giving the vinegar as a gift, or to identify a single herb vinegar, e.g., a sprig of tarragon in tarragon vinegar. Bottle close to the time you are giving so the herb or herb flower sprig(s) you add will retain their bright color(s). Once the herb is in the vinegar, the color will start to leach out.

ADDITIONS

You may add garlic, peppercorns, chili peppers, citrus peel or herb seeds to your vinegars. Use the hot method (see below) if adding any of these.

To add whole garlic cloves, arrange them on a wooden skewer, checking to make sure they will fit through the opening of your bottle. Peel citrus zest in one piece, using a vegetable peeler or knife; thread onto a wooden skewer. Insert skewer into jar before adding vinegar.

STORING

Label and date bottled vinegars. Store in a cool, dark place. Unopened, most vinegars will last a year or two. Once opened, use up within six months. If you are not sure if a vinegar is still usable, trust your taste. If it does not have a distinctive herb taste, chances are most of the flavor has been lost. Discard any vinegars that have fungus growth on the surface.

HOT METHOD (48 HOURS)

Rinse and pat dry herbs. Half fill a clean large glass jar (preferably a large canning jar) with chopped or torn herbs. Remove leaves from herbs with thick or woody stems, such as basil, rosemary or sage; leave very small herb leaves such as thyme on stems (too fussy to remove). Heat vinegar in the microwave or in a non-reactive saucepan. Whole spices, such as peppercorns, can be heated with the vinegar. Do not boil. Pour hot vinegar over herbs. Cool to room temperature; cover with plastic lids (vinegar will corrode metal lids) and infuse for 48 hours in a cool, dark place. Do not sit jars in a sunny window, as heat and light will destroy flavor.

The vinegar is now ready to use, but the flavor will continue to develop for another couple of weeks. Test for flavor and, if it is to your liking, strain (discard herbs) and pour into smaller bottles with a fresh sprig of herb in each. Seal with non-metallic lids; label and date bottles.

COLD METHOD (2 TO 3 WEEKS)

This method takes longer but produces a clear, mellow flavor. Prepare the herbs as you would for the hot method, but do not heat the vinegar. Check after two days. If herbs are not completely submerged, add more vinegar. Leave another three to four weeks, then strain into smaller jars or bottles. Insert a fresh sprig of herb in each jar or bottle. Seal with non-metallic lids; label and date.

RECIPES FOR HERB VINEGAR

GENERAL INSTRUCTIONS
Add 3 cups vinegar to any of the following recipes. Each recipe makes about 2-3/4 cups.

BASIL GARLIC VINEGAR
For salads, egg dishes, tomatoes, beef, chicken, cauliflower, broccoli:

6 to 8   fresh basil sprigs

4   large garlic cloves
(or 1/4 cup chopped garlic chives)

Black peppercorns (optional)

White wine vinegar

OREGANO GARLIC VINEGAR
For meat marinades, grilled vegetables, Italian dishes:

6 to 8   fresh oregano sprigs

4   large garlic cloves
(or 1/4 cup chopped garlic chives)

Black peppercorns (optional)

White wine vinegar

ROSEMARY GARLIC VINEGAR
For chicken, pork, lamb, potato salad:

3 or 4   fresh rosemary sprig

4   large garlic cloves
(or 1/4 cup chopped garlic chives)

Cider vinegar

ROSEMARY ORANGE VINEGAR
For chicken, pork, lamb:

3 or 4   fresh rosemary sprigs

Zest of 1 orange

White wine vinegar

LEMON TARRAGON VINEGAR
For fish, seafood and chicken:

4 to 6   fresh tarragon sprigs

Rind of 1 lemon

White wine vinegar

DILL LEMON VINEGAR
For fish/seafood, vegetables, potato salad:

4 to 6   fresh dill sprigs

Rind of 1 lemon

1 tsp   mustard seed

Rice wine vinegar

RED WINE HERB VINEGAR
For marinades, salads:

2 or 3   sprigs *each* of three of the following:
fresh basil, oregano, rosemary, thyme or
lemon thyme, marjoram, savory

Red wine vinegar

MIXED HERB VINEGAR

For chicken salad, fish and vegetables:

1 to 1-1/2 cups	finely chopped fresh herbs: basil, parsley, dill, thyme, tarragon, rosemary, summer savory, marjoram
2 to 3	garlic cloves (or 1/4 cup chopped garlic chives)
1 tsp	black peppercorns
	White wine or cider vinegar

ITALIAN HERB VINEGAR

For marinades, soups, stews, salads:

1/2 cup	*each*: chopped fresh rosemary and thyme
1/4 cup	*each*: chopped fresh chives and oregano
1	sprig fresh Italian parsley, chopped
1/2 cup	chopped shallots
12	black peppercorns
	White wine vinegar

FINES HERBES VINEGAR

For fish, seafood, vegetables:

1/2 cup	*each*: chopped fresh chervil, chives, parsley and tarragon
	White wine vinegar

LAVENDER VINEGAR

For marinating red meat, salad dressing:

4 tsp	fresh lavender flowers (or 2 tsp dried)
	White wine vinegar

OTHER COMBINATIONS

- cilantro, fresh ginger, chili pepper, rice wine vinegar
- oregano, sage, rosemary, lemon thyme, peppercorns, red wine vinegar
- oregano, mustard seeds, peppercorns, whole cloves, white wine vinegar
- tarragon, green peppercorns, white wine vinegar
- tarragon, dill and garlic, white wine vinegar
- rosemary, mint, red wine vinegar
- rosemary, lemon thyme, white wine vinegar

RECIPES USING HERB VINEGARS

SALAD DRESSINGS

1/3 cup	Herb Vinegar
1 cup	oil
1 tsp	*each*: granulated sugar, Dijon mustard

Whisk together in a small bowl or blend in food processor or blender. Makes about 1-1/3 cups.

CREAMY HERB DRESSING

1/3 cup	Herb Vinegar
2/3 cup	oil
1/3 cup	sour cream
1 tbsp	granulated sugar
1/2 tsp	*each*: dry mustard and paprika

Whisk together in a small bowl or blend in food processor or blender. Makes about 1-1/3 cups.

MARINADES

1/3 cup	*each*: Herb Vinegar, oil, wine

Whisk together in a small bowl and pour over meat in a glass dish or plastic bag. Cover and marinate in refrigerator. Makes about 1 cup.

HERBED MAYONNAISE

1	egg
3/4 cup	oil
2 tbsp	Herb Vinegar
1/4 tsp	dry mustard (or 1 tsp Dijon mustard)
1	clove garlic, minced (optional)
1/4 tsp	salt

In a food processor or blender, combine egg, 1/4 cup of the oil, Herb Vinegar, mustard, garlic (if using) and salt. Pulse 15 to 30 seconds to mix well. Very slowly drizzle in the remaining 1/2 cup oil in a thin stream until it thickens; scrape down sides. Store in a glass jar in refrigerator up to 4 days. Makes about 1 cup.

HERB OILS

The flavorful, volatile oils from herbs infuse nicely into cooking oils. Use herbs such as basil, cilantro, dill, marjoram, mint, oregano, rosemary, sage, savory, tarragon and thyme, by themselves or in combination. I prefer to make single herb oils, and then combine them when I am cooking. This allows for the most flexibility.

Herb oils have a concentrated flavor so only small amounts are needed. A little bit of herb oil will give a rich taste to low-fat meals. They add flavor to healthy foods like fish, vegetables and grains, which are typically low in fat to begin with.

Oils do not contain any cholesterol (cholesterol comes mainly from animal-source fats). Some oils have actually been found to assist in reducing the LDL-cholesterol in the blood and to maintain healthy levels of HDL-cholesterol. Fresh oils are a good source of unsaturated fat and essential fats, which must be obtained from food.

SUGGESTIONS FOR USING HERB OILS

- in marinades, mayonnaise, sauces
- in grain, bean or pasta salads, salad dressings
- drizzled over cooked or grilled vegetables
- to cook mushrooms or stir-fry vegetables
- with a little balsamic vinegar for dipping bread
- on pizza dough or drizzled over cooked pizza; to flavor pasta
- to flavor croutons for salads and soups
- brushed on toasted crostini for appetizers or to make breadcrumbs for gratins
- to marinate cheeses, such as goat cheese
- drizzled over tomato halves before broiling
- brushed over the top of bread, rolls, etc., before warming

MAKING HERB OILS

I like to use neutral-flavored oils such as safflower, sunflower, canola and light olive oil, for making herb oils. These oils allow the taste of the herb to shine through. However, regular olive oil or peanut oil may be suitable, depending on the end use of your oil. For Greek salad, you may wish to infuse olive oil with fresh oregano or, for a stir-fry, peanut oil with cilantro.

By using a good ratio of herbs to oil – about 1:2 – the oil will develop an intense flavor, and not as much oil will need to be used in your recipes and cooking.

Store oils in the refrigerator, covered, in a glass jar or bottle; use within a month. Oils may become cloudy when cold but will clear once they come to room temperature. Make small batches and use up as quickly as possible.

METHOD 1: INFUSING

1. Rinse herbs well with cold water and blot dry (they should be completely dry).
2. Tear or coarsely chop leaves and pack loosely into a sterilized, large wide-mouth jar, such as a large canning jar. (Remove large leaves like basil from their stems first.) Fill jar about half-full of herbs.
3. Pour oil over herbs to cover; seal and store in refrigerator for 1 week.
4. Pour off oil into a clean jar (or strain) and discard herbs. Taste oil. If a stronger flavor is desired, repeat, using new herbs. Once desired flavor is reached pour into decorative or other glass bottle with a cap. Store in refrigerator up to six months. (Refrigeration prevents rancidity. Rancid oil has a strong paint-like smell.)

METHOD 2: PURÉEING

1. Prepare herbs as in Method 1.
2. In a food processor, finely chop 1-1/2 cups loosely packed herbs; slowly pour in 2 cups oil with processor running.
3. Store in fridge; use within 1 week. To keep longer, strain out herbs, tightly cover and store in refrigerator up to a month.

METHOD 3: HEATING

This method is used when you are adding spices, fresh ginger or sun-dried tomatoes to the oil.

1. Prepare herbs as in Method 1.
2. Heat oil and spices in a small, heavy-bottom saucepan or in a large glass measuring cup in microwave, just until hot. DO NOT BOIL.
3. Stir in herbs; let stand at room temperature until cool. Strain through a fine sieve; discard solids. Pour oil into a clean glass jar or bottle; cover and refrigerate up to a month.

ADDITIONS

- dried chili peppers
- peppercorns
- whole spices such as cloves, cardamom, cinnamon stick, star anise
- ground spices such as ginger, saffron, cumin
- herb seeds such as dill seed, fennel, coriander and caraway

OIL BLENDS

Here are just a few suggestions to try. Customize your oils to suit your own tastes and uses.

DILL AND LEMON: fresh dill, dill seed, lemon rind

FINES HERBES: fresh chervil, chives, parsley and tarragon

ROSEMARY AND ORANGE: fresh rosemary, orange rind, hot red pepper flakes

ROSEMARY, THYME AND SAGE: fresh rosemary, thyme and sage, shallots, black peppercorns

SUN-DRIED TOMATO AND OREGANO: fresh oregano or marjoram, sun-dried tomatoes, garlic (also good made with fresh basil)

HERB MUSTARDS

Mustard is such a versatile and staple cooking ingredient that it is ideal for capturing the flavor of fresh herbs. Mustards can be used as sandwich spreads, added to hot and cold sauces, butters, marinades, salad dressings and devilled eggs, or simply used as a condiment to meats, such as sausages.

The easiest way to make herb mustards is to begin with a good quality mustard such as Dijon mustard, grainy mustard or deli-style mustard. Choose the mustard that has the sharpness or sweetness that you like. You can make your own from scratch using mustard seeds, but that is a lot more work, and will not be covered in this book.

To make mustards using dry mustard, combine equal amounts of dry mustard with white wine or herb vinegar to make a paste. Stir in minced garlic or shallots and some minced mixed herbs. If desired, add a little honey or brown sugar to taste.

Try small batches to start, using about 1 cup mustard. You can taste it to see if you like it, or make several to have on hand. I prefer to make single herb mustards, such as tarragon or dill, to use as ingredients in salad dressings, mayonnaise or sandwich spreads.

Soft-leaf herbs, such as basil, chervil, cilantro, dill, savory, sage and tarragon, can be minced and stirred into the mustard. The flavor will take several days to develop. Store in the refrigerator up to six months. Use only coated or plastic lids, as the vinegar in the mustard will corrode metal lids. Be sure to label with the herb used and the date.

BASIC RECIPE FOR MIXED HERB MUSTARD

MAKES ABOUT 1-1/4 CUPS

1 cup	Dijon mustard
2 tbsp	minced fresh parsley
1 tbsp	minced fresh tarragon
2 tsp	minced fresh basil
2 tsp	minced fresh dill
2 tsp	minced fresh oregano

1. In a small bowl, mix together all ingredients.

2. Place mixture in a jar; cover and refrigerate for 2 to 3 days before using.

RECIPES FOR HERB MUSTARDS

FINES HERBES MUSTARD

MAKES ABOUT 1 CUP

1 cup	Dijon mustard
1 tbsp	*each*: minced chives and parsley
2 tsp	*each*: minced chervil and tarragon

See method page 29.

ITALIAN MUSTARD

MAKES ABOUT 1 CUP

1 cup	Dijon mustard
2 tbsp	minced fresh basil
1 tbsp	minced fresh oregano
1 tsp	balsamic vinegar

See method page 29.

PESTO MUSTARD

MAKES ABOUT 1-1/4 CUPS

1 cup	Dijon mustard
1/4 cup	Basil Pesto (see page 162)

See method page 29.

LAVENDER MUSTARD

MAKES ABOUT 1/2 CUP

1/2 cup	Dijon mustard
2 tsp	fresh lavender flowers (or 1 tsp dried)
1 tsp	honey

See method page 29.

ROSEMARY TARRAGON MUSTARD

This method works better for tougher herbs such as rosemary.

MAKES ABOUT 1 CUP

1/4 cup	dry white wine
2 tbsp	minced shallots
1 tbsp	finely chopped fresh rosemary
1 tbsp	finely chopped fresh tarragon
1 cup	Dijon mustard

1. In a small saucepan, combine wine, shallots and herbs over high heat. Bring to a boil; reduce heat and simmer until the liquid has been reduced by half. Strain through a fine sieve; discard solids.

2. In a small bowl, mix mustard with herbed wine. Place in a jar; cover and refrigerate for 2 to 3 days before using.

HERB BUTTERS

Butter is another good medium for capturing the flavor of fresh herbs. Butters can be made for immediate use, but I like to freeze them too. Herbs frozen in butter keep their freshness better than if frozen on their own. Use salted or unsalted butter. If you wish, you can make herb butters using a good quality margarine (I prefer the non-hydrogenated types).

I am not suggesting that we slather our food with butter, but we can allow ourselves a little to add interesting herb flavors to low-fat foods such as vegetables, fish, chicken, lean pork and grilled meats.

Spread herb butters on fresh bread or rolls. They are excellent spread on French bread slices and heated in the oven for a few minutes. Or toss toasted bread cubes in melted herb butter for savory croutons. Use them to enhance the taste of vegetables by tossing a little onto hot vegetables and shaking to coat; see the chart of herbs and vegetables on page 192. Use chive, marjoram or rosemary butter on corn-on-the-cob or to top baked potatoes.

Butters may also be used to make pastry crusts for sweet or savory dishes, such as tarts or quiches.

MAKING HERB BUTTERS

Herb butters are quite easy to prepare. For large batches using 1 lb butter, use a food processor. First, chop the rinsed and well-dried herb leaves in the food processor, then add the butter and any additional ingredients, such as mustard, garlic, shallots, lemon juice, etc. Add a little olive or sunflower oil to the butter, if desired.

If you are using edible flowers for your butter (see Edible Flowers, page 38), stir in by hand for a prettier look. Flowers from herbs such as chives, garlic chives and basil are nice additions to butters.

For small quantities, finely chop herb leaves (removed from stems) and blend well into softened butter. I just stir them together in a medium bowl.

Butters may be packed into small plastic freezer storage containers. You can wrap them with plastic wrap in logs, and then over-wrap in plastic freezer bags or place in a rectangular storage container. Wrap them well so they do not pick up (or transfer) odors in your freezer.

STORAGE
Refrigerate for one to two weeks (unsalted butter is more perishable); freeze up to six months.

BUTTER
For convenience, use butter sold in sticks. Each stick is equivalent to 1/2 cup, 4 oz or one-quarter of a pound. Unwrap butter from foil paper while it is still cold and it will come off the paper easily. Place in bowl to soften.

BASIC RECIPE FOR HERB BUTTER

Prepare at least two hours ahead to allow flavors to blend. Makes about 1/2 cup.

1/2 cup	softened butter
2 tbsp	finely chopped fresh herbs
1 tbsp	finely chopped fresh parsley (optional)

1. In a medium bowl or food processor, mix together butter and herbs until well combined.

2. Spoon mixture onto a piece of plastic wrap or waxed paper. Shape into a log or cylinder about 1-1/2 inches in diameter, and twist ends to secure. Store in a plastic freezer bag or container; label.

3. Refrigerate until firm or freeze for later use.

To use, allow to soften a bit then slice 1/4 inch thick and place on top of food. The heat of the food will slowly melt the butter.

RECIPES AND USES FOR HERB BUTTERS

In place of the herbs in the Basic Recipe, add the following to 1/2 cup softened butter:

PARSLEY BUTTER (MAÎTRE D'HÔTEL BUTTER)

Use on any vegetables or grilled steak. For fish, use 2 tsp finely chopped shallots in place of garlic, or use finely chopped cilantro in place of parsley and omit garlic.

2 tbsp	finely chopped fresh parsley (Italian or curly)
1	clove garlic, crushed
2 tsp	lemon juice
Pinch	black pepper

FINES HERBES BUTTER

Use with fish, chicken or eggs; with vegetables such as peas, green beans, asparagus, potatoes.

1 tbsp	*each*: finely chopped fresh chervil, chives, parsley and tarragon
1 tbsp	finely chopped shallots (optional)

LEMON DILL BUTTER

Use with fish/seafood or vegetables such as asparagus, beets, potatoes, tomatoes, spinach.

2 tbsp	finely chopped fresh dill
2 tsp	lemon or lime juice

TARRAGON-DIJON BUTTER

Use on grilled steak (gives the taste of Béarnaise sauce) or fish; with vegetables such as green beans, carrots, asparagus, peas, tomatoes, mushrooms.

1 tbsp	finely chopped fresh tarragon
1 tbsp	finely chopped fresh parsley
1	clove garlic, crushed
1 tsp	lemon juice
1 tsp	Dijon mustard

BASIL-OREGANO-THYME GARLIC BUTTER

Excellent for garlic bread and croutons; use with eggs or vegetables such as roasted sweet peppers, eggplant, broccoli, zucchini, potatoes, tomatoes.

2 tbsp	finely chopped fresh basil
2 tsp	finely chopped fresh oregano
1/2 tsp	finely chopped fresh thyme
1	clove garlic, crushed

ROSEMARY BUTTER

Use with lamb, beef or chicken; with squash. For vegetables such as potatoes, cauliflower, mushrooms and squash, omit orange rind and pepper; add 1 tbsp *each* parsley and chives or garlic chives.

1 tbsp	finely chopped fresh rosemary
2 tsp	grated orange rind
1/2 tsp	coarsely ground black pepper

TOMATO MARJORAM BUTTER

Use with fresh vegetables, especially zucchini; with fish and lamb. For pasta, rice, chicken and fish, use 1 tbsp *each* basil and oregano in place of marjoram.

2 tbsp	finely chopped fresh marjoram
1 tbsp	tomato paste
1 tsp	lemon juice
1	small clove garlic, crushed
	Black pepper (optional)

BASIL SUN-DRIED TOMATO BUTTER

Spread on bread and broil until bubbly; serve with pasta or vegetables such as green beans, zucchini.

2 tbsp	finely chopped fresh basil
1 tbsp	minced, softened sun-dried tomatoes (softened)
1 tbsp	freshly grated Parmesan cheese
2 tsp	minced shallots
1	small clove garlic, crushed

ROASTED PEPPER OREGANO BUTTER

Use on pasta or vegetables such as cauliflower, cabbage, green beans, Brussels sprouts, zucchini.

2 tbsp	minced roasted sweet red or yellow peppers
1 tbsp	finely chopped fresh oregano or marjoram
1	small clove garlic, crushed
Pinch	hot red pepper flakes (optional)

PESTO BUTTER

Use for fish, shrimp or vegetables such as zucchini, grilled tomatoes, eggplant.

1/2 cup	Basil Pesto (see page 162)

SAGE BUTTER

Use with pork, chicken, turkey or veal; with vegetables such as cabbage, corn, sautéed onions, green beans, potatoes. For beef or vegetables such as asparagus, green beans, eggplant, peas, squash, use savory in place of sage.

2 tbsp	finely chopped fresh sage
1 tbsp	finely chopped fresh parsley
2 tsp	finely chopped shallots

CHIVE FLOWER BUTTER

Use to butter cucumber sandwiches or biscuits.

2 tbsp	chive flower florets
1 tbsp	finely chopped fresh parsley (optional)

CHIVE GINGER BUTTER

Use on squash or sweet potatoes. May also be made without fresh ginger and served with almost any vegetable.

2 tbsp	finely chopped fresh chives
1 tbsp	finely chopped fresh parsley or cilantro
1 tbsp	finely grated fresh ginger
1 tsp	lemon or lime juice
Pinch	black pepper

CILANTRO CHILI BUTTER

Use with chicken, pork, shrimp, eggs, rice or vegetables such as green beans, carrots, corn, potatoes, zucchini.

2 tbsp	finely chopped fresh cilantro
1 tbsp	finely chopped fresh parsley
2 tsp	minced jalapeño or other chili pepper (or 1/4 tsp hot red pepper flakes)
1/2 tsp	ground cumin

CILANTRO LIME BUTTER

Use with grilled fish/seafood, chicken or beef, or to butter corn-on-the-cob.

3 tbsp	finely chopped fresh cilantro
1 tbsp	lime juice
1/2 tsp	finely grated lime rind
Pinch	hot red pepper flakes (optional)

GARDEN HARVEST BUTTER

Use with beef, chicken, fish, eggs or vegetables such as carrots, tomatoes, potatoes.

1 tbsp	*each*: finely chopped fresh tarragon, parsley
2 tsp	finely chopped fresh thyme or lemon thyme
2 tsp	finely chopped fresh oregano
Pinch	black pepper

BASIL AND NUTMEG BUTTER

Use for vegetables such as cauliflower, squash, green beans, spinach. Use cinnamon basil or purple basil in place of regular basil; omit nutmeg.

2 tbsp	finely chopped fresh basil
1/4 tsp	ground nutmeg
Pinch	black pepper

MINT BUTTER

Use with lamb, swordfish or vegetables such as peas, grilled tomatoes, green beans, carrots.

2 tbsp	finely chopped fresh mint (see note on Mints, page 14)
1 tbsp	finely chopped fresh parsley
1	small clove garlic, crushed

HERB FLOWER BUTTER

Serve with poached or grilled fish such as salmon, trout or tuna.

1 tbsp	*each*: chive, basil, dill and rosemary flowers
1 tbsp	finely chopped purple basil leaves
1 tsp	lemon juice

EDIBLE FLOWER BUTTER

See page 38 for Edible Flowers. Use to butter scones, to make tart pastry or in shortbread cookies.

| 2 tbsp | chopped mixed edible flower petals |
| 2 tsp | liquid honey (optional) |

NASTURTIUM FLOWER BUTTER

Use this peppery-tasting butter with fish and any vegetables you wish.

| 1/2 cup | chopped nasturtium flower petals (orange, yellow, red) and leaves |
| 1 tbsp | minced shallots |

SPECIAL SERVING PRESENTATIONS

- Roll small balls of butter (about 2 tsp each) in finely chopped parsley or chives; chill.

- Use a melon baller to make rounds from semi-firm butters; drop into ice water. Remove from ice water, arrange on serving dish or freeze on a baking sheet then transfer to plastic freezer bags.

- Logs may be rolled in finely chopped parsley or chives, then sliced 1/4 inch thick and placed on waxed paper to chill. If using frozen logs, thaw slightly and parsley will stick more easily.

- For cut-out shapes, roll butter between two pieces of waxed paper to 1/4-inch thickness; chill until firm. Use small cookie or canape cutters to cut into decorative or festive shapes (hearts, maple leaves or flowers).

- Make butter in food processor, then use a pastry bag fitted with a large star tip to pipe onto a baking sheet lined with waxed paper; chill. Use a thin metal spatula to remove.

- Pack butter into small molds and chill. Tiny molds used for chocolate making are also good for this.

- Whip butter until light and fluffy, then spoon gently into small individual ramekins. Sprinkle with finely chopped parsley or chive flowers.

- Decorate serving plate with herb sprigs and edible flowers.

HERB HONEYS

Herb honeys are great to use in cooking, as well as to stir into hot drinks such as tea or cold drinks like lemonade, punch or champagne. When serving cold drinks, a few fresh lemon verbena or mint leaves can be added to the glass or frozen in ice cubes. Use herb honey to sweeten fruit salads, stir it into yogurt, add a small amount to a salad dressing or use it to replace regular honey in baking.

MAKING HERB HONEYS

Warm 1 cup honey in a small saucepan over low heat, or in a large glass measure in the microwave (a minute at a time). Stir occasionally until a thin consistency. Stir in about 1/4 cup finely chopped fresh herbs, such as lemon thyme, lemon verbena, lemon balm, cinnamon basil, orange mint, rosemary, sage, lavender flowers, and rose- or lemon-scented geranium. Allow to cool; cover and let rest at room temperature for about one week.

Taste honey. It may need to be left a few days longer or to be re-infused with more fresh herbs. If necessary to re-infuse to strengthen the flavor, re-warm as above and stir in about 2 tbsp chopped fresh herbs. When the desired flavor is reached, re-warm the honey in a saucepan or the microwave, stirring. Pour through a fine sieve; discard solids. Store in clean jar at room temperature.

HERB SYRUPS

Herb syrups can be used in much the same way as herb honey, but they can also be used to glaze the top of loaves, muffins, etc. After baking, let loaf cool in pan for about ten minutes. Brush syrup over top of loaf; turn loaf out onto cooling rack and cool completely.

Lavender syrup (see page 40) is great in sparkling wine with slices of strawberries. Add one vanilla bean, split lengthwise, to lavender syrup and use it to pour over fruit, such as peaches, raspberries, strawberries or blueberries.

Other herbs to use for syrups are the same as those used to make Herb Honeys (see page 36).

ROSEMARY SYRUP

MAKES ABOUT 2 CUPS

1-1/2 cups	water
1 cup	granulated sugar
1/3 cup	packed fresh rosemary leaves (or other herbs or herb flowers listed on page 36 under Herb Honeys)
	Whole spices such as cinnamon or cloves (optional)
	Lemon or orange rind (optional)

1. In a small saucepan, combine water, sugar and rosemary. Add spices and rind. Bring to a boil over high heat. Reduce heat; cover and simmer for 5 minutes. Remove from heat; let stand 30 minutes.

2. Strain through a fine sieve over a measuring cup; discard solids. Refrigerate in a glass bottle or jar up to 2 months. (For half the recipe, use 3 tbsp chopped fresh herbs.)

HERB SUGARS

Herbs will impart their flavors to sugar, too, which can then be used to make cookies, cakes, pies, etc.; sprinkled over fruit or cereal; used to top cookies, scones or muffins and to sweeten hot or cold drinks.

In a jar, layer whole herb leaves (cinnamon basil, mints, rosemary, lemon verbena, lemon balm, rose or lemon geranium, lavender, etc.) with about 3 to 4 tbsp granulated sugar (extra-fine if possible) between each layer. Cover; let rest at room temperature for a week. Sift through strainer to remove herbs. (Sugar may have hardened slightly.) Keep in covered glass jar up to a year.

HERB SALTS

Herb salts are made in a similar way to Herb Sugars. In a jar, layer whole leaves from herb (such as basil, rosemary, sage, savory or tarragon) with 2 tbsp salt between each layer. Cover and let rest at room temperature for a week. Keep in covered glass jar up to a year. Use salt, along with the dried herbs, to salt meats, vegetables, egg dishes, etc.

EDIBLE FLOWERS

Although the presence of flowers in a salad surprises many people, the use of wild and cultivated flowers in salads is one of the nicest traditions we have inherited from the past. The flowers do not impart a lot of flavor; however, the unexpected color adds interest to a salad.

There are lots of edible flowers available to the adventurous cook, but be sure to identify them accurately; if you are in doubt, leave them out of the salad altogether. Before using them in salad, wash flowers very lightly (swish in water to remove any garden pests); pat dry with paper towel.

It is preferable to use home-grown flowers, avoiding those that grow close to the road or are commercially sprayed with herbicides or pesticides. (Never use cut flowers from florists or fruit markets.) Many stores now carry edible flowers such as pansies or nasturtiums. Vibrant, healthy flowers will have the best flavor. To store flowers overnight, spray them with water and place in plastic bags in the refrigerator.

Edible flowers include:

Apple	Honeysuckle
Borage	Jasmine
Carnation	Lavender
Chrysanthemum	Lemon Blossom
Daisy	Lilac
Dandelion	Marigold
Daylily	Nasturtium and its leaves
Elderberry flowers	Pansy
Geranium	Rose
Gladioli	Tulip
Hibiscus	Violet and its leaves
Hollyhock	Flowers of culinary herbs

TIPS FOR USING EDIBLE FLOWERS

- Marigolds make a good, inexpensive substitute for saffron, and impart a lovely golden color to rice.
- Borage flowers, roses and violets make refreshing drinks. Soak flowers in chilled water for several hours; strain out flowers and serve with fresh blossoms floating in each glass.
- Freeze small flowers in ice cubes for drinks or in a ring mold to float in a punch bowl: fill ice-cube trays or a ring mold half-full with water, add flowers and freeze; add more flowers and water and freeze again.
- Carnations, chrysanthemums, nasturtiums or herb flowers are ideal for blending with butter, to make flower butters. Herb flowers add delicious flavor to breads; try rosemary, sage or thyme.
- Use edible flowers to garnish soups (chive and other herb flowers) and desserts (violets, roses, carnations, lavender).
- Include flowers in green salads, either whole or as confetti (mixed flower petals).

COOKING WITH LAVENDER

FLAVOR: Lavender is from the same family (Lamiaceae) as mint, rosemary, sage and thyme. It has a flavor that is floral and sweet with a hint of lemon and citrus. Described also as androgynous in flavor and aroma as it can be used in both sweet and savoury recipes. The most common lavenders for culinary use are English lavenders (*Lavendula angustifolia*), Munstead, Hidcote, Royal Velvet, Folgate, Melissa. Spanish and French lavenders have more camphor-pine, or turpentine overtones and are too strong and bitter to cook with.

GROWING AND HARVESTING: Lavenders grow well in the sun, in well-drained soil and with good air circulation. To harvest, pick lavender with the flower buds still closed. Grows well in Zones 5 through 8.

DRYING: The potency of the flavor increases with drying. Hang bunches upside-down and fasten with an elastic. (This allows for shrinkage as the stems dry.) Or, hang bunches inside a paper bag, scrunch bag opening around stems and wrap with elastic, poke bag with paring knife several times; the bag will catch the buds as it dries. Store in a glass jar away from heat and light.

CULINARY USES: Use only culinary grade (organic) lavender. The key to cooking with lavender is not to overdo it. Lavender can be used both fresh and dried,

flowers (sweet citrus), or leaves (less common). Pairs well with strawberries, raspberries, blackberries, blueberries, cherries, figs, peaches, nectarines, apples, pears, plums and oranges. Lemon is an excellent partner with lavender (lemon curd). Use lavender in dressings for salads with beets, goat cheese. To soften the "soapy" factor for savoury dishes, lightly toast buds in a dry skillet over medium heat. Partners well with other members of the mint family, including mint, lemon balm, sage, savory, thyme, rosemary, oregano, marjoram and basil. To substitute dried for fresh, use only a third of the amount of fresh lavender e.g. 1 tsp dried for 1 tbsp fresh. It will depend on what type of lavender you have, how long it has been dried, how it is stored (best in a glass jar) and what kind of dish you are using it in. Some recipes may call for half the amount of dried vs. fresh where you want the taste to be stronger.

INFUSIONS: Lavender flavor can be transferred to cream or milk to make whipped cream custards, crème brûlée, panna cotta, or ice cream, by heating lavender with the liquid, then straining out the buds. Infuse it into melted chocolate (then dip strawberries in it!) or add to white or dark chocolate bark. Lavender goes well with vanilla in desserts. Infuse lavender in alcohol for drinks (gin, vodka) or to make lavender extract.

LAVENDER SALT: Grind about 1 tsp dried lavender with 1/4 cup coarse salt, or layer in a jar. Toss with new potatoes and butter. Use on chicken, pork, and lamb.

LAVENDER MUSTARD: See page 30.

HERB SEEDS

Some of the fresh herbs of the *umbellifer* family – dill, parsley, cumin, coriander, caraway and fennel – produce flavorful seeds. The flowers, which resemble tiny umbrellas, turn into green berries, then dry to brown seeds within approximately ten days. These can then be picked and stored, preferably in a glass jar, and kept up to a year. Their flavor is more intense than the leaves due to the oils they contain. Some seeds, like coriander seed, have an entirely different flavor from the fresh herb (also known as cilantro, Chinese parsley or fresh cilantro). For a continuous supply of fresh cilantro, plant seeds at one-week intervals.

Herb seeds can be used to flavor pickles, breads, meats, fish and flavored oils.

Seeds may be planted to grow more fresh herbs for the next season. Plants will drop some of their seeds, which will come up on their own the next summer.

LAVENDER SUGAR: Add 2 tbsp dried buds to 1/2 cup sugar; grind finely in food processor. Store in a jar. Use sugar to sweeten hot tea or cold drinks; in baked goods such as cookies (shortbread, biscotti), pound cakes and scones; stir into fruit; use to make a fruit clafoutis or whip into meringues. Use a coffee grinder to finely grind.

LAVENDER SYRUP: Infuse a simple syrup with lavender. In small saucepan, heat together 1/2 cup water and 1/2 cup sugar. Bring to a boil, stirring to dissolve sugar. Remove from heat; stir in 2 tbsp fresh (or 1 tbsp dried) culinary lavender florets. Allow to infuse for about 30 minutes; strain out lavender. Store in refrigerator up to 2 weeks. Use to sweeten drinks such as lemonade, iced tea, mojitos, margaritas (especially fruit ones) and champagne cocktails (adding berries).

LAVENDER HONEY: Warm 1 cup of honey in a saucepan, or glass measure in the microwave. Stir in 2 tbsp dried lavender buds. Pour into a jar, cover and let stand for a few days. (Turn jar over if lavender floats to the top; repeat.) Warm honey again and pour through a fine sieve; discard buds. Store in covered jar in a dark cupboard. Stir into hot or cold drinks, drizzle over fruit, over toast with cream cheese, strawberries and pancakes/waffles.

METRIC EQUIVALENTS

Package sizes vary between countries; use the closest equivalent size.

BASIC MEASUREMENTS

1/4 tsp	1 mL		1/4 cup	50 mL
1/2 tsp	2 mL		1/3 cup	75 mL
1 tsp	5 mL		1/2 cup	125 mL
2 tsp	10 mL		2/3 cup	150 mL
3 tsp or 1 tbsp	15 mL		3/4 cup	175 mL
			1 cup	250 mL
			4 cups	1 L

OVEN TEMPERATURES

300°F	150°C		375°F	190°C
325°F	160°C		400°F	200°C
350°F	180°C		425°F	220°C

WEIGHTS

2 oz	60 g		16 oz/1 lb	500 g
3.5 oz	100 g		1-1/4 lb	625 g
4 oz	125 g		1-1/2 lb	750 g
5 oz	150 g		2 lbs	1 kg
6 oz	175 g		2-1/2 lbs	1.25 kg
7 oz	200 g		3 lb	1.5 kg
8 oz	250 g		4 lb	2 kg
10 oz	300 g		10 lb	5 kg
12 oz	375 g			

CAN SIZES

7.5 oz	213 mL
14 oz	398 mL
19 oz	540 mL
28 oz	796 mL

CARAWAY SEED

Warm, pungent, slightly bitter flavor with aniseed overtones. Complements cabbage, coleslaw, sauerkraut, potatoes, onions, carrots, pickles, cheese, goulash, pork, rye bread, cakes, biscuits and dumplings.

CORIANDER SEED

Mild, sweet, slightly pungent, citrus-like flavor with a hint of sage. Complements roast pork, poultry stuffing, curries, vegetables, pickles, lentils, Middle Eastern dishes, chutney, stewed fruit, cakes and biscuits.

DILL SEED

Similar to caraway in flavor. Complements pickles, soups, salads (cucumber, potato, and coleslaw), sauces, meats and fish, sauerkraut or boiled cabbage. For an interesting flavor, add a few seeds to an apple pie.

FENNEL SEED

Subtle, sweet anise-like flavor. Complements eggs, cheese, apples, pickles, rice, veal, pork, fish and potatoes/potato salad.

APPETIZERS

What a great place to start off a wonderful meal or gathering – by introducing the taste of fresh herbs in the first few bites! Herbs arouse the senses and get the appetite going. There are lots of recipes in this chapter, from amazing dips and spreads to sumptuous hors d'oeuvres that you can pop right into your mouth. It's worth hosting a cocktail party just so you can serve these delightful savory morsels.

Baked Brie with Pesto and Pine Nuts

This is an easy and elegant appetizer combining rich, smooth Brie and aromatic pesto.

1. Using a sharp knife, cut white rind off top of Brie, leaving sides and bottom intact. Place Brie cut side up in a glass pie plate or small baking pan.

2. Spread pesto over top of Brie; sprinkle with pine nuts.

3. Bake in a 400°F oven for 8 to 10 minutes or until heated through. (Or microwave on high for 1 to 2 minutes.) Serve immediately with assorted crackers.

MAKES 4 SERVINGS

1	round (4 oz) Brie cheese
2 tbsp	Basil Pesto (see page 162)
1 tbsp	pine nuts

VARIATION

Use walnuts to make pesto then top with 1/4 cup chopped walnuts. Walnuts grown in California have the best flavor.

Tomato Bruschetta

Pronounced "bru-sketa," this popular restaurant appetizer is a cinch to make at home. Make sure to add it to the menu in mid-summer when tasty, locally grown tomatoes and basil are in abundance.

1. Halve tomatoes; squeeze out seeds. Dice and place in a medium bowl.

2. Stir in basil, onion, 1 tbsp of the olive oil, garlic, season with salt and pepper. Let stand at room temperature for one hour. Taste and adjust seasoning.

3. Brush bread with remaining olive oil, if desired. Place on baking sheet; toast bread on both sides under broiler (watch carefully). Spoon tomato mixture on top and serve immediately.

   NOTE: Can be made with Roma tomatoes which have thick walls and a meaty texture. Quantity will vary with the size.

   TIP: Add a pinch of granulated sugar to tomato mixture when tomatoes are out of season.

MAKES 4 SERVINGS

1 lb	red or heirloom tomatoes (about 3 large)
3 tbsp	thinly sliced fresh basil
2 tbsp	finely chopped red onions or shallots
2 tbsp	olive oil, divided
1	clove garlic, minced or crushed
	Salt and pepper, to taste
16	1/2-inch diagonal slices Italian ciabatta or French stick

VARIATION

If desired, slice bread stick in half horizontally, then in diagonal slices. Each piece will have a crust on the bottom. Pieces will also be a bit thicker. Toast cut side up.

Mushroom Bruschetta

Here's a twist on popular tomato bruschetta for mushroom lovers! You can use your favorite mix of cultivated wild mushrooms. Serve as a party appetizer or with the salad course.

1. In a medium bowl, mix together mushrooms, green onions, cheese, parsley, thyme, 2 tbsp of the oil and vinegar.

2. Slice bread into slices 1/2 inch thick. Brush tops with the remaining 1 tbsp of the oil; toast under broiler until golden.

3. Top with mushroom mixture; broil until hot and bubbling. Serve hot.

MAKES 6 SERVINGS

8 oz	mushrooms (button or cremini), coarsely chopped
1/2 cup	chopped green onions
1/2 cup	grated Parmesan cheese
1/4 cup	finely chopped fresh parsley
2 tsp	finely chopped fresh thyme or lemon thyme
3 tbsp	olive oil, divided
1 tbsp	balsamic or red wine vinegar
1	baguette or French stick, about 18 inches long

Creamy Chive and Garlic Dip

To serve this dip as a spread, decrease sour cream to 1/4 cup. If dip is too thick, add more sour cream to reach desired consistency. Garnish with chive florets if desired.

1. In food processor, purée all ingredients until smooth. Chill for several hours to allow flavors to blend.

2. Serve with chopped raw vegetables or crackers.

   VARIATION: You may omit the garlic and substitute chives with 2 tbsp garlic chives.

MAKES ABOUT 1 CUP

1	pkg (8 oz) cream cheese, softened
1/2 cup	sour cream or plain yogurt (or Greek yogurt)
2	cloves garlic, minced
1/4 cup	chopped fresh chives
1/4 cup	chopped fresh parsley
	Pepper, to taste

Classic Spinach Dip in a Pumpernickel Bowl

Serve this dip with assorted raw vegetables, such as carrot and celery sticks, broccoli and cauliflower florets, mushrooms, and sweet pepper strips.

1. In a large bowl, mix together spinach, sour cream, mayonnaise, parsley, chives, dill, sweet pepper and lemon juice. Refrigerate for at least 1 hour to allow flavors to blend.

2. Slice top off bread; tear top into chunks. Remove center of bread in chunks, leaving a 1-inch thick crust to form bowl. Reserve bread chunks.

3. Just before serving, spoon dip into bread bowl. Place on serving platter; surround with bread chunks and raw vegetables.

MAKES 10 TO 12 SERVINGS

1	pkg (10 oz) frozen chopped spinach thawed and well drained
1 cup	sour cream or plain yogurt (or Greek yogurt)
1 cup	mayonnaise or creamy salad dressing
1/2 cup	chopped fresh parsley
1/4 cup	snipped fresh chives
2 tbsp	chopped fresh dill
2 tbsp	minced sweet red or yellow pepper
1 tbsp	lemon juice
1	round pumpernickel bread, unsliced

Creamy Tuna Dill Dip

This easy-to-make recipe can be doubled. Serve with carrot and celery sticks, sweet pepper and zucchini strips, and bread sticks.

1. In food processor, place tuna, cream cheese, onion, lemon juice, Worcestershire sauce and garlic. Process until smooth, scraping down sides with spatula.

2. Add mayonnaise and dill; pulse until well combined. Refrigerate up to two days.

MAKES 1 CUP

1	can (6 oz) flaked white tuna, well drained
1	pkg (4 oz) cream cheese, softened
1 tbsp	minced onion
1 tsp	lemon juice
1/2 tsp	Worcestershire sauce
1/2 tsp	minced garlic
2 tbsp	mayonnaise
2 tbsp	finely chopped fresh dill

VARIATIONS

- May also be made with flaked salmon, crab or chopped shrimp.
- Use 1 tbsp chopped fresh savory in place of dill.

Guacamole Dip

Serve guacamole as an accompaniment to Mexican dishes, such as tostadas, enchiladas, quesadillas and nachos.

1. Pit and peel avocados; mash with fork until chunky or smooth, as desired.

2. Stir in tomato, onion, lime juice, jalapenos and cilantro. Cover with plastic wrap; wrap should be directly on surface to avoid discoloration of avocado. Refrigerate until serving. Garnish with cilantro sprigs.

   NOTE: A ripe avocado gives to a gentle squeeze in your palm and is darker, almost black in color. If green and firm, it will take a few days to ripen. Refrigerating will slow the ripening process. It is a myth that putting the pit in the guacamole will keep it from browning. Sealing it from the air is best.

   The average avocado tree can produce about 150 fruits per year, some up to 500! Rudolph Hass from California is credited with planting the first tree in 1935 in his front yard! That chance seedling became the Mother Tree that he patented and sold graftings from.

MAKES ABOUT 2-1/2 CUPS

3	ripe large avocados
1	medium tomato, seeded and diced
1/4 cup	diced sweet onion
1 tbsp	lime juice
1 tbsp	minced jalapeño peppers
1 tbsp	finely chopped fresh cilantro (or to taste)
	Cilantro sprigs, for garnish

TIP

To remove the pit from the avocado, slice lengthwise into halves, then halve the half with the pit again (from the skin side) and pull the pit out. Scoop out flesh with spoon.

VARIATIONS

- Stir in diced sweet peppers, chopped chipotle peppers, diced mango, roasted corn, or roasted garlic (see Herb Roasted Garlic, page 203).

- Replace cilantro with chopped mint.

- Top with toasted green pumpkin seeds (pepitas), crumbled bacon, chopped chives, green onion, grated cotija cheese or feta cheese.

Hot Salsa and Cheese Dip

This quick dip is great for warming up from the inside after cool-weather outdoor activities, whether it's touch football, skating, skiing, tobogganing or a brisk walk. Or for a summer barbecue.

1. In a small saucepan over medium heat, place cream cheese, cream and salsa. Heat, stirring constantly, until cream cheese melts and all ingredients are blended.

2. Add Monterey Jack cheese; stir until smooth.

3. Remove from heat; stir in cilantro and chives. Serve warm with taco chips.

MAKES 4 TO 6 SERVINGS

1	pkg (8 oz) cream cheese
1 cup	table cream (18%)
1 cup	commercial salsa, (mild, medium or hot)
1 cup	shredded Monterey Jack cheese
2 tbsp	chopped fresh cilantro
1 tbsp	snipped fresh chives
	Taco chips

Salsa Dip

Serve this dip with corn tortilla chips, spoon it over baked potatoes, use it as a dip for cooked shrimp or serve with quesadillas.

1. Using electric mixer, beat cream cheese until smooth. Beat in sour cream.

2. Stir in salsa and cilantro.

MAKES ABOUT 1-1/2 CUPS

4 oz	cream cheese, softened
1/2 cup	sour cream
1/2 cup	salsa (store-bought or homemade, mild, medium or hot)
1/4 cup	chopped fresh cilantro

Zesty Bean Dip or Spread

Beans are an excellent source of fiber. This hummus-like dip/spread is lower in fat than recipes that use tahini (sesame-seed paste). It can be scooped up with crackers or dipped into with raw vegetables or Tortilla Crisps (see recipe below). To make a thinner dip, stir in about 1/4 cup plain low-fat yogurt.

1. In food processor, mince garlic. Add beans, oil, savory, lemon juice, salt, cumin and paprika; process until smooth. To make a thinner dip, stir in about 1/4 cup plain low-fat yogurt or a little water.

2. Spread onto a large plate (or spoon into a shallow bowl). Sprinkle top lightly with paprika; add parsley around edge to garnish.

3. Serve at room temperature. (May be made ahead and refrigerated up to 48 hours.)

MAKES 1-1/2 CUPS

2	cloves garlic
1 can	(14.5 oz or 19 oz) white kidney beans (cannellini) or white beans, drained and rinsed
1 tbsp	olive oil
1 tbsp	finely chopped fresh savory or dill
1 tbsp	lemon juice
1/4 tsp	*each*: salt, ground cumin, paprika
	Paprika and chopped fresh parsley, for garnish
	Tortilla Crisps (recipe follows)

Tortilla Crisps

1. Lightly brush both sides of each tortilla with a little olive oil. Cut each tortilla into 8 wedges; place in a single layer on a baking sheet.

2. Bake in a 375°F oven for 6 to 8 minutes, turning once, until crisp. Let cool. If desired, store in tightly covered container up to 24 hours. Re-crisp in warm oven if necessary.

MAKES 32 PIECES

4	large flour tortillas (any flavor)
2 tsp	(approx.) olive oil

VARIATIONS

- Substitute white pea beans, navy beans, black beans or chickpeas for the cannellini beans.

- Use fresh basil in place of savory, top with diced sun-dried tomatoes and toasted pine nuts.

- To increase the heat, add minced jalapeño peppers, hot pepper sauce or cayenne pepper.

- Substitute chopped fresh cilantro for the parsley.

Roasted Beet and Dill Hummus

I tasted a beet hummus and really liked it. Here is my rendition flavored with dill. Great way to get the goodness of beets and the hummus is high in fiber.

MAKES 2 CUPS

2	medium beets
1	small clove garlic
1 can	(14.5 oz or 19 oz) chickpeas, drained and rinsed
1/4	cup lemon juice
3 tbsp	tahini (sesame seed paste)
1 tbsp	*each*: sunflower oil, water
4 tsp	chopped fresh dill
1/2 tsp	onion powder
1/2	tsp salt
	Pepper, to taste

1. Cut tops off beets, leaving about 1 inch of the stem. Wrap individually in foil. Place on baking sheet; roast in a 375°F oven for about 1-1/2 hours, or until tender when pierced with knife. Let cool; slip off skins. Chop beets.

2. In food processor, chop garlic. Add beets, chickpeas, lemon juice, tahini, oil and water. Add more water if using for a dip vs. a spread. Purée until very smooth.

3. Pulse in dill, onion powder, salt and pepper. Refrigerate up to 3 days. Serve on crackers, as a dip for raw vegetables or as an addition to "Buddha bowls."

   NOTE: Serving suggestion – reserve 2 tbsp of the chickpeas and use to decorate top of hummus, along with chopped fresh dill and a drizzle of oil.

Cheddar Chive Spread

I developed this spread for crackers and soon discovered that it is terrific as a baked potato topping and as an alternative to cheese sauce on boiled cauliflower or broccoli. It's also a "cheese and celery sticks" spread for grown-ups.

1. In food processor, blend all ingredients until smooth. Keeps in refrigerator up to a week.

MAKES ABOUT 3/4 CUP

1-1/2 cups	shredded sharp (old) Cheddar cheese (about 5 oz)
1/4 cup	butter, softened
1/2 tsp	Dijon mustard
1 tbsp	finely chopped fresh chives

VARIATIONS

Lemon Dill Havarti Spread
Use Havarti cheese in place of Cheddar, add 1 tbsp chopped fresh dill and 1 tsp grated lemon zest. Toss with cooked pasta and shrimp, or vegetables.

Monterey Jack Cilantro Spread
Use Monterey Jack or Tex-Mex cheese in place of Cheddar, replace chives with 2 tbsp chopped fresh cilantro. Serve with tortilla crisps.

Herbed Chèvre Spread

This tasty spread was a hit at my herb cooking classes. Try it stuffed in blanched snow pea pods as an interesting appetizer.

1. In a medium bowl, mix together chèvre, ricotta and garlic until smooth.

2. Stir in parsley, basil and tarragon; season with pepper. Refrigerate for about 1 hour. To serve, bring to room temperature.

   NOTE: If the spread is too salty for your taste, add a bit more ricotta.

   VARIATION: For a dip, thin with a little milk to desired consistency.

MAKES ABOUT 2 CUPS

1-1/4 cups	chèvre cheese (at room temperature)
1/2 cup	ricotta cheese
2	cloves garlic, minced
1/4 cup	chopped fresh parsley
2 tbsp	chopped fresh basil
2 tbsp	chopped fresh tarragon
	Pepper, to taste
Pinch	cayenne pepper (optional)

Greek Red Pepper and Feta Spread

This spread has a rich satisfying flavor. Use as a dip or to stuff chicken breasts.

MAKES ABOUT
1-1/3 CUPS

2 tbsp	olive oil
1	large sweet red pepper, chopped
1/4 tsp	hot red pepper flakes
2 tsp	chopped fresh thyme or marjoram
8 oz	feta cheese, crumbled

1. In a large skillet over medium heat, heat oil. Add sweet pepper and pepper flakes. Cook, stirring often, until peppers are very soft, about 10 minutes.

2. Stir in thyme; cook for 1 minute. Remove from heat; let cool.

3. Scrape pepper/oil mixture from skillet into bowl of food processor; add feta. Pulse on and off until smooth. Transfer to serving bowl. Store, covered, in refrigerator up to a week. Bring to room temperature for serving. Serve with crackers or pita triangles.

VARIATION: Replace fresh peppers with 1 cup chopped roasted red peppers and cook for only 2 to 3 minutes.

Herbed Cream Cheese

This is similar to Boursin and Rondelé brands of herb spreads. It's great on bagels and crackers or with crusty bread, olives, sliced Italian salami and raw vegetables. Other ideas for using this spread: in scrambled eggs; on baked potatoes; as a stuffing for cherry tomatoes or blanched pea pods; stuffed into mushroom caps and baked; stirred into warmed heavy cream and sprinkled with Parmesan cheese as a sauce for pasta; as a spread for roast beef (see tarragon variation), chicken or turkey sandwiches.

1. In food processor, place cream cheese, butter and garlic; process until smooth. (May also be beaten with electric mixer in medium bowl.)

2. Add an herb mix; pulse several times until well mixed, scraping down sides. (If making in a bowl, stir in herbs.) Season with pepper (if using).

3. Refrigerate for several hours to blend flavors. Let rest at room temperature for about 30 minutes to soften to spreadable consistency. Keeps up to 5 days.

MAKES 1 CUP

1	pkg (8 oz) cream cheese, softened
2 tbsp	soft butter
1 or 2	cloves garlic, crushed (see page 92 about crushed garlic)
	Herb Mix (see list below)
	Coarsely ground pepper (optional)

VARIATIONS

(all finely chopped fresh herbs)

- 1 tbsp *each*: basil, chives and dill.

- 1 tbsp *each*: basil, marjoram and parsley

- 1 tbsp *each*: lemon thyme, oregano and parsley

- 1 tbsp *each*: parsley and chives and 2 tsp *each*: chervil and tarragon

- 2 tbsp chopped fresh parsley or chervil and 1 tbsp chopped chives

- Add 4 oz soft goat cheese such as chèvre.

- Omit butter, mix in 2 tbsp Olive and Sun-Dried Tomato Tapenade (see page 65) or Basil Pesto (see page 162).

- Use 1/2 tsp Herbes de Provence (see page 3), 1 tbsp chopped fresh parsley and 1 tsp red wine vinegar.

- Mix 1 tbsp finely chopped fresh dill and 1 tsp lemon juice and add to cream cheese; serve on bagels or pumpernickel bread with smoked salmon topped with thinly sliced red or sweet onion and capers.

Herb-Marinated Goat Cheese

Chèvre is a smooth goat cheese from France, but very good locally made renditions are quite delicious too. Herbs and garlic are a wonderful accent to its tangy flavor. Serve with crusty French bread (and a glass of French wine!) for an appetizer or snack. Use to make Baked Herbed Chèvre Salad (see page 90).

MAKES 4 TO 6 SERVINGS

8 oz	chèvre log
1/2 cup	olive oil (or Herb Oil, see page 27)
1/4 cup	chopped fresh basil
2 tsp	minced fresh rosemary, oregano or marjoram
1 tsp	minced fresh thyme or lemon thyme
1	clove garlic, minced
1/4 tsp	coarsely ground black pepper

1. Place chèvre log in freezer for about 30 minutes to make firm for easier slicing. Slice into 1/2-inch thick rounds. Place in shallow baking dish in single layer.

2. In a small bowl, whisk together oil, basil, rosemary, thyme, garlic and pepper. Pour over cheese; turn cheese to coat on both sides. Cover and refrigerate for at least 8 hours or overnight. Store up to 1 week in refrigerator. Bring to room temperature before serving.

VARIATIONS

- Use 1 tbsp Herbes de Provence (see page 3) instead of fresh herbs and add 1 tsp lemon juice.

- In a small saucepan over medium heat, heat the oil, garlic, 6 whole peppercorns, 1 bay leaf and pinch hot red pepper flakes, just until mixture bubbles. Remove from heat; stir in herbs and let cool. Pour over cheese.

- Place cheese rounds on toasted French stick rounds (slices). Place on baking sheet under broiler (about 6 inches from heat) until golden brown and bubbling.

- Marinated Feta Cheese: Use 1/2-inch cubes of feta instead of goat chèvre.

TIP

Use dental floss or fishing line to slice chèvre. Stretch floss between hands and press down on cheese log to make clean round slices.

Marinated Mushrooms

These mushrooms make a tasty addition to an antipasto platter or as an appetizer at a barbecue. To serve as a side salad, use larger mushrooms and thinly slice them or cut them into quarters.

1. Wash mushrooms well; trim stems.

2. In a large bowl, whisk together oil, lemon juice, salt, parsley, chives, thyme and a few grinds of pepper.

3. Add mushrooms; toss to coat well. Cover and refrigerate for 1 hour.

1 lb	small button mushrooms (about 1-inch diameter)
1/4 cup	oil
2 tbsp	lemon juice
1/4 tsp	salt
2 tbsp	finely chopped fresh parsley
1 tbsp	finely chopped chives
1 tsp	finely chopped fresh thyme or lemon thyme
	Pepper, to taste

Stuffed Mushroom Caps with Stilton and Bacon

I first tasted a recipe like this in London, England (hence the Stilton), served as an elegant starter. I could have eaten two!

1. Wipe mushrooms clean with a damp paper towel. Trim stem ends, then remove stems from caps with knife; finely chop stems and set aside. Remove brown gills with a spoon. Brush outside of caps with a little oil and place top down on a baking sheet; set aside.

2. In a large skillet over medium heat, cook bacon, onion and garlic for about 3 minutes, until bacon is partially cooked. Stir in chopped mushroom stems and thyme; cook until onion and mushrooms are soft. Stir in grated Parmesan cheese and parsley.

3. Fill mushroom caps with filling, top each with a slice of the Stilton and the shavings or thin slices of Parmesan cheese.

4. Bake in a 400°F oven for 10 to 12 minutes until caps are tender and cheese melts. Serve immediately.

   VARIATIONS: Fill with cooked quinoa in place of mushroom stems. Replace blue cheese with Gruyère. For vegetarian, omit bacon.

MAKES 4 SERVINGS

4	portobello mushrooms
	Olive oil
2	slices bacon, diced
1/4 cup	finely chopped onion or shallots
1	clove garlic, minced
1 tsp	finely chopped thyme, lemon thyme or rosemary (or 1/4 tsp Herbes de Provence, see page 3)
2 tbsp	grated Parmesan cheese
2 tbsp	finely chopped fresh parsley
4 oz	Stilton cheese, or other blue cheese
2 oz	Parmesan cheese, in shavings or thinly sliced

Mini Salmon Cakes
WITH LEMON DILL MAYONNAISE

These mini salmon cakes are a popular party hors d'oeuvre. Take to work for lunch or enjoy as a healthy snack.

1. Place salmon fillets skin side down on piece of foil or parchment paper large enough to enclose. Wrap and place on baking sheet. Bake in 425°F oven for 12 to 15 minutes or until salmon flakes in centre. Let cool slightly then lift salmon with spatula onto plate; remove skin and discard. Flake completely with fork.

2. In medium bowl, beat egg. Stir in salmon, mayonnaise, chives and cracker crumbs. Season with salt and pepper. Stir until well combined. Form, using heaping tablespoons, into small patties about 1-3/4 inches in diameter and 1/2 inch thick. Place on waxed paper.

3. Heat 2 tbsp oil in large non-stick skillet over medium heat. Fry patties in small batches for 1-1/2 minutes on each side until golden brown. Add more oil as needed. Place on paper towel; keep warm.

4. Serve as an appetizer topped with a dollop of Lemon and Dill Mayonnaise and a small sprig of dill for garnish. For casual fare, place mayo in bowl for dipping and surround with salmon cakes.

   VARIATION: Replace salmon with about 3 cups cooked crab meat.

MAKES 18 TO 20 MINI PATTIES OR 4 LARGE PATTIES FOR BURGERS

4	salmon fillets (6 oz each)
1	egg
1/4 cup	mayonnaise
1/4 cup	finely chopped fresh chives
12	soda crackers, crushed (or about 1/2 cup panko crumbs or dry breadcrumbs)
	Salt and pepper
2 to 4 tbsp	oil

Lemon and Dill Mayonnaise

1. In small bowl, whisk together mayonnaise, lemon rind and juice and dill. Refrigerate until ready to use. (May be made ahead and rewarmed.)

2/3 cup	mayonnaise
1 tsp	finely grated lemon rind
1 tbsp	lemon juice
1 tbsp	finely chopped fresh dill

Rosemary and Thyme Marinated Olives

In the Mediterranean, olives are set out as appetizers in bowls, or served with a lunch of bread and cheese or fruit. Use a variety of olives such as green or Kalamata.

1. In a large bowl, whisk together olive oil and lemon juice. Stir in garlic, rosemary, thyme and pepper. Stir in olives. Refrigerate for 1 or 2 days to blend flavors, stirring a few times.

2. Serve with pita, French, Italian or other bread. Can be stored in the refrigerator for several weeks.

   TIP: Give a jar of these olives as a host/hostess gift. Place a few sprigs of rosemary on the inside of the jar against the glass.

MAKES 4 CUPS

1/4 cup	extra-virgin olive oil
2 tbsp	fresh lemon juice
4	cloves garlic, cut into slivers
4 tbsp	chopped fresh rosemary
1 tbsp	chopped fresh thyme
	Pepper, to taste
4 cups	mixed olives

Mini Greek-Style Lamb Burgers

I call these mini burgers "lamb-burg-inis"; they are great to serve at a barbecue.

1. In a medium bowl, break up lamb using the back of a wooden spoon. Add breadcrumbs, egg, onion, parsley, mint, cinnamon, salt, pepper and garlic (if using; you may want to omit garlic if serving burgers with tzatziki). Stir until well combined.

2. Form mixture into 20 meatballs; flatten to form 1/2-inch thick patties. If not cooking immediately, arrange on a platter with waxed paper between layers; refrigerate, covered, up to 4 hours.

3. Preheat barbecue. Place burgers on oiled barbecue grill; grill over medium-high heat with lid closed for about 10 minutes, turning once halfway through cooking, until burgers are no longer pink inside.

4. With sharp knife, slit open each mini pita (or large pitas cut into quarters) to make pocket. Place a burger and a spoonful of tzatziki into each pocket.

VARIATION: Make into a sandwich, placing two burgers into large pita halves and adding shredded veggies and lettuce, or coleslaw.

MAKES 20

1 lb	ground lamb
1/3 cup	dry breadcrumbs
1	egg, beaten
1/4 cup	grated onion (1 small)
1/4 cup	*each*: chopped fresh parsley and mint
1/2 tsp	cinnamon
1/2 tsp	salt
1/4 tsp	black pepper
1	clove garlic, minced (optional)
20	mini pitas or mini burger buns, or 10 regular pitas
	Tzatziki (see page 165)

Olive and Sun-dried Tomato Tapenade

This tasty spread from Provence, in southern France, derives its name from the French word for capers. For an Italian *olivada*, omit capers and sun-dried tomatoes; use lemon juice in place of balsamic vinegar.

1. In food processor, place all ingredients. Pulse on and off until almost smooth.

2. Transfer to a serving bowl. Let rest at room temperature for about an hour to let flavors develop. Serve at room temperature with crackers or Crostini (recipe follows). To store, cover surface with thin layer of olive oil and plastic wrap; refrigerate up to 2 weeks.

MAKES 1 CUP

1 cup	pitted Kalamata olives
1/4 cup	chopped sun-dried tomatoes
1 or 2	cloves garlic
2 tbsp	olive oil
2 tbsp	finely chopped fresh curly or Italian parsley
1 tbsp	capers (optional)
2 tsp	finely chopped fresh rosemary
1 tsp	finely chopped fresh thyme or lemon thyme
1 tsp	balsamic vinegar
	Pepper, to taste

Crostini (little toasts)

1. Slice a baguette or French stick into 1/2-inch thick rounds. Arrange on a baking sheet. Bake in a 350°F oven for about 8 minutes on each side, until golden brown. While still warm, rub one side of each toast with a cut clove of garlic, then brush with a little olive oil. (If making ahead, store in an airtight container overnight at room temperature. Re-crisp in a 350°F oven for a few minutes before serving.)

TIP

Stir together equal amounts of tapenade and mayonnaise and serve with hard-cooked eggs, tomatoes, chicken, turkey or fish.

Smoked Salmon Terrine

My friend Rose brings this wonderful terrine to parties. There are never any leftovers and there are lots of requests for the recipe. Serve with rice crackers or small slices of pumpernickel bread.

1. In a medium bowl, mix together butter and mayonnaise. Add garlic, lemon juice, salt and pepper; mix well.

2. Drain salmon; remove skin and bones and flake with fork. Add salmon, dill, parsley, basil and chives to mayonnaise mixture; mix well.

3. Using kitchen scissors, snip smoked salmon into small bits; stir into canned salmon mixture.

4. Line a 2-cup bowl or mold with plastic wrap, leaving about 3 inches of wrap overhanging. If desired, place a sprig of dill in the bottom of the bowl. Pack mixture into bowl, flattening the surface. Refrigerate for at least 4 hours or up to 24 hours.

5. To serve, place plate over bowl; quickly turn plate and bowl over. Remove bowl and plastic wrap. If refrigerated for 24 hours, let stand at room temperature for 30 minutes before serving. Garnish plate with dill sprigs and lemon slices.

MAKES 8 TO 12 SERVINGS

1/4 cup	butter, softened
1/4 cup	mayonnaise
2	cloves garlic, minced
1/2 tsp	lemon juice
1/4 tsp	*each*: salt and pepper
1	can (7.5 oz) salmon
3 tbsp	*each*: finely chopped fresh dill and parsley
2 tbsp	*each*: finely chopped fresh basil and chives
4	slices smoked salmon (about 1/4 lb total)
	Dill sprigs and lemon slices, for garnish

Basil Pesto Torte

Bring this to your next party or make it for guests – they'll all want the recipe! Serve with water crackers as they are plain tasting and firm.

1. In food processor or a medium bowl, mix together cream cheese, chèvre and butter until well blended.

2. In a 7-inch springform pan, begin with a layer of half of the cheese mixture (just over 1-1/4 cups). Refrigerate for about 20 minutes to firm it up. Spread with pesto. Add dollops of remaining cheese. Carefully spread to cover pesto but not disturb it. Cover and refrigerate to firm it up.

   (If you do not have a springform pan, line a straight-sided bowl, of similar diameter, or a round casserole with plastic wrap. After chilling, invert torte onto a plate; remove plastic. Or leave if in a clear bowl.)

3. Arrange pine nuts on top in a spoked wheel pattern; fill in between spokes with sun-dried tomatoes. Garnish center with fresh basil sprig. Remove sides of pan and serve torte with assorted crackers.

MAKES 42 TO 54
APPETIZER SERVINGS

1	pkg (8 oz) cream cheese, softened
8 oz	chèvre (goat cheese), softened
1/2 cup	butter, softened
1 cup	Basil Pesto (see page 162)
1/2 cup	toasted pine nuts
1/2 cup	diced oil-packed, sun-dried tomatoes, (drain and blot on paper towel)
	Basil sprig, for garnish

TIP

Allow to warm at room temperature a bit before serving so that it is spreadable.

Mediterranean Tarts

This recipe has been adapted from the original, courtesy of the International Olive Oil Council. The flavorful vegetable filling for these tarts can be made a couple of days ahead. For speedy assembly, start with tiny pre-baked tart shells. If they are not available, make Toast Cups (recipe follows).

1. In a large skillet, heat oil over medium heat. Add onion, garlic and sweet peppers. Season with a little salt and pepper. Cook, stirring often, for about 30 minutes until onions and peppers are very soft.

2. Stir in oregano, rosemary and thyme; cook for 5 minutes longer.

3. Stir in basil and parsley; cook for 2 minutes longer. Remove from heat and stir in olives. Taste and adjust seasoning. (Mixture can be prepared up to 2 days ahead; keep refrigerated. Bring to room temperature to serve.)

4. To serve, spoon room-temperature mixture into tart shells or toast cups; garnish with small oregano sprigs or lemon thyme.

MAKES 3 DOZEN

3 tbsp	olive oil
1	large red onion, thinly sliced
2	cloves garlic, minced
1	*each*: sweet red and yellow pepper, thinly sliced
	Salt and pepper
1 tsp	*each*: minced fresh oregano, rosemary and thyme
1/3 cup	slivered fresh basil
2 tbsp	minced fresh parsley
1/4 cup	coarsely chopped pitted Kalamata olives
36	small baked tart shells (1-1/2-inch rounds)
	Small sprigs of fresh oregano, for garnish

Toast Cups

1. Cut crusts from 9 thin slices of white bread. Using a rolling pin, roll out bread flat; cut each slice into quarters. Press into greased mini-tart tins. (Or roll out enough bread to cut into rounds with a cookie cutter to fit mini-tart tins.) Brush lightly with olive oil. Bake in a 350°F oven for 5 to 7 minutes, or until crisp and golden. Let cool before filling. (Can be stored in an airtight container for several days.)

Tomato Tarts

Two great summer tastes – local-grown or home-grown tomatoes and fresh herbs! For appetizers, cut each tart into four squares or triangles after baking.

1. In a small bowl, mix together basil, marjoram, oil and garlic. Let stand.

2. On a floured surface, roll out each half of the pastry to a 10-inch square. Cut each into four 5-inch squares, to make 8 squares. Place on a large baking sheet.

3. Stir herb mixture and spread evenly over pastry squares. Top with tomato slices (about 3 per tart), overlapping slightly. Season with pepper and sprinkle with a little chèvre or Parmesan cheese.

4. Bake in a 400°F oven for 20 to 25 minutes or until pastry is crisp and golden. Serve warm.

   VARIATION: Before baking, drizzle with balsamic vinegar and top with chopped sun-dried tomatoes or black olives.

MAKES 8 TARTS OR 32 APPETIZERS

2 tbsp	finely chopped fresh basil
1 tbsp	finely chopped fresh marjoram
2 tsp	olive oil
1/2 tsp	crushed garlic
1	pkg (17.3 oz/450 g) butter puff pastry, thawed according to package directions
4	medium tomatoes, sliced very thinly
	Pepper, to taste
1/3 cup	crumbled chèvre or freshly grated Parmesan cheese

SOUPS

Herbs can be used in a bouquet garni to flavor stock, cooked directly into the soup, added at the end of cooking, or used to garnish the soup. A garnish may be as simple as a sprinkling of chopped fresh parsley, chiffonade of basil, blades or snips of chives, a sprig of dill, a swirl of pesto or pistou in vegetable soup, herbed croutons in a creamed soup, or edible flowers floating on a chilled summer soup.

Carrot, Orange and Thyme Soup

"Keep your cool" when you serve this delicious chilled soup. For a flavor switch, use fresh cilantro, chervil, dill, fennel, tarragon or lemon thyme.

1. In a large saucepan, heat oil over medium-low heat. Stir in carrots and onions; cover and cook for 8 minutes, stirring occasionally.

2. Add stock, thyme and bay leaf. Increase heat to high and bring to a boil. Reduce heat; cover and simmer for 15 to 20 minutes or until carrots are tender. Discard bay leaf.

3. Using a slotted spoon, transfer vegetables to food processor or blender; purée with a little soup stock until smooth. Return to saucepan.

4. Stir in orange juice. Season with salt and pepper; chill for at least 1 hour. (May be made a day ahead and refrigerated.) If desired, serve in chilled glass bowl.

5. Garnish with a drizzle or dollop of yogurt and a sprig of thyme, or sprinkle with chopped chives, chive florets or parsley.

MAKES 6 SERVINGS

3 tbsp	oil (or a mixture of oil and butter)
5 cups	sliced carrots
2	medium onions, sliced
4 cups	chicken or vegetable stock
2 tbsp	fresh thyme
1	bay leaf
1 cup	orange juice
	Salt and pepper, to taste
	Plain yogurt (such as Greek) or sour cream
	Thyme sprigs, chopped fresh chives, chive florets, chervil or parsley, for garnish

Cauliflower and Potato Soup

The fresh taste of the herbs really comes through when they are added just before serving. When chives are in flower, add a few florets to the herb mixture for added color.

1. In a Dutch oven, heat oil over medium heat. Add onions and celery (if using); cook for 7 minutes or until softened.

2. Add garlic, potatoes and bay leaf; cook, stirring, for about 2 minutes.

3. Stir in stock, cauliflower and carrots; increase heat to high and bring to a boil. Reduce heat; simmer for about 10 minutes or until all vegetables are tender.

4. Remove bay leaf. Remove about 3 cups of the vegetables and a small amount of the soup liquid. In food processor or blender, purée until smooth. Stir back into soup. Season with salt and pepper.

5. In a small bowl, mix together chives, dill and parsley. To serve, sprinkle each serving with mixed herbs.

   VARIATION: Use purple basil or marjoram in place of dill.

2 tbsp	oil
1	large onion, chopped
1/4 cup	diced celery (optional)
1	clove garlic, minced
2 cups	peeled, diced potatoes
1	bay leaf
6 cups	chicken or vegetable stock
6 cups	cauliflower florets
1 cup	diced carrots
	Salt and pepper, to taste
2 tbsp	*each:* finely chopped fresh chives, dill and parsley

Chicken Tortilla Soup
WITH CILANTRO

This delicious soup from Mexico is also popular in the U.S. southwest. I first tried it in Arizona. Cilantro is a must to give it the authentic taste. If desired, add jalapeño peppers to increase the heat.

1. In a large Dutch oven or large saucepan, heat oil over medium heat. Add onion, cook for about 5 minutes to soften. Add garlic; cook for 1 minute.

2. Add chicken and lightly brown.

3. Stir in spices; season with salt and pepper.

4. Stir in liquid, tomatoes and juice, beans, corn and salsa. Bring to boil. Reduce heat and simmer for 5 minutes to heat everything through. (Add more stock if using smaller can size for tomatoes.)

5. Place tortilla strips in large soup bowls; ladle soup on top. Add toppings of cilantro, avocado, cheese, and a squeeze of lime juice. Garnish with cilantro sprig if desired.

MAKES ABOUT
10-1/2 CUPS

1	tbsp oil
1	large onion, chopped
1	large clove garlic, minced
2	chicken breasts or thighs (boneless, skinless), chopped into bite-size pieces
1 tsp	*each:* ground cumin, chili powder, paprika or smoked paprika
	Salt and pepper, to taste
4 cups	chicken stock
1	can (14.5 oz or 19 oz) Petite Cut Tomatoes, including juice
1	can (14.5 oz or 19 oz) cooked black beans, drained and rinsed
1-1/2	cups frozen corn (canned corn, or barbecue roasted fresh corn)
1	cup mild salsa (or to taste)
	Tortilla Strips (commercial brands such as: Southwest or Chili Lime, made from corn tortillas) or see preparation on page 75.
	Toppings: chopped fresh cilantro (or parsley), diced avocados, shredded Monterey Jack or Cheddar cheese, or crumbled queso fresco or cow's milk feta and lime wedges.
	Cilantro sprigs, for garnish (optional)

Corn Tortilla Crisps

1. Cut tortillas in half then into 1/4-inch wide strips. (This is easy using kitchen scissors.)

2. Heat oil in medium saucepan over medium-high heat. Cook strips in batches, stirring, until light golden; remove with slotted spoon to paper towel-lined plate.

   Alternately, the strips can be baked at 350°F for about 10 minutes.

   VEGETARIAN: Use vegetable broth in place of chicken broth (add more to desired consistency). Add more salsa and cheese to replace the chicken, or use a vegetarian Chick'n substitute.

   VARIATIONS: In place of chicken, use leftover turkey. Add leftover cooked rice and increase the amount of broth.

6   six-inch corn tortillas

1/2   cup vegetable oil

Cool Cucumber Mint Soup

Serve this refreshing chilled soup as an appetizer or starter, topped with colorful chive blossoms. It has eye *and* appetite appeal, and is low-fat and quick to prepare.

1. Cut cucumber into chunks and place in food processor or blender with garlic; process until cucumber is well chopped.

2. Add stock, yogurt, mint and lemon juice; process until smooth. Season with salt and pepper. Chill for at least 3 hours. Serve chilled in a chilled glass or glass bowl; garnish with mint leaves, chopped chives or chive flowers.

   TIP: Soup may be made with regular cucumber. Peel and remove seeds first.

   NOTE: English cucumbers have soft skins and do not need to be peeled.

MAKES 4 SERVINGS

1	English cucumber
1	clove garlic
1 cup	chicken or vegetable stock, chilled
1 cup	plain yogurt
1/4 cup	chopped fresh mint
1 tsp	lemon juice
	Salt and pepper, to taste
	Mint leaves, chopped fresh chives or chive florets, for garnish

Gazpacho

This cool summer soup is best made when tomatoes are in season and at their best. This dish has its origin in Andalusia in southern Spain. Gazpacho recipes often don't include breadcrumbs, but it is the secret ingredient that keeps the soup from separating. Choose some of the interesting toppings listed below to serve in small bowls with the soup. It's a fun starter to serve at parties.

1. In blender or food processor, combine tomatoes, onions, cucumber, green pepper, garlic and olive oil; purée to desired consistency (chunky or smooth).

2. Add breadcrumbs, basil, lemon juice, vinegar, and Worcestershire and hot pepper sauces. Pulse to blend in. Season with salt and pepper. If desired, add more hot pepper sauce.

3. Chill for at least 1 hour before serving to allow flavors to develop. Serve with small bowls of toppings.

   VARIATION: Use fresh cilantro or dill in place of basil. Use herb vinegar (basil, tarragon, dill) in place of red wine vinegar.

MAKES 4 TO 6 SERVINGS

3 cups	peeled, seeded chopped tomatoes
1/2 cup	finely chopped sweet onions or shallots
1	field cucumber, peeled and seeded
1	sweet green pepper, chopped
1	clove garlic, minced
3 tbsp	olive oil
1 cup	soft fresh breadcrumbs
3 tbsp	chopped fresh basil
1 tbsp	lemon or lime juice
2 tbsp	red wine vinegar
1/2 tsp	Worcestershire sauce
1/4 tsp	hot pepper sauce or cayenne pepper
	Salt and pepper, to taste
	Toppings: diced red onions, sliced green onions, chopped tomato, chopped sweet yellow pepper, chopped cucumber, chopped hard-cooked egg, Parsleyed Croutons (see page 101)

Green Pea Soup
WITH MINT

This soup has just a hint of mint to set off the fresh taste of the peas. It is great served hot or cold.

1. In a Dutch oven or large saucepan, heat butter and oil over medium heat until butter foams. Stir in leeks; cook, stirring, for 5 minutes.

2. Stir in potatoes; cook for 3 minutes.

3. Stir in flour; cook for 2 minutes, stirring often.

4. Stir in stock, peas and bay leaf. Increase heat to high and bring to a boil. Reduce heat; cover and simmer for 15 minutes.

5. Remove bay leaf; stir in mint.

6. In food processor, purée in batches until smooth. If serving hot, return to pot and heat through. Serve with a drizzle of whipping cream and croutons. If serving cold, refrigerate for at least 1 hour and serve with a dollop of sour cream or yogurt. Garnish with mint sprigs or chives.

MAKES 6 TO 8 SERVINGS

2 tbsp	butter
1 tbsp	oil
2 cups	chopped leeks, white and light green parts only
1 cup	peeled, diced potato
2 tbsp	all-purpose flour
6 cups	chicken or vegetable stock
5 cups	fresh or frozen peas
1	bay leaf
2 tbsp	finely chopped fresh mint
	Whipping cream, sour cream or plain yogurt
	Parsleyed Croutons (see page 101)
	Fresh mint sprigs or chives, for garnish

VARIATION

Use fresh chervil in place of thyme.

Minestrone

Here's a quick and hearty vegetable and pasta soup, with a touch of herbs. Serve with thick slices of whole grain bread for a satisfying dinner.

1. In a large saucepan or Dutch oven, heat oil over medium heat. Add onion and cook, stirring often, for 7 minutes or until softened.

2. Stir in garlic and zucchini; cook, stirring often, for 3 minutes.

3. Stir in stock, tomatoes (with juice), mixed beans, green beans and oregano. Increase heat to high and bring to a boil. Reduce heat and simmer for 10 minutes.

4. Stir in orzo; simmer 5 minutes. Stir in basil and parsley. Season with salt and pepper.

5. Sprinkle 1 tbsp Parmesan cheese over each serving.

   VARIATION: Serve with a dollop of homemade Basil Pesto (see page 162); omit basil and parsley.

   NOTE: Orzo is a small, rice-shaped pasta. Use in soups or to replace rice in salads.

MAKES 6 SERVINGS

2 tbsp	olive oil
1	large onion, chopped
2	cloves garlic, minced
1	medium zucchini, quartered lengthwise and sliced
6 cups	chicken or vegetable stock
1	can (14.5 or 19 oz) diced tomatoes
1	can (15.5 or 19 oz) mixed beans, drained and rinsed (or 2 cups cooked beans, such as Romano, chickpeas, red or white kidney beans)
2 cups	frozen cut green beans
1/2 tsp	dried oregano or 1 tbsp chopped fresh marjoram
1/3 cup	orzo or small soup pasta
1/3 cup	*each*: chopped fresh basil and parsley
	Salt and pepper, to taste
6 tbsp	grated Parmesan cheese

Soupe au Pistou

A thick, hearty vegetable soup that is Provence, France's take on Minestrone. Its finishing touch is a refreshing and garlicky dollop of pistou, which is like pesto but without the pine nuts, and sometimes without cheese. Provence borders on Italy, close to Genoa where basil and pesto are popular, so no wonder there are similarities. Seconds anyone? Mais oui!

1. In a large saucepan or Dutch oven over medium heat, heat oil. Add onion and cook, stirring often, for 7 minutes or until softened.

2. Stir in stock, potatoes, zucchini, carrots, bay leaf and thyme. Increase heat to high and bring to a boil. Reduce heat, cover and simmer for 8 minutes.

3. Stir in green beans, tomatoes and white beans. Cover and cook 5 minutes more or until all vegetables are tender. Season with salt and pepper. Serve with a dollop of Pistou in the centre.

MAKES ABOUT 12 CUPS

1 tbsp	oil
1-1/2 cups	diced onion or chopped leeks (white and light green parts)
6 cups	vegetable or chicken stock
2 cups	chopped peeled potatoes (1/2-inch pieces)
2 cups	chopped zucchini or yellow summer squash (1/2-inch pieces)
1 cup	diced carrots
1	dried bay leaf
1 tsp	finely chopped fresh thyme leaves (or 1/2 tsp dried)
1 cup	fresh or frozen green beans (cut in 1-inch lengths)
1	can (14.5 oz or 19 oz) petite cut tomatoes or (2 cups diced tomatoes and 1/2 cup more stock)
1	can (15.5 oz or 19 oz) cooked white beans or navy beans (drained and rinsed)
	Salt and pepper, to taste
	Pistou (see page 81)

Pistou

Pistou originates in Provence, France which borders with Liguria, Italy. Genoa is the birthplace of pesto which is similar to pistou but uses pine nuts. Traditionally this would be made with a mortar and pestle: crush garlic with a pinch of salt. Then grind in basil until in small bits. Blend in cheese and olive oil to a smooth texture.

1. In a food processor, finely chop garlic. Add basil; process until finely chopped.

2. Blend in olive oil. Add cheese, if using. Texture should be a bit runny. Add more olive oil if necessary.

2	large cloves garlic
1-1/2 cups	lightly packed fresh basil leaves
1/3 cup	olive oil
1/3 cup	grated Parmesan, Compté or Gruyère cheese (optional)

Squash and Sweet Potato Chowder

Here's a great soup to warm up with on chilly fall days. If desired, drizzle with a little sage oil (see page 27 for making herb oils) before serving.

1. In a large saucepan, heat oil over medium heat. Stir in onion, garlic and potatoes. Cook until onions are soft, stirring occasionally.

2. Add stock, thyme and bay leaf. Increase heat to high and bring to a boil. Reduce heat; cover and simmer 7 minutes or until potatoes are soft.

3. Stir in squash, beer and salt; season with pepper. In blender or food processor, purée soup until smooth. Heat through and serve garnished with chives, Parsleyed Croutons or Fried Sage Leaves.

MAKES 4 TO 6 SERVINGS

2 tbsp	vegetable oil
1	large onion, chopped
1	clove garlic, minced
3 cups	diced peeled sweet potatoes or potatoes
3 cups	chicken or vegetable stock
1 tsp	chopped fresh thyme
1	fresh or dried bay leaf
2 cups	cooked mashed butternut squash or pumpkin (or 14 oz canned pumpkin)
1/2 cup	beer or milk
1/4 tsp	salt
	Pepper, to taste
	Snipped fresh chives
	Parsleyed Croutons (see page 101) or Fried Sage Leaves (see page 139), for garnish

Tortellini Soup

Buy ready-made frozen tortellini to have on hand for this soup. It's quick to make and makes a delicious meal served with a loaf of fresh Italian bread. *Mangia!*

1. In a large saucepan, heat oil over medium heat. Add onion and carrots; cook for 7 minutes or until carrots are softened.

2. Add zucchini and green pepper; cook for 3 minutes.

3. Add tomatoes (with juice) and stock. Increase heat to high; bring to a boil.

4. Stir in tortellini; reduce heat and simmer for 15 to 18 minutes or until tortellini are tender (take one out to test).

5. Stir in parsley and basil. Pour into serving bowls; sprinkle with Parmesan cheese.

MAKES 8 SERVINGS

2 tbsp	olive oil
1	medium onion, chopped
1 cup	chopped carrots
2 cups	chopped zucchini
1/2 cup	diced green pepper
1	can (28 oz) tomatoes
5 cups	chicken or vegetable stock
2 cups	frozen tortellini (meat- or cheese-filled)
1/2 cup	chopped fresh parsley
1/4 cup	chopped fresh basil
	Grated Parmesan cheese, to taste

Tuscan Tomato and Bread Soup
(PAPPA ALA POMODORO)

My friend Sandra introduced me to this yummy soup. For us this is dinner! She loves all types of soups and we have enjoyed many bowls together. Make it with fresh tomatoes in summer but it is also good made with canned tomatoes in winter. Her tip for extra flavor is to add the leftover rind of the block of Parmesan once it has been all grated (remove before serving).

1. In a large Dutch oven, heat oil over medium heat. Add onion, cook, stirring occasionally until softened, about 5 minutes. Add garlic; cook for 1 minute.

2. Stir in tomatoes, broth, brown sugar, thyme and pepper flakes. Use potato masher to crush tomatoes a bit. When hot, stir in bread and rind of Parmesan cheese, if using. Cover and reduce heat to simmer until the bread is completely soft but small pieces remain, about 30 minutes.

3. Stir in basil. Simmer uncovered for about 5 minutes more. Remove rind. Season with salt and pepper. Soup will be thick and porridge-like.

4. Ladle into bowls. Top with cheese and garnish with basil, if desired.

MAKES 4 SERVINGS

2 tbsp	olive oil
1 cup	diced onion
1 tbsp	finely chopped garlic
3 cups	diced peeled Roma tomatoes, or 1 can (28 oz) diced tomatoes and juice
3 cups	chicken or vegetable broth
2 tsp	brown sugar
1-1/2 tsp	finely chopped fresh thyme (or 1/2 tsp dried)
	Pinch crushed red pepper flakes
2 cups	torn small pieces, stale sourdough, Italian or French bread
1/4 cup	chopped fresh basil
	Salt and pepper, to taste
1/2 cup	grated Parmesan or Asiago cheese
	fresh basil leaves, for garnish

Zesty Tomato and Dill Soup

When local tomatoes are abundant, make this soup using 3 cups chopped tomatoes and increase stock to 2 cups. I enjoy making it all year long. It's a great starter soup too.

1. In a large saucepan, heat oil over medium heat. Stir in onion; cook for 7 minutes or until soft. Stir in garlic; cook for 1 minute more.

2. Stir in tomatoes (with juice), stock, chili sauce, sugar and hot pepper sauce. Increase heat to high; bring to a boil. Reduce heat; cover and simmer for 10 minutes.

3. Stir in fresh dill and season with pepper. Remove about 2 cups of the soup and purée in blender or food processor until smooth; stir back into soup.

4. Serve soup hot with 1 tbsp of sour cream in the center of each serving; or chopped fresh dill for a garnish.

   VARIATION: Use fresh basil in place of dill; garnish with sprig of basil. Replace sour cream with grated Parmesan cheese.

MAKES 4 SERVINGS

1 tbsp	oil or butter
1	medium onion, chopped
1	clove garlic, minced
1	can (28 oz) diced tomatoes
1 cup	chicken or vegetable stock
1/2 cup	commercial chili sauce
1 tsp	brown sugar
1/2 tsp	hot pepper sauce, or to taste
2 tbsp	finely chopped fresh dill
	Pepper, to taste
4 tbsp	sour cream
	Dill sprigs or chopped fresh dill, for garnish

Wild Mushroom Soup
WITH THYME

Dried wild mushrooms are easy to find in supermarkets nowadays. They come packaged as individual types as well as mixed. This soup has a rich, earthy taste, sure to be savored by mushroom aficionados.

1. Trim any tough stems from the dried mushrooms. Rinse and soak dried mushrooms in hot water for 30 minutes. Drain, reserving liquid; chop mushrooms.

2. In a large saucepan over low heat, melt butter. Add onions; cover and cook for 10 to 12 minutes or until very tender and golden.

3. Add garlic; cook for 2 minutes. Stir in flour; cook for 1 minute.

4. Stir in dried mushrooms and reserved liquid, fresh mushrooms, stock and thyme. Increase heat to high; bring to a boil. Reduce heat; cover and simmer for 40 minutes or until mushrooms are tender.

5. Strain soup, reserving 3 cups of liquid. Purée soup until smooth. Return purée and reserved liquid to saucepan. Stir in cream; season with salt and pepper. Garnish with parsley and thinly sliced mushrooms, or with Parsleyed Croutons.

MAKES 4 SERVINGS

1 oz	mixed dried mushrooms (such as porcini, chanterelle, and morel)
1/4 cup	butter
2	medium onions, chopped
1	small clove garlic, minced
3 tbsp	all-purpose flour
1 lb	sliced fresh mushrooms
5 cups	chicken or vegetable stock
1 tbsp	finely chopped fresh thyme
1 cup	whipping cream (35%)
	Salt and pepper, to taste
2 tbsp	finely chopped fresh parsley
	Thinly sliced mushrooms, Enoki mushrooms or Parsleyed Croutons (see page 101), for garnish

NOTE

Thyme is the ideal herb for cooked mushrooms and mushroom dishes.

Zucchini Basil Soup

This soup is a favorite of mine to make in the summer when zucchini and fresh basil are both plentiful, but it is enjoyable year-round.

1. In a large saucepan or Dutch oven, heat oil over medium heat. Add onion and cook, stirring often, for 7 minutes or until softened.

2. Add garlic and zucchini; cook, stirring occasionally, for 3 minutes.

3. Stir in stock, lemon juice and sugar. Increase heat to high; bring to a boil. Reduce heat and simmer, uncovered, for about 15 minutes, or until zucchini is tender. Stir in basil; simmer for 1 minute longer.

4. In blender or food processor, purée soup in small batches until smooth. Return to saucepan to heat through.

5. Spoon into serving bowls. Spoon 1 tbsp of the yogurt in the center of each serving; garnish with a sprig of basil and a sprinkle of paprika.

MAKES 4 SERVINGS

1 tbsp	oil
1	medium onion, chopped
2	cloves garlic, minced
5	medium zucchini, chopped
4 cups	chicken or vegetable stock
1 tbsp	lemon juice
2 tsp	granulated sugar
1/3 cup	chopped fresh basil
4 tbsp	plain yogurt or sour cream
	Basil sprigs and paprika, for garnish

TIP

Use food processor to shred zucchini to save preparation and cooking time.

SALADS AND DRESSINGS

Herbs are eaten fresh in salads, either as an ingredient in the salad itself or to flavor the dressing. Salads range from fresh leafy greens to crisp colorful vegetables, from bread and pasta salads to mixtures of hearty grains and legumes, and can be served as appetizers or main courses. Edible flowers and herb flowers can be used to accent visual appeal.

Baked Herbed Chèvre Salad

This is a delicious starter salad, topped with warm cheese rounds.

1. Lift cheese from marinade and coat well in breadcrumbs, pressing to coat on both sides. Transfer cheese rounds to baking sheet; bake in a 425°F oven for 4 to 6 minutes, or until cheese softens and crumbs are golden.

2. Place about 2 cups salad greens on each of four individual plates. Top with cheese rounds. Sprinkle with chives, or chive florets, if using. Drizzle with Vinaigrette and serve immediately.

MAKES 4 SERVINGS

	Herb Marinated Goat Cheese (see page 59)
1/3 cup	fine dry breadcrumbs
8 cups	mixed salad greens (mesclun): radicchio, watercress, arugula, endive, etc.
	Chopped chives, or chive florets (optional)
	Vinaigrette (recipe follows)

Vinaigrette

1. Whisk together all ingredients.

MAKES 1/2 CUP

1/3 cup	olive oil
2 tbsp	red wine or herb vinegar
1 tsp	Dijon mustard
1 tsp	granulated sugar
1/2 tsp	paprika
1	clove garlic, minced
	Salt and pepper, to taste

Bean Salad

Ever-popular bean salad is especially nice in the summer made with garden-fresh beans. It's commonly made with kidney beans, but these can be replaced with other types of beans or legumes, such as Romano or cannellini beans, chickpeas or bean mixtures.

1. In a small bowl, whisk together oil, vinegar, sugar, lemon juice, garlic, hot pepper sauce and a little salt and pepper; set aside.

2. In a large bowl, mix together green beans, kidney beans, sweet pepper, onion and savory. Pour dressing over salad; taste and adjust seasoning. Cover and refrigerate for at least 2 hours to allow flavors to blend.

MAKES 4 TO 6 SERVINGS

1/3 cup	olive oil
2 tbsp	red wine or cider vinegar
1 tsp	granulated sugar
1 tsp	lemon juice
1	clove garlic, crushed
	Hot pepper sauce, to taste
	Salt and pepper, to taste
1 lb	crisp-cooked green beans (or half green and half yellow beans), chopped
1	can (15.5 or 19 oz) kidney beans, drained and rinsed
1/2 cup	chopped sweet yellow or red pepper
1/2 cup	chopped red onion
1 tbsp	finely chopped fresh savory

Chicken Cobb Salad
WITH CREAMY TARRAGON-CHIVE DRESSING

This legendary salad was created by Robert Cobb at Hollywood's Brown Derby restaurant in the late 1930's (it closed in 1985). The tarragon and chive dressing brings it to new heights.

1. Grill or oven-roast chicken; slice into strips. In large skillet, fry bacon pieces until crisp; drain on paper towel.

2. Divide lettuce among four large plates. Arrange chicken, tomatoes and hard-cooked eggs on lettuce. Sprinkle salads with avocado, bacon bits and blue cheese. Drizzle salad with dressing.

MAKES 4 SERVINGS

1 lb	boneless, skinless chicken breasts or turkey
6	slices bacon, cut into 1/2-inch pieces
10 cups	torn lettuce pieces (romaine, Boston, iceberg or a mixture)
20	cherry or grape tomatoes, halved
4	hard-cooked eggs, quartered
1	large, semi-firm avocado, diced
4 oz	blue cheese, crumbled
	Creamy Tarragon-Chive Dressing (recipe follows)

Creamy Tarragon-Chive Dressing

This dressing also makes a tasty dip for shrimp. If desired, add 4 oz crumbled blue cheese to the dressing and use as a delicious sauce for steak, or dip for chicken wings.

1. In a medium bowl, mix together mayonnaise, sour cream, vinegar, honey and garlic until smooth.

2. Stir in chives and tarragon.

MAKES ABOUT 1-1/2 CUPS

3/4 cup	mayonnaise
1/2 cup	sour cream
2 tbsp	red wine or cider vinegar
1 tbsp	honey
1	large clove garlic, crushed
3 tbsp	chopped fresh chives
1	tbsp chopped fresh tarragon

TIP

To make garlic into more of a paste, after mincing it, sprinkle with a bit of salt while on cutting board. Press edge of a large knife into it to grind into a paste.

Couscous and Chickpea Salad

This is a great salad for summer barbecues, or to take along for a pot-luck. Feel free to add your own variations. If desired, add 2 cups cooked chicken in place of chickpeas; omit currants and stir in 1-1/2 cups diced mango. If desired, use 1/2 cup chopped fresh basil or cilantro in place of mint.

Dressing
1. Whisk together all ingredients; set aside.

Salad
1. In a medium saucepan over high heat, bring stock and butter (if using) to boil. Remove from heat; stir in couscous. Cover and let stand for 10 minutes. Fluff with fork.

2. In a large bowl, mix together couscous, currants and remaining ingredients, except pine nuts. Stir in dressing until well mixed. Cover and let stand at room temperature for about 1 hour. (May be refrigerated overnight; bring to room temperature before serving.) Just before serving, stir in pine nuts.

   TIP: Plump currants by placing them in a small dish, pour boiling water over to just cover; let stand for 5 minutes. Drain well; pat dry on paper towel.

MAKES ABOUT 12 SIDE-DISH SERVINGS

DRESSING

1/2 cup	olive oil
1/2 cup	lemon juice
1 tsp	minced garlic
1/2 tsp	ground cumin
2 to 4 drops	hot pepper sauce
	Salt and pepper, to taste

SALAD

3 cups	chicken or vegetable stock
2 tbsp	butter (optional)
2 cups	couscous
2/3 cup	currants (plump in boiling water for 5 minutes; blot on paper towel
1	can (19 oz) chickpeas, drained and rinsed
2/3 cup	diced sweet red or yellow pepper
1/2 cup	sliced green onions (about 4)
1/2 cup	chopped parsley
1/4 cup	chopped fresh mint
1/3 cup	toasted pine nuts

Greek Salad

The Greek Islands are known for oregano, and its taste comes through in this popular salad. Traditional recipes do not include lettuce; replace lettuce with additional cucumber and tomatoes, if desired. Add 1 tsp dried oregano to the dressing if you cannot get fresh.

1. In a large salad bowl, combine lettuce, tomatoes, cucumber, red pepper, onion, oregano, mint and parsley (if using) and olives. Cover and refrigerate until serving.

2. In a small glass measuring cup, whisk together vinegar and lemon juice. Slowly whisk in olive oil. Set aside.

3. When ready to serve, whisk dressing and pour desired amount over salad; toss to coat well. Season with salt and pepper. Top with feta cheese.

   NOTE: Oregano, which translates as "joy of the mountain", was grown first in Greece then adopted by the Romans. It became popular in North America when it was brought back from Italy in the 1940's by soldiers after the war.

   VARIATION: Replace cucumbers with about 2 cups cubed watermelon. Add just before serving as it will release juices.

MAKES 4 SERVINGS	
4 cups	torn iceberg lettuce or mesclun mix
4	large, ripe tomatoes, cut into wedges (or 3/4 lb cherry tomatoes, halved)
1	medium English cucumber (unpeeled), thinly sliced or chopped
1	large sweet red or yellow pepper, chopped into large chunks
1/2 cup	thinly sliced sweet onion
2 tbsp	chopped fresh oregano
2 tbsp	chopped fresh mint leaves (optional)
1 tbsp	chopped fresh parsley (optional)
16	Kalamata olives
2 tbsp	red wine vinegar
1/2 tsp	lemon juice
6 tbsp	olive oil
	Salt and pepper, to taste
4 oz	feta cheese, crumbled or broken into small pieces

Green Goddess Dressing

Serve this on a salad of greens, topped with avocado slices, shrimp and/or hard-cooked eggs.

1. In food processor, blend tarragon, parsley, chives and garlic, if using. Add sour cream, mayonnaise, oil, lemon juice, anchovy paste and a little salt and pepper; purée just until smooth. Chill for several hours to thicken.

2. Taste and adjust seasoning. Use within 3 days.

MAKES ABOUT 1-2/3 CUPS

1/2 cup	*each*: loosely packed fresh tarragon and parsley
1/2 cup	snipped fresh chives or garlic chives
1	small clove garlic (optional)
1/2 cup	*each*: sour cream and mayonnaise
4 tbsp	olive oil
2 tbsp	lemon juice
2 tsp	anchovy paste
	Salt and pepper, to taste

Herb Salad

Basil, tarragon and chervil all have anise or licorice undertones, making them ideal salad companions. They are used here with the perfect backdrop of mild-tasting lettuces. Substitute with 12 cups mesclun mix, if desired. Make use of herb flowers or other edible flowers for the finishing touch.

Salad

1. Tear lettuce leaves into bite-size pieces and place in large bowl. Toss with herbs; refrigerate until serving.

2. Just before serving toss with a little Vinaigrette to taste. Garnish with herb flowers and other edible flowers.

Vinaigrette

1. In a small bowl, whisk together vinegar, mustard, sugar, salt and pepper.

2. Slowly whisk in oil. Store in refrigerator up to 4 weeks.

   NOTE: All flowers of culinary herbs are edible. The flavor will be similar to the herb it comes from. In some cases, such as with chive flowers, the taste will be quite strong, so separate the flower heads into small florets.

SALAD

1	head red leaf lettuce
1	head Boston lettuce
2 cups	coarsely chopped fresh basil or purple basil
1 cup	coarsely chopped fresh tarragon
1 cup	coarsely chopped fresh chervil
1 cup	chopped fresh chives
	Vinaigrette (recipe follows)
	Herb flowers and other edible flowers (see Edible Flowers, page 38), for garnish

VINAIGRETTE

1/4 cup	white wine or herb vinegar (such as chive blossom, purple basil or tarragon)
1 tsp	Dijon mustard or Herb Mustard (see page 29)
1/2 tsp	granulated sugar
1/4 tsp	salt
	Pepper, to taste
1 cup	sunflower oil

Herbed Asparagus Salad

This salad is a perfect side dish for grilled fish or chicken – crispy, barely cooked fresh asparagus spears in a tangy herb vinaigrette. When fresh local asparagus is in season, here's a new way to enjoy!

Salad

1. Put asparagus in a medium saucepan of boiling water; return to boil and cook for 3 to 4 minutes or just until tender. Drain asparagus; chill in cold water. Drain again; dry on paper towel.

2. In a medium bowl, mix together asparagus, water chestnuts and onion.

Dressing

1. In a small bowl, whisk together oil, vinegar, dill, mustard, sugar, garlic and salt and pepper.

2. Pour over salad; toss to coat well. Salad may be made up to 4 hours ahead and refrigerated.

SALAD

1 lb	asparagus, cut into 1-1/2-inch pieces
3/4 cup	sliced water chestnuts
1/4 cup	diced red onion (or cut into slivers)

DRESSING

2 tbsp	*each*: oil and white wine vinegar
1 tbsp	finely chopped fresh dill or tarragon
1 tsp	Dijon mustard
1/4 tsp	granulated sugar
1	small clove garlic, crushed
	Salt and pepper, to taste

Marinated Vegetable and Chickpea Salad

This is a great make-ahead salad that is full of crunchy vegetables. The chickpeas add a boost of fiber. Serve with roasted or grilled chicken, pork kebabs or sausage.

1. In a large saucepan of boiling water, cook cauliflower and carrots until tender crisp, about 2 minutes. Drain and plunge into cold water; drain well and place in large bowl. Add zucchini, peppers and chickpeas.

2. Whisk together marinade ingredients, pour over vegetables and toss. Cover tightly with plastic wrap or transfer to large zip-lock bag. Refrigerate for at least 4 hours or up to 2 days. Stir mixture or turn bag occasionally.

MAKES ABOUT 10 CUPS

SALAD

3 cups	bite-size pieces of cauliflower
2 cups	thinly sliced carrots
2	small zucchini, sliced
1	red pepper, cut into bite-size pieces
1	green pepper, cut into bite-size pieces
1	can (15.5 or 19 oz) chickpeas, drained and rinsed

MARINADE

1/2 cup	olive oil
1/4 cup	red wine vinegar
2	cloves garlic, minced
2 tbsp	*each*: finely chopped fresh basil and parsley
1 tbsp	finely chopped fresh oregano, marjoram or savory (or 1 tsp dried)
1 tsp	granulated sugar
	Salt and pepper, to taste

Mesclun Salad
WITH HEIRLOOM TOMATOES AND PESTO DRESSING

With basil's affinity for tomatoes, this pesto dressing brings out the best. There are many types of heirloom tomatoes available in supermarkets now, so choose a variety of different ones.

1. Divide salad mix, tomatoes, sun-dried tomatoes and pine nuts between 4 serving plates. (Or combine in a salad bowl).

2. Pour some of the Pesto Dressing over each salad and top with shaved Parmesan. (Or toss dressing with salad in bowl and top with shave Parmesan).

   VARIATION: If desired, substitute some of the mesclun mix with arugula.

MAKES 4 SERVINGS

8 cups	mesclun salad mix
4	heirloom tomatoes, chopped
1/4 cup	chopped sun-dried tomatoes
1/4 cup	toasted pine nuts
1/2 cup	shaved Parmesan cheese
	Pesto Dressing (recipe follows)

Pesto Dressing

1. In a small bowl or glass measuring cup, whisk together pesto, vinegar and oil.

MAKES 1/2 CUP

2 tbsp	Basil Pesto (see page 162)
1 tbsp	white wine vinegar
1/4 cup	olive oil

Orzo Salad

Orzo is a tiny rice-shaped pasta that works well in this Greek-style salad. Serve with lamb, pork or chicken kebabs.

1. In a large saucepan of boiling, salted water, cook orzo just until tender; drain. Rinse with cold water and drain well.

2. In a large bowl, mix together orzo, sun-dried and cherry tomatoes, peppers, feta, onion, basil, parsley and oregano.

3. Whisk together vinegar and oil; pour over salad and toss. Garnish with olives.

   NOTE: Oregano, sometimes called wild marjoram, comes from Greek, meaning "joy of the mountain." It has a pungent, earthy taste which is even nicer dried. It has an affinity for tomato dishes such as sauces for pizza and pasta common to Italian cooking, as well as Greek, Turkish and Mexican dishes.

MAKES 6 SERVINGS

1-1/2 cups	orzo
1/3 cup	chopped, soft sun-dried tomatoes
12	cherry tomatoes, quartered
1/2 cup	*each*: diced sweet red and yellow pepper
1/2 cup	crumbled feta
1/3 cup	diced red or Vidalia onion (or other sweet onion)
1/4 cup	*each*: finely chopped fresh basil and parsley
1 tbsp	finely chopped fresh oregano (or 1 tsp dried)
1/4 cup	red wine vinegar
2 tbsp	olive oil
12 to 15	Kalamata olives

Parsleyed Croutons

So much better than store-bought croutons! Crunchy on the outside and soft on the inside. Use for salads or to garnish soups.

1. In a large skillet over medium heat, melt butter. Stir in bread cubes; immediately toss to coat well.

2. Stir in parsley; sprinkle with seasoning salt. Cook, stirring often, until lightly browned and crisp. Reduce heat if they begin to get too brown. Remove to paper towel and let cool. Best served fresh.

MAKES ABOUT 2 CUPS

2 tbsp	butter
2 cups	cubed stale bread (French, Italian, pumpernickel, etc.), crusts removed, cut into 3/4-inch cubes
3 tbsp	finely chopped fresh parsley (or 2 tbsp parsley and 1 tbsp chopped sage or lemon thyme)
	Seasoning salt, to taste

Herbed Garlic Croutons

This recipe makes a small batch but feel free to double it. I like the texture the airy ciabatta bread gives these croutons. You may be tempted to nibble them! Try these in a Caesar salad.

1. In a large skillet, heat oil over medium heat. Add garlic; stir until it turns golden; remove with a slotted spoon. Stir in bread cubes; immediately toss to coat well.

2. Stir in rosemary and thyme; sprinkle with seasoning salt. Cook, stirring often, until lightly browned and crisp. Reduce heat if they begin to get too brown. Remove to paper towel and let cool. Best served fresh.

MAKES ABOUT 1 CUP

1 tbsp	olive or sunflower oil
1	clove garlic, sliced
1 cup	cubed ciabatta bread or buns, cut into 3/4-inch cubes
1/2 tsp	very finely chopped fresh rosemary
1/4 tsp	very finely chopped fresh thyme
	Seasoning salt, to taste

Panzanella

This is the great bread salad from Tuscany, Italy. It's a must to make at the peak of tomato season. If desired, add any of the following: artichoke hearts, asparagus, cannellini (white kidney) beans, cubed mozzarella and finely chopped capers.

1. In a small bowl, whisk together oil, vinegar, lemon juice and a little salt and pepper. Stir in parsley; reserve.

2. In a large bowl, mix together bread, tomatoes, cucumbers, onion, garlic, basil and olives. Add reserved dressing and toss well. Taste and season with more salt and pepper if desired. Serve immediately.

MAKES ABOUT 4 SERVINGS

1/3 cup	olive oil
2 tbsp	*each*: red wine vinegar and lemon juice
	Salt and pepper, to taste
1/4 cup	minced fresh parsley
3 cups	torn day-old Italian bread
3	large ripe tomatoes, chopped
2 cups	peeled, seeded and chopped cucumbers
1 cup	chopped or sliced red onion
1	large clove garlic, crushed
1/2 cup	sliced fresh basil
1/3 cup	Kalamata olives

VARIATIONS

Replace dressing with Pesto Dressing
(see page 99). Add arugula or grilled chicken.

Bread Salad from Crete
Add 2 tbsp *each*: chopped fresh oregano and
mint. Add 3/4 cup feta cheese.

Fattoush (Lebanese)
Omit red wine vinegar and use total of 3 tbsp
lemon juice. Use torn pita bread in place of
Italian bread. Use 2 tbsp chopped mint or
cilantro in place of basil; omit olives. Add 1 cup
cooked drained chickpeas (optional). Add 2 tsp
Za'atar (see page 4) mix to the dressing.

Potato Salad
WITH DILL-CHIVE VINAIGRETTE

Contrive your own delicious version of this salad to enjoy for summer barbecues and picnics. Add any of the following: chopped firm avocado, chopped sun-dried tomatoes, wedges of hard-cooked eggs, cooked peas, chopped sweet red or yellow peppers (roasted, if desired), sliced celery or radishes, or crisply cooked asparagus tips. Yeah, okay...bacon bits too.

1. Halve or quarter potatoes. In a large saucepan of boiling salted water, cook potatoes for 8 to 10 minutes or until tender. Drain; let cool.

2. In a large bowl, mix together potatoes, onion and parsley. Gently stir in enough vinaigrette to coat potatoes. Season with salt and pepper.

MAKES 8 SERVINGS

3 lbs	medium or small red-skinned potatoes
1/3 cup	diced white or red onion (or sliced green onions)
1/4 cup	chopped fresh parsley
1/2 to 3/4 cup	Dill-Chive Vinaigrette (recipe follows)
	Salt and pepper, to taste

Dill-Chive Vinaigrette

This is a very versatile dressing. Pour it over tender-crisp cooked green beans, peas or cauliflower. Serve over a salad of asparagus, new potatoes, hard-cooked eggs or tomato wedges, cold shrimp or tuna.

1. In a small bowl, whisk together vinegar, lemon juice, mustard and sugar.

2. Gradually whisk in oil. Stir in dill and chives. Season with salt and pepper. Refrigerate up to 1 week. Shake or stir before using.

MAKES 1-1/4 CUPS

1 tbsp	white wine vinegar
1 tbsp	lemon juice
1 tbsp	Dijon mustard
1/2 tsp	granulated sugar
1 cup	oil
1/3 cup	chopped fresh dill
1/4 cup	chopped fresh chives
	Salt and pepper, to taste

TIP

To prepare dressing in food processor, combine all ingredients except oil; pulse to mix. With machine running, slowly pour oil down feed tube. Process until well combined and slightly thickened.

Roasted Beet Salad
WITH DILL-CHIVE VINAIGRETTE

This is a scrumptious and colorful little salad that is sure to impress. The beets have a wonderful sweet taste that is accented by the orange and dill.

MAKES 4 SERVINGS

3 to 4	medium beets, such as golden or candy cane
1	head Boston or red leaf lettuce
2	large oranges, peeled and sliced
4 tbsp	toasted walnut pieces (optional)
	Dill-Chive Vinaigrette (see page 104)
	Dill sprigs, for garnish
	Optional: top with crumbled feta or chèvre cheese.

1. Cut greens off beets, leaving about 1 inch of stem. Wrap individually in foil. Place on baking sheet; roast in a 375°F oven for about 1-1/2 hours, or until tender when pierced with knife. Let cool; slip off skins. (This may be done ahead; wrap beets in plastic wrap and refrigerate up to 2 days.)

2. Slice beets about 1/4 inch thick. Arrange lettuce on 4 individual serving plates. Place beet and orange slices on lettuce, alternating each.

3. Just before serving, top each serving with 1 tbsp walnuts (if using); drizzle with Dill-Chive Vinaigrette. Garnish with dill sprigs.

    VARIATIONS: Replace lettuce with Belgian endive or add endive (Belgian or curly) to the greens mix. Replace lettuce with mesclun mix, add Belgian or curly endive, or escarole to the lettuce. Replace oranges with sliced apples or pears.

Spinach Salad
WITH CREAMY HERB YOGURT DRESSING

This tasty salad can be served as a starter, or for the main course with a nice loaf of grainy bread.

1. Divide spinach among 4 individual plates. Top each with 1/4 cup of the sliced mushrooms.

2. Sprinkle eggs over each salad; top with bacon bits.

3. Refrigerate until ready to serve. Drizzle with dressing.

MAKES 4 SERVINGS

8 cups	torn spinach leaves
1 cup	thinly sliced button or cremini mushrooms
3	hard-cooked eggs, chopped
1/3 cup	bacon bits
	Creamy Herb Yogurt Dressing (recipe follows)

Creamy Herb Yogurt Dressing

For a super low-fat dressing, use no-fat yogurt and low-fat mayonnaise.

1. In a small bowl, whisk together yogurt, mayonnaise, lemon juice, garlic and paprika until smooth.

2. Stir in basil, tarragon and chives, if using. Season with salt and pepper.

3. Chill dressing until ready to serve. Can be made 1 to 2 days ahead; store in the refrigerator.

MAKES ABOUT 1-2/3 CUPS

1 cup	plain yogurt
1/2 cup	mayonnaise
2 tsp	lemon juice
1	clove garlic, crushed
1/4 tsp	paprika
1 tbsp	*each*: chopped fresh basil and tarragon
1 tbsp	chopped fresh chives (optional)
	Salt and pepper, to taste

Spinach Salad
WITH GRILLED ASPARAGUS, PARMESAN AND MINT

This salad would make a wonderful light lunch or supper when served with fresh bread.

1. Line up asparagus spears in a row; skewer through center using metal or soaked bamboo skewers. Lightly brush with oil; sprinkle with salt and pepper.

2. Barbecue over medium heat for 3 to 6 minutes or until tender. Cut into 2-inch pieces.

3. In a small bowl, whisk together 1/4 cup oil, mint, lemon juice, mustard, garlic and a little salt and pepper.

4. In a large bowl, place asparagus, spinach, onion and prosciutto. Toss with just enough mint dressing to coat. Divide among 4 to 6 individual serving plates. Top each serving with a little Parmesan cheese.

MAKES 4 TO 6 SERVINGS	
12 oz	asparagus, trimmed
	Olive oil for brushing
	Salt and pepper, to taste
1/4 cup	olive oil
1/4 cup	finely chopped fresh mint
2 tbsp	lemon juice
1 tbsp	honey mustard
1	clove garlic, minced
8 cups	fresh spinach, trimmed and torn into bite-size pieces
1/2 cup	thinly slivered red onion
2	slices prosciutto, chopped
1/4 cup	shaved Parmesan cheese (or 2 tbsp grated)

VARIATIONS

Replace spinach with mesclun mix. Replace prosciutto with cooked, crumbled bacon or pancetta. Replace Parmesan with asiago cheese. Replace dressing with Creamy Tarragon-Chive Dressing (see page 92).

Strawberry and Melon Salad
WITH MINTED YOGURT DRESSING

This very light, refreshing summertime salad is perfect to serve as an appetizer or a luncheon main course with grainy bread and cold chicken or fish. The low-fat dressing is slightly sweet, with a hint of lemon and fresh mint.

1. Tear lettuce leaves into bite-size pieces; divide among salad plates.

2. Top lettuce with melon and cantaloupe pieces and strawberries.

3. Drizzle each with a little dressing.

   VARIATIONS: Replace strawberries with blueberries.

MAKES 4 TO 6 SERVINGS

1	head Boston lettuce
1	honeydew melon, cut into bite-size chunks
1	cantaloupe, cut into bite-size chunks or made into small balls using melon baller
1 cup	sliced strawberries
	Minted Yogurt Dressing (recipe follows)

Minted Yogurt Dressing

1. In a small bowl, whisk together yogurt, honey and lemon juice.

2. Stir in mint and lemon rind. Cover and refrigerate up to 1 day.

MAKES ABOUT 2/3 CUP

1/2 cup	low-fat plain yogurt
2 tbsp	liquid honey
2 tsp	lemon juice
2 tsp	finely chopped mint
1 tsp	finely grated lemon rind

Tabbouleh Salad

Middle Eastern in origin, this crunchy grain salad is a natural for fresh herbs, especially lots of parsley. It has a minty cool, fresh taste, perfect for summertime meals. Serve with barbecued chicken or lamb and Haydari Sauce (see page 211).

1. In a large bowl, place bulgur; stir in boiling water. Cover and let stand for 30 minutes. Drain well, using spoon to press out excess water; let cool to room temperature.

2. Mix together bulgur, cucumber, tomatoes, parsley, chives and mint.

3. In a small bowl, whisk together oil, lemon juice and garlic; pour over salad and mix well. Season with salt and pepper. Refrigerate for at least an hour or up to 6 hours. Remove from refrigerator 15 minutes before serving.

   NOTE: Bulgur is partially cooked, cracked whole wheat and is high in fiber.

MAKES 6 SERVINGS

1 cup	bulgur
2 cups	boiling water
1 cup	seeded, diced English cucumber
14	cherry tomatoes, quartered
1/2 cup	finely chopped fresh parsley (curly or Italian)
1/4 cup	snipped fresh chives
2 tbsp	finely chopped fresh mint
4 tbsp	olive oil
2 tbsp	lemon juice
1	small clove garlic, minced
	Salt and pepper, to taste

VARIATIONS

Substitute with 2-3/4 cups cooked barley, or other whole grains or rice. Add cooked chickpeas or green lentils. Substitute mint with orange mint. Use to stuff Belgian endive for an appetizer. If desired, add toasted pine nuts.

Tangy Thai Coleslaw

This low-fat, vitamin-packed coleslaw is a favorite of food specialist and cookbook author Dana McCauley. She recommends serving it with grilled lean flank steak. I also think it would be great with grilled chicken breast or oven-roasted chicken.

1. In a small bowl, whisk together orange juice, soy sauce, vinegar, ginger, sugar, orange rind and hot pepper sauce. Whisking constantly, drizzle in sesame oil until well combined. Reserve.

2. In a large bowl, mix together cabbage, carrots, snow peas, mango, onion, bean sprouts and cilantro. Add dressing; toss until well combined. Taste and adjust seasoning if necessary. If desired, transfer to serving bowl; garnish with cilantro sprig.

   VARIATIONS: Substitute half of the cabbage with red cabbage.

DRESSING

2 tbsp	orange juice
1 tbsp	light soy sauce or tamari
1 tbsp	rice wine vinegar
1 tsp	minced fresh ginger
1/2 tsp	*each*: granulated sugar and grated orange rind
Dash	hot pepper sauce
2 tsp	sesame oil

SALAD

2 cups	finely shredded Napa or Savoy cabbage
1/2 cup	*each*: coarsely shredded carrots, thinly sliced snow peas and finely diced mango
1/4 cup	*each*: thinly sliced red onion, bean sprouts
2 tbsp	chopped fresh cilantro
	Cilantro sprig, for garnish

Tarragon and Caper Mayonnaise

Serve with cold potatoes, asparagus, shrimp, hard-cooked eggs, crab or lobster.

1. In food processor, combine egg yolks, vinegar, chives, tarragon, parsley, mustard, capers and garlic. Season with salt and pepper; process until smooth.

2. With food processor running, slowly drizzle in oil. Refrigerate up to 4 days.

   NOTE: For food safety, use fresh eggs that have been kept refrigerated.

MAKES ABOUT 1-1/4 CUPS

2	egg yolks
3 tbsp	white wine vinegar
1 tbsp	*each*: finely chopped fresh chives, tarragon and parsley
1 tbsp	Dijon mustard
2 tsp	capers
1	small clove garlic, crushed
	Salt and pepper, to taste
1 cup	oil

Basil Mayonnaise

Great with eggs or to top a chicken, turkey or vegetarian burgers.

1. Mix all ingredients together in a small bowl. Refrigerate up to 1 week.

MAKES ABOUT 1/2 CUP

1/2 cup	mayonnaise
1/2 tsp	Dijon mustard
1/4 tsp	finely minced garlic
1 tbsp	finely chopped fresh basil
	Salt and pepper, to taste

VARIATIONS

Tarragon Mayonnaise
Replace basil with finely chopped tarragon. Use as a spread for roast beef sandwichs with roasted red peppers.

Chive Mayonnaise
Replace basil with 2 tbsp chopped fresh chives and 1 tbsp finely chopped sweet red peppers. Use with cold shrimp or other seafood.

Pesto Mayonnaise
Omit garlic and basil, stir in 2 tbsp pesto. Serve with cold shrimp or hard-cooked eggs.

Thai Mango Salad

I first tried this salad at a Thai restaurant called The Green Mango and fell in love with it. My preference is to make it with Atulfo mangoes, ones that are under-ripe, so they are a bit tart. Goes well with grilled chicken, shrimp and pork tenderloin and other Thai dishes.

1. In medium bowl, combine mango, red pepper, onion and cilantro.

2. In small bowl, mix together lime juice, sugar, soy sauce and pepper flakes until sugar dissolves. Whisk in oil. Stir into mango mixture. Cover and refrigerate for at least one hour to allow flavors to blend.

3. Just before serving, transfer to serving dish; sprinkle with cashews. Garnish with whole cilantro leaves.

MAKES 4 TO 6 SERVINGS

SALAD

3 cups	thin strips peeled, firm mango (about 2 large)
1 cup	thin strips sweet red pepper
3/4 cup	thinly sliced red onion
1/3 cup	chopped fresh cilantro or mint
1/4 cup	cashews or chopped peanuts, lightly toasted
	Cilantro leaves, for garnish

DRESSING

1/4 cup	lime or lemon juice
1 tbsp	granulated sugar
1 tbsp	soy sauce (preferably naturally brewed) or fish sauce
1/4 tsp	crushed red pepper flakes or chili-garlic paste
3 tbsp	peanut or sunflower oil

Tomato Salad
WITH BASIL CREAM DRESSING

I always make this salad mid-summer when my cherry tomato "trees" are overflowing with these little, red, so-sweet jewels. You can also make a salad of garden leaf lettuce, topped with regular tomato wedges, sliced onions or snipped chives, and basil; drizzle with a dressing of sour cream and vinegar.

1. In a medium bowl, combine tomatoes, onion and basil.

2. In a small bowl, whisk together sour cream and vinegar; pour over salad and stir to combine well. Cover and let stand for an hour to allow flavors to develop.

   NOTE: A *chiffonade* is a French term to define a method of slicing plant leaves and herbs, to cut into little ribbons. It is done by laying leaves flat, one on top of the other, then rolling up like a cigar. Then it is sliced perpendicular to the roll in thin strips. In the case of herbs, like basil, it keeps them from bruising too much and it looks nice when sprinkled over the top of foods like pasta sauce and salads.

MAKES 4 SERVINGS

3 cups	halved cherry tomatoes or grape tomatoes
1/4 cup	diced or thinly sliced red onion or green onions
1/4 cup	chiffonade of fresh basil (see page 3)
1/4 cup	sour cream
1 to 2 tbsp	red wine vinegar or balsamic vinegar

Tomatoes and Bocconcini
WITH BASIL AND BALSAMIC

This recipe was a favorite of cookbook author and magazine food editor, the late Carol Ferguson (see book dedication and acknowledgments) and appeared in her *The New Canadian Basics Cookbook* (Penguin Books Canada Ltd., 1999). She said "This makes a beautiful salad platter for a hot summer day when garden tomatoes and fresh basil are at their peaks. Serve with crusty Italian bread. Be sure to use top-quality cheese and olive oil."

1. On a large platter or 4 individual salad plates, alternate tomato and cheese slices, overlapping slightly.

2. Sprinkle lightly with salt and a few grindings of fresh pepper. Sprinkle with basil and chives.

3. Drizzle with oil and vinegar.

MAKES 4 SERVINGS

4	ripe tomatoes, sliced
1/2 lb	sliced bocconcini cheese
	Salt and pepper, to taste
1/2 cup	chiffonade of fresh basil (see page 3)
1/4 cup	snipped fresh chives (or 2 tbsp chopped Italian parsley)
6 tbsp	extra-virgin olive oil
2 tbsp	balsamic or red wine vinegar

VARIATIONS

- Use halved cherry or grape tomatoes and whole baby bocconcini in place of sliced.

- Use Pesto Dressing (see page 99) in place of oil and drizzle with 1 tbsp balsamic vinegar.

- Use crumbled feta cheese in place of bocconcini; sprinkle over tomato slices.

- Instead of basil and chives, sprinkle with 2 tbsp *each* finely chopped basil and oregano (or marjoram) and 1 tsp finely chopped thyme or lemon thyme. Excellent served as a side dish for grilled chicken.

Watermelon and Cucumber Salad
WITH MINT

This cooling summer salad may be laid out on a platter using slices of the watermelon and cucumber. Mint and lime flavors are the perfect accents.

1. Cut peeled watermelon into slices or cubes. In a large bowl, combine watermelon, cucumber, feta, onion, olives and mint. If making ahead, drain any liquid before adding dressing.

2. Dressing: in a small bowl, mix together lime rind and juice and sugar; stir to dissolve sugar. Slowly pour in oil while whisking. Pour over salad and stir to coat. Season with salt and pepper.

3. Transfer to serving bowl. Serve with garnish of mint spring.

VARIATIONS: Replace mint with chopped basil, cilantro or dill. Add 2 tbsp chopped chives, if desired, in place of onion. Replace olives with a handful of pomegranate seeds.

NOTES: Newer round mini watermelons have very thin skins and few soft seeds. Sweet onions grown in Vidalia, Georgia or Walla Walla, Washington, are uniquely sweet in flavor due to the low sulfur soil in the areas they are grown.

MAKES ABOUT 6 CUPS

4 lb	small seedless watermelon (cut in half; reserve half for another use or if doubling recipe)
1	English cucumber (about 2 cups chopped)
3/4 cup	feta cheese
1/3 cup	thinly sliced red or sweet onion
1/3 cup	Kalamata olives
2 tbsp	finely chopped fresh mint (or sliced chiffonade, see page 3)

LIME DRESSING

1 tsp	finely grated lime rind
2 tbsp	lime juice
1 tsp	granulated sugar (or other sweetener)
4 tbsp	sunflower oil
	Salt and pepper, to taste
	Mint spring, for garnish

MEAT, FISH/SEAFOOD, EGGS AND VEGETARIAN BURGERS

Herbs give a flavor infusion to marinades for meats, add a splash of excitement to fish and seafood and naturally go with eggs. Use herbal oils, vinegars and mustards in marinades. Fresh herbs in mustards, sauces and salsas accent meat and seafood dishes. Douse eggs with almost any fresh herb. Place a dab of herb butter over meats, fish or seafood just before serving – the warmth of the food melts the butter and releases the flavor. Chopped fresh parsley can be added to any dish to add lively color.

Focaccia Sandwiches

These sandwiches "stack up" great taste! The tarragon in the mayonnaise complements the beef very well.

1. Slice bread in half horizontally. Spread bottom half generously with Tarragon and Caper Mayonnaise (see page 111).

2. Layer meat on top of the mayonnaise; add arugula, peppers, tomatoes and onion.

3. Replace top of bread. Secure with toothpicks; cut into wedges or rectangles.

   NOTE: If you do not have time to make the Tarragon and Caper Mayonnaise, stir 1 tbsp finely chopped fresh tarragon into 1/2 cup store-bought mayonnaise.

1	large loaf focaccia bread
1/2 cup	Tarragon and Caper Mayonnaise (see page 111)
1 lb	sliced roast beef, turkey or chicken
1	bunch arugula
2	large roasted sweet red or yellow peppers, sliced
2	large tomatoes, thinly sliced
1	small red onion, thinly sliced

VARIATIONS

- Use grilled eggplant in place of the meat.

- Use pesto in place of the mayonnaise and roasted or grilled chicken.

- Use Remoulade Sauce (see page 143) in place of Tarragon and Caper Mayonnaise.

Cherry Chicken
WITH ROSEMARY AND ORANGE

Cherries partner well with poultry. This recipe is a delicious combination of savory and sweet. Serve with mashed potatoes or a mixture of white and wild rice.

1. Flatten or cut chicken to 1/2-inch thickness; season with salt and pepper and dredge in flour. In a large skillet, heat 1 tbsp of the butter over medium heat. Cook chicken until golden, for about 3 minutes on each side; remove from pan.

2. Put remaining 1 tbsp butter in the pan. Add shallots and rosemary; cook for 3 minutes or until softened. Stir in wine, marmalade and mustard.

3. Return chicken to pan; add cherries. Reduce heat; simmer for about 10 minutes or until sauce is thickened. Serve with cherry sauce spooned over chicken. Garnish with rosemary sprigs.

MAKES 4 SERVINGS

1 lb	boneless skinless chicken breast
	Salt and pepper, to taste
2 tbsp	all-purpose flour
2 tbsp	butter
1/2 cup	finely chopped shallots
1 tbsp	minced fresh rosemary
3/4 cup	dry white wine
1/3 cup	orange marmalade
2 tsp	Dijon mustard
2 cups	sweet cherries, pitted and halved
	Rosemary sprigs, for garnish

Chicken Breasts Provençal

The Provence region of southern France is known for its use of garlic, tomatoes, olives and olive oil in its cooking. A dash of wine and a handful of herbs and you'll almost feel like you are there! I have tried this dish with a little crumbled feta cheese added to it just before serving and it was terrific.

1. In a large skillet over medium-high, heat 2 tbsp of the oil. Dredge chicken in flour; sprinkle with salt and pepper. Cook for 2 to 3 minutes per side to brown; remove from pan.

2. Reduce heat to medium-low; add remaining 1 tbsp oil to pan. Stir in onions and garlic; cook for 3 to 5 minutes or until softened.

3. Stir in wine, scraping up browned bits from the bottom of the pan. Stir in tomatoes, olives and brown sugar, if using.

4. Return chicken and juices to pan. Cover; simmer for 15 minutes.

5. Remove lid. Increase heat to medium; cook, uncovered, for 10 to 12 minutes to thicken sauce.

6. Stir in marjoram, rosemary and tarragon; cook for 3 minutes. Serve sprinkled with parsley.

MAKES 4 SERVINGS

3 tbsp	olive oil
4	boneless, skinless chicken breasts (or 8 skinless thighs)
1/4 cup	all-purpose flour
	Salt and pepper, to taste
1/2 cup	diced onions or shallots
2	cloves garlic, minced
1/2 cup	white wine
3 cups	chopped tomatoes (3 or 4 large), or 28 oz can diced tomatoes, drained
16	black olives, halved and pitted
1 tbsp	packed brown sugar (optional)
1 tbsp	chopped fresh marjoram or oregano
2 tsp	*each*: finely chopped fresh rosemary and tarragon
1 tbsp	chopped fresh parsley

VARIATIONS

- Use shrimp in place of chicken, but cook sauce alone, uncovered, over medium heat for about 8 to 10 minutes, to thicken. Then add 1 lb peeled, deveined large shrimp; cook for 2 to 3 minutes, until shrimp is just cooked through (do not overcook). Serve with rice.

- Use 1 tsp dried Herbes de Provence mixture (see page 3) in place of fresh marjoram, rosemary and tarragon. Add in step 3.

Chicken Piccata

Tender chicken in a light lemon and caper sauce (more of a glaze) with a hint of tarragon is quick to prepare. Serve with steamed broccoli or green beans and rice.

1. Flatten chicken breasts using a meat mallet. Season with a little salt and pepper. Dredge chicken in flour, shaking off excess.

2. In a large non-stick skillet, heat butter and oil over medium heat. Add chicken; cook for about 3 minutes per side or until lightly browned.

3. Add wine, capers, if using, tarragon and lemon juice to pan, turning chicken to coat. Cover; cook for 2 to 3 minutes. Garnish plate with lemon slices and small tarragon sprigs.

MAKES 4 SERVINGS

4	boneless, skinless chicken breasts
	Salt and pepper, to taste
1/4 cup	all-purpose flour
1 tbsp	*each*: butter and oil
1/3 cup	dry white wine or chicken broth
1/4 cup	drained capers (optional)
1 tbsp	chopped fresh tarragon
1 tbsp	lemon juice
	Lemon slices and tarragon sprigs, for garnish

Chicken Tikka Masala

This is a delicious East Indian dish full of exotic spices and accented with fresh herbs – cilantro and mint. Go easy on the hot chiles if you like it mild. Serve with Raita (see page 165) for a touch of coolness. Add cooked basmati rice and warmed naan bread to complete the meal.

1. In food processor, place chopped onions, 2 cloves garlic, tomato paste, lemon juice, ginger, coriander, cumin and chili powder. Add a little salt and pepper. Process until smooth.

2. Cut chicken into 1-1/2-inch cubes. In a large bowl, mix together chicken and marinade. Cover and refrigerate for at least 2 hours or overnight.

3. In a large skillet over medium heat, heat oil. Add sliced onion; cook for about 7 minutes or until softened. Stir in garlic and chili pepper; cook for 1 minute.

4. Drain excess marinade from chicken; add chicken to skillet. Cook, stirring, for 5 minutes or until chicken is cooked through.

5. Stir in tomatoes, yogurt and coconut milk. Reduce heat; cover and simmer for about 20 minutes.

6. Remove from heat; stir in cilantro and mint. Garnish with mint sprigs.

MAKES 4 SERVINGS

1 cup	chopped onions
2	cloves garlic, crushed
1/4 cup	tomato paste
1/4 cup	lemon juice
1 tbsp	grated fresh ginger
1 tsp	*each*: ground coriander, cumin and chili powder
	Salt and pepper, to taste
1-1/2 lb	boneless skinless chicken breast
2 tbsp	oil
1	large onion, halved and sliced
2	cloves garlic, crushed
1	chopped green chili pepper, or to taste
1 cup	drained diced tomatoes (fresh or canned)
1/2 cup	*each*: plain yogurt and coconut milk
1 tbsp	*each*: finely chopped fresh cilantro and mint
	Mint sprigs, for garnish

Cranberry Orange and Rosemary Stuffed Chicken or Turkey Breast

Chicken or turkey breast is stuffed with an orange and herb cream cheese filling, coated in herbed crumbs and baked. These are a super-easy alternative to serving a whole turkey when you have a small group.

1. In a medium bowl, mix together cream cheese, cranberries, juice concentrate, chives, 1 tbsp of the parsley and garlic until well combined; chill to firm up slightly.

2. Place chicken between two pieces of waxed paper; pound to flatten, until 1/4 inch thick. Divide filling among chicken breasts, placing at one edge; fold in sides and roll up, sealing completely. Wrap rolls tightly with plastic wrap and refrigerate for at least 30 minutes.

3. In a medium bowl, combine breadcrumbs, melted butter, parsley, rosemary and seasoning salt. Dip each roll in eggs then in breadcrumb mixture, pressing to coat well. Place on a lightly greased baking sheet. Bake in a 375°F oven for 25 to 30 minutes, until golden and tender.

VARIATIONS

- Chicken Kiev: Make Fines Herbes Butter (see page 32), omitting chervil and shallots. Divide butter into 6 portions; form into small logs and chill or freeze until firm. Use this butter in place of the cream cheese filling.

- Use goat cheese (chèvre) in place of cream cheese.

- Omit dried cranberries and orange juice concentrate, replace orange rind with lemon rind.

- Replace rosemary with 1 tbsp lemon thyme.

MAKES 6 SERVINGS

1	pkg (8 oz) cream cheese, softened
1/4 cup	chopped dried cranberries
4 tsp	orange juice concentrate
1 tbsp	finely chopped fresh chives
1 tbsp	chopped fresh parsley
1 tsp	grated orange rind
1	clove garlic, finely chopped
6	boneless, skinless chicken or turkey breasts (6 oz each)

CRUMB COATING

2 cups	fresh breadcrumbs
1/4 cup	butter, melted
1/4 cup	chopped fresh parsley
2 tbsp	minced fresh rosemary
1 tsp	seasoning salt or salt
2	eggs, beaten

Herb-Roasted Chicken
WITH ROASTED GARLIC

This is a dish you will want to make over and over. The herb flavors penetrate the meat to give a wonderful taste. Serve with mashed potatoes and roasted squash, green beans, Brussels sprouts or carrots.

1. Rinse chicken and pat dry with a paper towel. Sprinkle inside of cavity with salt and pepper. Place 2 or 3 sprigs of each herb in cavity.

2. Gently peel skin away from breast of chicken. Reserving 2 sprigs of sage, tuck remaining sprigs of herbs between flesh and skin; pull skin over top.

3. Place chicken on a rack in a roasting pan; surround with garlic cloves and leaves from the reserved 2 sprigs of sage. Brush chicken with olive oil and drizzle some over the garlic. Cover with foil.

4. Roast in a 375°F oven for 30 minutes. Remove foil; roast for 45 to 60 minutes longer, basting occasionally, until chicken is golden brown and juices run clear when thigh is pierced with the point of a sharp knife.

5. Slice chicken, discarding the herbs from under the skin. Serve with roasted garlic (squeeze softened garlic from cloves) and sage.

MAKES 4 SERVINGS

1	whole roasting chicken, about 4 lb
	Salt and pepper, to taste
4 to 6 sprigs	*each*: fresh rosemary, sage, savory, thyme or lemon thyme
2	heads garlic, separated into cloves
	Olive oil

TIP

To remove garlic from papery skins, press through a strainer.

NOTE

Herbs sprigs should be about 4 inches in length. Sage sprigs with have 4 to 6 leaves on each.

Lemon Herb Grilled Chicken

Chicken thighs grill well, staying moist. Some of the delicious lemon and herb marinade is reserved and brushed on after grilling to add extra yum. This chicken goes very well with a Greek Salad (see page 94) or Panzanella (Tuscan bread salad, see page 102).

1. Blot chicken dry with paper towel. If skin is on, score with knife in several places. Place in a zipper lock freezer bag or in a large bowl.

2. Place in a glass measuring cup, combine oil, lemon rind and juice, garlic, rosemary, thyme and salt and pepper; whisk together and reserve 3 tbsp in a small bowl. Pour the rest of the marinade into the bag (or toss with chicken in bowl.) Seal the bag (cover bowl with plastic wrap). Massage marinade into the chicken. Leave at room temperature for about 30 minutes, or if longer, refrigerate 8 to 10 hours or overnight.

3. Place skin side down (if skin is on), over medium-high heat, cook for 5 to 6 minutes per side, depending on the thickness of the meat, until it reaches an internal temperature of 165°F.

4. Remove from grill to a platter. Brush reserved marinade over the chicken. Cover loosely with foil and let sit for 5 minutes.

To oven bake:
Place chicken on foil-lined baking sheet, skin side down. Bake in a 425°F oven for about 20 minutes; flip over and cook for another 15 to 20 minutes or until nicely browned and internal temperature is 165°F. Continue with Step 4.

Grilled Lemons
Cut 1 whole lemon in half (through middle not ends). Trim off ends. Place cut sides down onto grill. Cook for about 5 minutes or until nicely browned. Cut in half through ends (now have 4 pieces); serve with chicken.

MAKES 4 SERVINGS

2 lbs	boneless, skinless chicken thighs (or 2-1/2 lbs with skin-on)
1/3 cup	olive oil
1 tbsp	grated lemon rind
4 tbsp	lemon juice
2	large cloves garlic, minced
1 tbsp	finely chopped fresh rosemary
2 tsp	finely chopped fresh thyme or lemon thyme
	Salt and pepper, or seasoning salt
	Lemon wedges or grilled lemons (see below), optional

VARIATIONS

- Use chicken breast in place of thighs. When ready to serve, cut into slices on the diagonal and spread slices slightly on plate.

- Use *Herbes de Provence* mixture (see page 3) in place of rosemary and thyme and add 2 tsp Dijon mustard to marinade.

- Use 2 tbsp *Za'atar* mixture (see page 4) in place of herbs.

Lemon and Thyme Chicken
WITH MUSHROOM COUSCOUS

This is a very quick and satisfying dish to make. If using lemon thyme in place of the regular thyme, omit the lemon rind.

1. Lightly coat chicken with flour. In a very large skillet, heat 1 tbsp of the oil over medium heat. Add chicken; cook, stirring frequently, until lightly browned.

2. Add 1/4 cup of the stock; stir in thyme. Cook until most of the liquid has evaporated. Transfer mixture to a bowl; cover and keep warm.

3. In the same skillet, heat remaining 1 tbsp oil over medium heat. Add onion and garlic; cook for 2 minutes. Add mushrooms, yellow pepper and lemon rind; cook for 3 to 5 minutes or until mushrooms are softened.

4. Add remaining 1-1/4 cups stock. Increase heat to high; bring to a boil. Stir in couscous and roasted red peppers. Cover; remove from heat. Let rest for 5 minutes.

5. Stir in reserved chicken; season with salt and pepper.

   NOTE: Couscous is not a grain but very tiny pasta-like steamed balls made from wheat semolina. It cooks very quickly, absorbing hot liquid.

MAKES 4 SERVINGS

2	boneless chicken breasts, thinly sliced
2 tbsp	all-purpose flour
2 tbsp	olive oil
1-1/2 cups	chicken or vegetable stock
1 tbsp	chopped fresh thyme or lemon thyme
1/2 cup	finely chopped red onion
1	clove garlic, minced
1/2 lb	brown mushrooms, sliced
1/2 cup	diced sweet yellow pepper
2 tbsp	grated lemon rind
1 cup	couscous
1/4 cup	finely chopped roasted red peppers
	Salt and pepper, to taste

Marinated Chicken or Turkey Kebabs

Serve kebabs with rice and grilled vegetables such as sweet peppers, zucchini and onion wedges. If desired, serve with Tzatziki (see page 165) or Haydari Sauce (see page 211).

1. In a medium bowl, whisk together oil, lemon juice, garlic, rosemary, oregano and thyme. Reserve 1 tbsp in a small bowl for brushing on chicken during cooking.

2. Cut chicken into large even pieces; add to marinade and toss. Cover and refrigerate for 1 to 2 hours.

3. Thread chicken onto skewers. (If using wooden skewers, soak them in water for 30 minutes before using.)

4. Grill over medium-high heat on barbecue for 3 minutes on each side. Brush with reserved marinade while cooking. (Or broil in oven about 5 inches from heat.)

VARIATION: Use 1 tbsp minced fresh cilantro instead of the other herbs.

MAKES 4 SERVINGS

1/4 cup	olive oil
2 tbsp	lemon juice
1	clove garlic, minced
2 tsp	*each:* minced fresh rosemary and oregano
1 tsp	minced fresh thyme or lemon thyme
1 lb	boneless skinless chicken or turkey breast

Roast Leg of Lamb
WITH MINT SAUCE

Herbs, garlic and lamb all seem to go together so well. Serve with Mint Sauce, fluffy mashed potatoes, baby carrots and green beans.

MAKES 6 SERVINGS

4 lb	leg of lamb (bone-in, short shank)
3 or 4	cloves garlic, slivered
2 tbsp	olive oil
1 tbsp	lemon juice
2 tbsp	finely chopped fresh rosemary
2 tsp	finely chopped fresh thyme or lemon thyme
1/4 cup	fresh lavender flowers (or 1 tbsp dried lavender), optional
	Salt and pepper

1. Remove outer membrane from lamb. Using the tip of a sharp knife, make small slits all over lamb; insert garlic slivers.

2. In a small bowl, mix together oil, lemon juice, rosemary, thyme, lavender (if using) and a little salt and pepper. Brush over lamb; place in a glass baking dish. Cover and refrigerate for about 8 hours, or up to 24 hours.

3. Place lamb in a shallow roasting pan; let stand for 30 minutes at room temperature.

4. Roast in a 425°F oven for about 15 minutes; reduce heat to 350°F for 1 to 1-1/2 hours or until lamb has reached an internal temperature of 130°F for rare, or 140°F for medium-rare (insert thermometer in thickest part of lamb).

5. Transfer to a cutting board; cover loosely with foil and let rest for 10 minutes before slicing. Serve with Mint Sauce (recipe follows).

    VARIATION: Use 2 tbsp Herbes de Provence (see page 3) instead of fresh herbs.

Mint Sauce

MAKES ABOUT 1/2 CUP

1 cup	finely chopped fresh mint
2 tbsp	granulated sugar (or icing or brown sugar)
1/4 cup	vinegar (white or red wine, cider, malt or balsamic)

1. In a medium bowl, place mint; add sugar and stir to crush leaves against the sugar.

2. In a small saucepan over high heat, heat vinegar. Bring to a boil; stir into mint until sugar is dissolved. Let stand for 1 hour. Store in refrigerator up to 1 week.

    VARIATION: Mint-Cilantro Sauce – Replace half of the mint with chopped fresh cilantro.

Braised Lamb Shanks
WITH ROSEMARY

These lamb shanks are slow-cooked with wine, lemon and herbs until the meat is falling off the bones. Thanks to my friend Pat, also a recipe developer, for her recipe creation. Serve with Polenta with Herbs (see page 188), or Roasted Garlic Mashed Potatoes (see page 203).

1. Combine flour, salt and lemon pepper in a shallow dish. Pat lamb dry; coat with flour mixture. In a Dutch oven, heat oil over medium-high heat. Working in batches, add shanks to pot and cook until brown on all sides, for about 8 minutes. Transfer shanks to bowl.

2. Add onion, carrots, celery and garlic; cook for 5 minutes, stirring frequently.

3. Stir in broth, wine, rosemary, thyme, bay leaves, lemon peel and parsnip. Return shanks to pot, pressing down to submerge. Cover and cook in a 350°F oven for 2-1/2 hours or until shanks are tender.

4. Using a slotted spoon, transfer meat and vegetables to platter; discard bay leaves and lemon peel. Cover and keep warm.

5. In a small bowl, stir together water and cornstarch; stir into sauce. Bring to a boil, reduce heat and simmer about 3 to 5 minutes until thickened, stirring constantly. Spoon sauce over lamb shanks and vegetables. Sprinkle with parsley.

MAKES 4 SERVINGS

1/4 cup	all-purpose flour
1/2 tsp	*each*: salt and lemon pepper
4	lamb shanks, (about 3 lb)
1	medium onion, chopped
3	carrots, peeled, chopped
2	stalks celery, chopped
3	cloves garlic, minced
2 cups	low-sodium beef broth
1 cup	dry white wine
1 tbsp	chopped fresh rosemary leaves
4	sprigs fresh thyme leaves
2	fresh or dried bay leaves
2	strips lemon peel (3 x 1-inch)
1	parsnip, peeled and chopped
1/4 cup	cold water
2 tbsp	cornstarch
2 tbsp	chopped fresh Italian parsley

Pork Tenderloin Medallions

Pork tenderloin is a tender cut that needs little cooking time. In this recipe, thin slices are coated with a creamy Dijon and rosemary sauce.

1. Slice tenderloins into slices 3/4 inch thick medallions. Place between waxed paper; pound to 1/4-inch thickness.

2. In a medium bowl, mix together flour, salt and pepper. Dip each medallion to coat; shake off excess.

3. In a large skillet over medium-high heat, melt butter. Add medallions; cook on each side until lightly browned, about 2 minutes per side. Remove to a plate.

4. Using additional butter or oil if necessary, cook shallots and garlic for 2 to 3 minutes or until softened. Add stock; cook, stirring to scrape browned bits from the bottom of the pan, for 1 to 2 minutes. Stir in mustard and rosemary.

5. Return medallions and juices to skillet. Reduce heat; cover and simmer for about 5 minutes.

6. Stir in cream and parsley. Cook for 1 minute to heat through.

MAKES 4 SERVINGS

2	pork tenderloins (about 2 lbs total weight)
1/4 cup	all-purpose flour
1/4 tsp	*each*: salt and pepper
4 tsp	butter or olive oil
1/2 cup	chopped shallots
1	clove garlic, minced
1 cup	chicken stock or dry white wine (or half stock and half wine)
2 tbsp	Dijon mustard
2 tsp	minced fresh rosemary or Herbes de Provence (see page 3)
3 tbsp	table cream (18%)
2 tbsp	finely chopped fresh parsley

Oven-Baked Pork Tenderloins

Whole pork tenderloins are marinated in a garlicky mustard and herb baste, then baked. They make an attractive presentation with slices laid overlapping on the plate, garnished with fresh rosemary sprigs. Serve with mashed potatoes or a wild rice blend and green beans, Brussels sprouts or carrots.

MAKES 4 SERVINGS

2	pork tenderloins (about 3/4 lb each)
2	cloves garlic
1 tbsp	*each*: finely chopped fresh sage (or savory), thyme and rosemary
2 tbsp	Dijon mustard
1 tbsp	oil
2 tsp	coarsely ground pepper
1/4 tsp	salt

1. Trim any fat or silverskin from tenderloins; tuck ends under and tie with kitchen string. Place on large piece of plastic wrap.

2. In food processor, place garlic, sage, thyme and rosemary; pulse until finely chopped. Add mustard, oil, pepper and salt. Purée until smooth, scraping down sides with a spatula. Brush generously over tenderloins. Cover with plastic wrap; refrigerate for about 1 hour.

3. Unwrap tenderloins; place in a shallow roasting pan. Roast in a 400°F oven for 25 to 30 minutes, or until meat thermometer inserted in center registers 160°F.

4. Remove tenderloins to cutting board; tent loosely with foil and let stand for 10 minutes. Remove string; slice thinly on the diagonal.

Steak "Bowls"
WITH QUINOA, EDAMAME AND VEGETABLES

This is a take-off on Buddha bowls – originally vegetarian one-bowl meals that Buddhist monks ate. Tofu, meats or fish/seafood, vegetables and legumes can be piled onto rice, quinoa or noodles. Serve hot, or cold like a salad. Prep veggies before you start cooking.

1. Cook quinoa: place quinoa in a bowl, cover with water; soak 2 minutes. Drain and rinse well (removes bitter saponin from the exterior). Place in medium saucepan. Add 2 cups of water and 1/2 tsp of salt. Bring to a boil; reduce heat, cover and simmer for about 15 minutes or until liquid has been absorbed and grain is tender. Do not stir. Turn heat off; let rest for 5 minutes. Fluff with fork. Stir in parsley, if using.

2. Take steaks out of refrigerator; let steak rest at room temperature for about 30 minutes.

3. Cook vegetables: Boil or steam green beans until tender-crisp; drain, remove and keep warm. In large non-stick skillet, heat 1 tsp of the oil over medium heat. Cook carrots and sweet peppers (separated on each half of the pan), stirring occasionally until tender-crisp. Remove and keep warm. In same skillet, add remaining oil. Add mushrooms, thyme and seasoning salt; cook until soft, stirring occasionally. Remove and keep warm. Warm edamame in microwave if desired.

4. Blot steaks well with paper towel. Brush on both sides with about 1 tsp of the oil; season generously with salt and pepper. In a large skillet, heat the remaining oil over medium-high heat. When pan is hot, add steaks and cook for 3 minutes on each side. Remove to a plate and cover loosely with foil. Let rest for about 10 minutes. Slice steak into 1/4-inch slices.

MAKES 4 SERVINGS

1 cup	uncooked quinoa (or 3 cups cooked)
2 tbsp	chopped fresh parsley (optional)
	each: salt and pepper

STEAKS

2	strip loin steaks (about 10 oz each)
1 tbsp	oil
	Salt and pepper, or seasoning salt
1 tbsp	oil
1 tbsp	butter
1	large clove garlic, minced
1 tbsp	finely chopped fresh rosemary

VEGETABLES

1 lb	green beans, stem ends removed
1 tbsp	oil
1 cup	matchstick-cut carrots
3/4 cup	thinly sliced sweet red or yellow peppers
8 oz	white or cremini mushrooms (about 3 cups sliced)
2 tsp	finely chopped fresh thyme
1/4 tsp	seasoning salt
1 cup	shelled edamame
3 tbsp	chopped fresh chives

5. Add butter to same skillet (do not clean) over medium heat. When melted, add garlic and rosemary; cook for one minute. Add sliced steak and cook, stirring, until warmed through and to desired doneness.

6. Assemble bowls: into each bowl, spoon 3/4 cup quinoa, top with steak in centre. Arrange 1/4 of each of the other vegetables around the edges. Sprinkle with chives.

VARIATIONS

- Use roasted sweet potatoes cubes or cauliflower slices in place of carrots; spinach or broccoli in place of green beans; chickpeas in place of edamame.

- Substitute chicken or shrimp for the beef.

- For vegetarian, replace meat with slices of tofu (reduce the cooking time).

TIP

Serve with a drizzle of Green Goddess Dressing (see page 95) or Remoulade (see page 143).

Béarnaise Sauce

This delicious, velvety sauce is named for the Béarn region in the southwest of France. Béarnaise Sauce is also delicious over asparagus eggs (Eggs Benedict) or with seafood.

MAKES ABOUT 1 CUP

1/4 cup	white wine vinegar (or tarragon vinegar), or half white wine
3 tsp	finely chopped fresh tarragon
2 tsp	finely chopped fresh chervil (optional)
1 tbsp	finely chopped shallots
3	peppercorns, crushed
Pinch	salt
4	egg yolks
1/2 cup	butter, softened, or melted (or clarified: milk solids removed if desired)

1. In a small saucepan over high heat, mix together vinegar, 2 tsp of the tarragon and 1 tsp of the chervil (if using), shallots, pepper and salt. Bring to a boil; reduce heat and simmer, uncovered, for about 5 minutes, until liquid is reduced by half. Strain; discard solids.

2. In the top of a double boiler (not over heat), place egg yolks. Whisk in herbed vinegar mixture well.

3. Place double boiler over pot of simmering water. Gradually whisk in butter a little at a time (if using melted or clarified butter, add a few drops at a time); whisk until sauce thickens.

4. Remove from heat; stir in remaining 1 tsp *each* of the tarragon and chervil, if using. Keep warm until ready to use: transfer to a glass measuring cup. Place in a bowl of boiling hot water; stir occasionally.

   NOTE: If you do not have a double boiler, use a heat-proof bowl placed on top of a saucepan with a small amount of boiling water.

TIP

My method for reheating Béarnaise Sauce if you wish to refrigerate any leftovers. (Do NOT microwave.)

Place sauce in a 2 cup glass measure; set it in a medium bowl. Pour boiling water into the bowl, about halfway up the side of glass measure, or the level of the sauce. Cover with plastic wrap and let rest for 10 minutes, stirring once or twice. Discard cooled water and add new boiling water; repeat resting, stirring for another 10 minutes, until sauce reaches desired temperature (about 130°F). This will keep the sauce from separating.

Grilled Steak
WITH BÉARNAISE SAUCE

Meats don't always have to be marinated to get the taste of herbs. Béarnaise is a classic herb sauce to serve with steak, and is not that hard to make. A very good alternate to use is Tarragon-Dijon Butter (see page 33) placed on top of a steak just before serving.

1. Let steaks rest, covered, at room temperature, for 30 minutes. Cut garlic in half lengthwise (if using); rub over surface of steaks. Season with a few grinds of pepper (do not add salt).

2. Place on heated barbecue grill or grill pan on top of stove over medium-high heat. Grill, turning every 1 to 2 minutes for even cooking. Serve with Béarnaise Sauce in a side dish.

   NOTE: Salt tends to draw the water out of the meat, toughening it; add salt after cooking if desired.

MAKES 4 SERVINGS

4   filet mignon or boneless sirloin steaks, 6 to 8 oz each; or New York steaks, about 1 inch thick

1   clove garlic (optional)

    Freshly ground pepper

    Béarnaise Sauce (see page 134)

DONENESS – TOTAL TIME

Rare	Cook 5 to 7 minutes
Medium-rare	7 to 9 minutes
Medium	9 to 11 minutes
Medium-well	11 to 13 minutes
Well	13 to 15 minutes

Veal Saltimbocca alla Romana

Saltimbocca Roman-style, which means "jumps in the mouth" in Italian, is traditionally made with veal, but is equally delicious with chicken or turkey. Just use boneless, skinless chicken or scaloppine of turkey breasts and flatten them with a mallet; use dry white wine instead of Marsala. Serve with mashed potatoes and green beans, or asparagus when in season. This is one of my favorite dishes.

MAKES 4 SERVINGS

1 lb	thinly sliced veal scaloppine (8 pieces)
8	slices prosciutto
16	whole fresh sage leaves
4 oz	Parmesan cheese, thinly sliced
1 tbsp	*each*: butter and olive oil
3/4 cup	Marsala wine
1 tbsp	lemon juice
1 to 2 tbsp	chopped fresh parsley

1. Pound veal to 1/8 inch thickness. Top each veal slice with a slice of prosciutto; place 2 large sage leaves on top. Top with a slice of Parmesan.

2. Roll up each assembled piece, securing with a strong toothpick. Or tie with kitchen string.

3. In a large skillet, heat butter and oil over medium heat. Add veal rolls; cook for 6 to 8 minutes until well browned on all sides. Remove from pan; keep warm. Remove toothpicks or string.

4. Add wine to pan; stir with wooden spoon to scrape browned bits from the bottom of the pan. Stir in lemon juice; simmer until reduced and thickened (almost syrupy).

5. Place 2 veal rolls on each individual plate; drizzle with sauce and sprinkle with parsley.

   NOTE: If desired, place veal back in pan and spoon sauce over; remove pan and keep warm. Or, place in oven dish, pour sauce over top; cover with foil and warm in oven. Careful not to overcook.

Veal Osso Bucco
WITH GREMOLATA

This classic Italian dish is made from veal shanks simmered in an herb, wine and tomato sauce until tender. The marrow found inside the bone is considered a delicacy. Serve with mashed potatoes, rice or Polenta with Herbs (page 188).

1. In a large skillet, heat 1 tbsp of the oil over medium heat. Add carrots, onion and celery; cook for about 7 minutes, until carrots are almost soft. Add garlic, thyme and bay leaves; cook for 2 minutes. Transfer to large oven-proof casserole.

2. Add remaining 2 tbsp of the oil to skillet and increase heat to medium-high. Season veal with salt and pepper, coat with flour. Cook veal for about 4 minutes on each side or until browned. Transfer to baking dish containing vegetables.

3. Add wine and stock to skillet; bring to a boil, stirring to loosen browned bits. Pour over veal; stir in tomatoes, including juice. If necessary, add more broth to almost cover veal.

4. Cover and bake in a 375°F oven for about 1-1/2 hours, or until meat is very tender and starting to separate from bones. Before serving, remove bay leaves. If necessary, boil sauce on stovetop to reduce slightly. Place veal on plate, spoon sauce over top and sprinkle with Gremolata (recipe follows).

MAKES 4 TO 6 SERVINGS

3 tbsp	olive oil
2 cups	diced carrots (4 or 5 carrots)
1-1/2 cups	diced onion
2	stalks celery, diced
3	large cloves garlic, minced
3 tbsp	chopped fresh thyme
3	bay leaves
6	veal shanks (about 3 lb/1.5 kg)
	Salt and pepper, to taste
1/4 cup	all-purpose flour
1 cup	dry white wine
1 cup	beef stock (approx.)
1	can (28 oz) diced tomatoes

Gremolata

This tasty mixture is great on many cooked meat or fish dishes, or on roasted vegetables.

1. In a small bowl, mix together all ingredients.

   NOTE: Sauté 1/2-inch slices of yellow summer squash or zucchini in a little olive oil until tender. Toss with a little Gremolata, to taste.

1/2 cup	chopped fresh parsley
1 tbsp	grated lemon rind
2	cloves garlic, minced

Roasted Garlic Stuffing
WITH SAGE AND THYME

The mellow taste of roasted garlic updates this traditional herbed bread stuffing. It can be cooked separately in a casserole dish or used to stuff a 3-lb chicken. Triple recipe to stuff a 10 lb turkey. To cook with turkey breast, mound stuffing in a baking dish and place breast on top; cover with foil.

1. In a non-stick skillet over medium heat, melt butter. Add onion and celery; cook for 7 minutes or until softened. Stir in roasted garlic; cook for 1 minute.

2. In a 6- to 8-cup baking dish, combine bread cubes, apple, parsley, sage, thyme and onion mixture. Pour in enough chicken stock to just moisten bread. Season with a little salt and pepper.

3. Cover and bake in a 350°F oven for about 25 minutes or until apple is softened and stuffing is heated through.

   *ROASTED GARLIC: Trim about 1/4 inch from the top of a whole head of garlic. Place garlic head on a piece of foil; drizzle with a little olive oil and close foil. Bake in a 325°F oven for 50 to 60 minutes or until very soft. Let cool; squeeze softened garlic from papery skins.

MAKES 4 SERVINGS

2 tbsp	butter
1	medium onion, chopped
1	stalk celery, chopped
1	whole head of roasted garlic*
4 cups	dry bread cubes
1	tart apple, peeled and chopped
2 tbsp	*each*: chopped fresh parsley and sage
1 tbsp	chopped fresh thyme
1/4 to 1/2 cup	chicken stock or apple juice
	Salt and pepper

Fried Sage Leaves

Serve with pork, chicken or turkey as a crunchy, edible garnish, or to garnish Polenta with Herbs (see page 188).

1/2 cup	oil (such as sunflower or canola)
	Large sage leaves
	Seasoning salt (optional)

1. In a large skillet, heat oil over medium heat until a drop of water sizzles when dropped in.

2. Test one sage leaf; fry for 10 to 15 seconds or until it shrivels slightly. Remove; drain on a paper towel. Once cool, test for crispness. If soft, add another 5 seconds to cooking time. Fry remaining sage leaves, several at a time.

3. Sprinkle with seasoning salt, if using. Serve immediately.

VARIATION

Fried Parsley Leaves
Use same method as for sage but fry large clumps of fresh curly parsley. Serve with cubes of deep-fried Camembert or Brie cheese, or as a crispy garnish for soups and meats, or fish/seafood dishes.

Salmon
WITH DILL SAUCE

This sauce is the perfect accompaniment for fish such as grilled salmon or tuna, and broiled rainbow trout. For a lower-fat sauce, use low-fat sour cream or plain no-fat Greek yogurt, and low-fat mayonnaise.

1/2 cup	sour cream or plain yogurt
1/2 cup	mayonnaise
1 tbsp	finely chopped dill
1 tsp	Dijon or Herb Mustard (see page 29)
3 tsp	lime juice
4	salmon fillets, each about 4 to 6 oz
	Salt and pepper, to taste
2 tbsp	oil
	Dill sprigs, for garnish

1. In a small bowl, mix together sour cream, mayonnaise, dill, mustard and 1 tsp of the lime juice. Cover and refrigerate until ready to serve.

2. Place salmon, skin side down, on a plate. Sprinkle with remaining 2 tsp lime juice. Let stand for about 5 minutes. Season well with salt and pepper.

3. In a large skillet or grill pan heat, oil over medium heat. Place salmon in pan, skin side down. Cook for 3 to 5 minutes. Carefully turn over; remove skin. Cook on all sides for 3 to 5 minutes or until salmon is lightly browned and flakes. (Check the thickest part to see if salmon is opaque and flakes.)

   TO BARBECUE: Place salmon, skin side down, on oiled barbecue grill. Brush generously with oil. Cook on all sides over medium-high heat with lid down, and do not remove skin until salmon is completely cooked.

4. To serve, place salmon on individual serving plates. Garnish with dill sprigs. Serve with sauce.

   VARIATION: Use 2 tsp finely chopped fresh tarragon in place of dill.

Broiled Snapper
WITH LEMON AND TARRAGON BUTTER

Here's a super-easy fish dish that cooks up quickly under the broiler. Try using sole, tilapia, catfish (or basa fish) or haddock fillets instead of red snapper. Serve with rice and green beans, broccoli or peas, and carrots.

1. Rinse fish and pat dry with a paper towel. Place on a baking sheet that has been lined with foil and then lightly oiled.

2. In a small bowl, mix together butter, shallots, parsley, tarragon, lemon rind and juice; brush over fish.

3. Place fish under pre-heated broiler about 2 inches from heat. Broil for about 5 minutes, or until fish flakes with fork. To serve, garnish with tarragon sprigs and lemon slices.

   VARIATIONS: Use about 3 tbsp prepared herb butter in place of tarragon butter mixture. (See Herb Butters, page 31.)

MAKES 4 SERVINGS

4	red snapper fillets (about 8 oz each)
2 tbsp	melted butter
1 tbsp	minced shallots
1 tbsp	finely chopped fresh parsley
2 tsp	finely chopped fresh tarragon
2 tsp	finely grated lemon rind
1 tsp	lemon juice
	Tarragon sprigs and lemon slices, for garnish

Herb-Stuffed Trout

A whole trout or salmon is stuffed full of herbs, garlic and lemon. Use individual herbs such as cilantro, dill, lemon basil or tarragon, or a combination such as basil/tarragon, rosemary/lemon thyme or rosemary/oregano.

MAKES 4 SERVINGS

4	whole rainbow trout (10 to 12 oz each), or 1 whole salmon, about 3 to 4 lb)
1 tbsp	lemon juice or white wine
1 tbsp	butter or olive oil
1	clove garlic, minced
1/4 cup	chopped fresh chives
4	6-inch sprigs fresh basil
4	6-inch sprigs fresh tarragon

1. Cut 3 or 4 diagonal slashes on both sides of fish. Place each fish in center of a piece of foil large enough to fold over. Inside fish cavity, sprinkle each fish with one-quarter of each of the lemon juice, butter, garlic and chives. Place one sprig of each herb inside each fish; measure fish at thickest part, to determine cooking time. Fold foil over fish to seal.

2. Place on barbecue grill over high heat; close lid. Cook for 10 to 12 minutes per inch of stuffed thickness turning once. To check for doneness, open foil and look into slashes. Fish is done when flesh has just become opaque and flakes easily.

   TO OVEN BAKE: Place wrapped fish on baking sheet. Bake in a 450°F oven for 20 to 25 minutes for trout; up to 30 minutes for salmon.

3. Unwrap fish; remove head and tail, cut skin along spine. Fold fish back from center of cavity; discard herbs. Remove spine and bones in one piece. Remove skin if desired. May be served hot or cold.

Scallops
WITH REMOULADE SAUCE

Remoulade is a French sauce that also made its way to Louisiana and is used on cold shrimp, crab or lobster, cold meats, and fried seafood. It is also excellent with vegetables such as fresh tomatoes, avocado, or cooked asparagus; hard-cooked eggs; Po' Boy sandwiches (beef or fried seafood on a baguette or ciabatta bun); fish tacos or burgers; blackened fish, shrimp or crab cakes; to dip raw veggies (crudité) and to dress salads of carrots and celeriac (celery root), as well as alongside roast beef. It has a great many variations. Add Cajun seasoning in place of paprika, use the ketchup and omit the capers to make it more New Orleans-style vs. traditional French.

1. Remoulade: In a medium bowl, mix together all sauce ingredients until well combined. Cover and refrigerate for a couple of hours or up to 3 days.

2. Blot scallops well with paper towel. Season with salt and pepper.

3. Heat 2 tbsp of the butter and oil in large skillet over medium-high heat. When hot, add some of the scallops, placing them in pan so there is room around each. (May need to do in two batches.) Sear scallops for about 2 minutes on the first side, until they are lightly browned. Add 1 tbsp butter to pan. Turn scallops and cook for about 1 to 2 minutes more. Remove and keep warm. Cook remaining scallops, adding remaining 1 tbsp butter for the last turn. Serve with Remoulade (there may be sauce leftover). Garnish with Fried Parsley (see page 139).

VARIATION: Instead of serving with Remoulade on the side, after all the scallops are cooked (and removed), stir in 1 tsp finely chopped thyme or lemon thyme and 1 tbsp lemon juice. Stir until very hot. Pour sauce over scallops before serving. Garnish with thyme sprigs.

NOTE: Gherkin pickles may be used in place of cornichons if you are using dill in the recipe.

MAKES 4 SERVINGS

REMOULADE SAUCE
MAKES ABOUT
1-1/2 CUPS

1 cup	mayonnaise
1/4 cup	finely diced shallots
2 tbsp	finely chopped dill pickle (or cornichons), or dill pickle relish
1 tbsp	Dijon or whole grain mustard (or Creole mustard)
1 tbsp	lemon juice or vinegar
1 tbsp	ketchup (optional)
1	large clove garlic, finely minced
2 tsp	capers, drained and finely chopped (optional)
1 tsp	paprika (or 1/4 tsp smoked paprika)
1 tbsp	chopped fresh tarragon
1 tbsp	finely chopped fresh chives
	Pinch cayenne pepper, or to taste
	Salt and pepper, to taste

SCALLOPS

1 lb	dry sea scallops (untreated)
	Salt and pepper
4 tbsp	butter
2 tbsp	olive oil

Shrimp
WITH MARJORAM AND ORANGE

These shrimp have the delightful taste of herbs and orange. Serve hot or cold.

1. In a large skillet, heat oil over medium-high heat. Add shrimp and garlic; cook, stirring often, for 1 or 2 minutes, just until shrimp turns pink.

2. Add orange rind and juice; bring to a boil. Cook, stirring, for 1 or 2 minutes or until juice thickens slightly.

3. Stir in marjoram, parsley and marigold petals (if using); season with salt and pepper.

   VARIATION: Instead of oil, use 2 tbsp Herb Butter (see page 31); replace orange rind and juice with 2 tsp lemon juice and omit other herbs.

   NOTE: Marigolds add a peppery flavor to this dish.

MAKES 4 SERVINGS

2 tbsp	olive oil
1 lb	large shrimp, peeled and deveined
1	clove garlic, minced
2 tsp	finely grated orange rind
1/2 cup	orange juice
1 tbsp	finely chopped fresh marjoram or oregano
1 tbsp	finely chopped fresh parsley
1 tbsp	finely chopped marigold petals, optional (see Edible Flowers, page 38)
	Salt and pepper, to taste

Pesto Shrimp

This pesto shrimp was once described by my mentor, Carol Ferguson (see acknowledgments), as the "little black dress" of dishes as it is so simple and so good. Enjoy as an appetizer with pieces of fresh baguette to dip in the sauce, or as a main course with rice or pasta. Serve with a glass of the same white wine used in the recipe.

1. In a large skillet, heat pesto over medium-high heat. Add shrimp, wine and lemon juice; cook, stirring, for 2 to 3 minutes, until the shrimp just turns pink. Serve immediately.

MAKES 4 MAIN COURSE OR 6 TO 8 APPETIZER SERVINGS

1/2 cup	Basil Pesto (see page 162)
1 lb	large shrimp, peeled and deveined
1/3 cup	white wine
1 tsp	lemon juice

Devilled (Stuffed) Eggs

Most people love to eat stuffed eggs but seldom make them. Take these interesting versions to a party and they will be a hit. Stuffed eggs are a nutritious snack to have on hand for after school or work and on weekends. Egg yolks are rich in many vitamins and minerals, including all the fat-soluble vitamins D, E, A and K.

1. In a medium bowl, mash egg yolks with a fork. Stir in mayonnaise, mustard, chives, tarragon and a little salt and pepper. (If the mixture is not moist enough, add a little more mayonnaise to desired consistency.)

2. Refill egg whites with yolk filling, using small spoons or a pastry bag fitted with a star tip. Garnish with parsley or chive florets. Serve immediately, or cover and refrigerate up to 2 days.

MAKES 12

6	hard-cooked eggs, peeled and cut in half lengthwise
3 tbsp	mayonnaise
1 tsp	Dijon mustard or Herb Mustard (see page 29)
1 tbsp	minced chives
1 tsp	minced fresh tarragon (or 2 tsp minced fresh dill)
	Salt and pepper, to taste
	Parsley or chive florets, for garnish

VARIATIONS

Salmon or Shrimp
Add 2 tbsp mashed smoked salmon or finely chopped cooked shrimp; use dill instead of tarragon. Garnish eggs with small shrimp and or dill sprigs.

Sun-dried Tomato and Basil
Add 1 tbsp minced sun-dried tomatoes and use 1 tbsp minced fresh basil instead of chives and tarragon. Garnish with very small basil leaves.

Olive and Lemon Thyme
Add 1 tbsp minced Kalamata olives and 1/2 tsp finely chopped fresh lemon thyme (or 1/4 tsp finely chopped fresh thyme).

Olive and Sun-dried Tomato
Add 2 tbsp Olive and Sun-dried Tomato Tapenade (see page 65). Garnish with small sprigs of fresh parsley.

Garnishes
Small herb leaves (basil, chervil, cilantro, thyme) or short blades of chives, slices of olives (green or black), slices of gherkin pickles or radish halves, small thin slices of sweet or hot peppers, tomatoes, bacon bits or diced ham or prosciutto strips, capers, alfalfa sprouts, crumbled feta or blue cheese.

Egg Salad

This egg salad has a subtle touch of herbs — a nice change from the old stand-by. Use filling to make small sandwiches for a "tea" party. If desired, serve open-faced on bread and garnish tops with choice of dill sprigs, finely chopped chives, slice of radish, alfalfa or other sprouts, thin slices of sweet peppers, etc.

1. In a medium bowl, chop eggs using a pastry blender or fork.

2. Stir in mayonnaise, chives, tarragon and vinegar; mix until well combined. Season with salt and pepper.

3. Serve on buttered whole grain bread or croissant with a few lettuce leaves, if desired.

MAKES 2 SERVINGS

4	hard-cooked eggs, peeled
2 tbsp	mayonnaise
1 tbsp	finely chopped chives
1 tsp	minced fresh tarragon or chervil
1 tsp	vinegar or tarragon vinegar (see Herb Vinegars, page 22)
	Salt and pepper, to taste
4	slices whole grain bread or 2 croissants
	Lettuce leaves (optional)

TIP

Use older eggs rather than fresh for hard-cooking as they will peel more easily (simmer, do not "boil" eggs). After cooking, crack egg shells all over, then roll eggs between your hands. Begin peeling from the rounder end.

Eggs Benedetto

This is my version of Eggs Benedict (Bennie) Italian-style. Meat is layered on fried Polenta with Herbs (see page 188) and topped with poached eggs and bruschetta (bru-sketta) topping. Bellissimo!

1. Bruschetta Tomatoes: In a medium bowl, combine tomatoes, basil, 1 tbsp of the olive oil and garlic. Set aside.

2. Cut Polenta with Herbs (version made in a 13 × 9-inch pan) into 3 × 3-inch squares (approximately). Prepare this ahead. Heat about half of the remaining oil in large skillet. Fry polenta (in batches) until lightly browned on both sides. Keep warm in low oven.

3. Fry pancetta to desired crispness. Drain on paper towel. Keep warm in low oven.

4. Poach eggs in pot of boiling water, in batches. For each serving, layer two slices of fried polenta with pancetta slices and poached eggs; top with bruschetta tomato mixture. Garnish with small basil leaves.

VARIATION: Use prosciutto in place of pancetta (do not fry it); fold over onto polenta.

MAKES 6 SERVINGS

4	large Roma Tomatoes, seeded and diced
2 tbsp	chopped fresh basil
2 tbsp	olive oil
1	garlic clove, crushed
	Salt and pepper, to taste
	Polenta slices (3-inch squares)
12	slices pancetta or thinly sliced Genoa salami
12	eggs
	Basil leaves for garnish

Herb-Baked Eggs

Treat yourself to a lingering Sunday morning breakfast; sip coffee or juice while you read the paper and let the eggs bake.

1. Butter a 7-inch baking dish. Break eggs into dish; top with basil, parsley, chives, tarragon and chervil, if using. Drizzle with cream.

2. Bake in a 350°F oven for about 7 minutes. Sprinkle with cheese. Bake for 3 to 5 minutes longer or until yolks are set to your liking. Season with salt and pepper. Serve immediately.

NOTE: Chervil, widely used in French cooking, has the taste of anise (licorice notes), pepper and parsley, a bit like a cross between tarragon and parsley. It can be hard to find in stores so it is one to grow yourself. It is a component of Fines Herbes (see page 3). For more uses, see Herb Directory (page 6).

NOTE: Gruyère cheese has a lovely nutty flavor that goes well with herbs.

MAKES 1 SERVING

2	eggs
1 tbsp	*each*: finely chopped fresh basil and parsley
1 tbsp	snipped fresh chives
1 tsp	finely chopped fresh tarragon
1 tsp	chopped fresh chervil (optional)
2 tbsp	whipping cream (35%)
2 tbsp	shredded Gruyère cheese, or freshly grated Parmesan cheese
	Salt and pepper, to taste

Akoori

(INDIAN-STYLE SCRAMBLED EGGS)

These spiced eggs are a popular breakfast in India but can be eaten any time of the day. Serve with warm Naan bread and plain yogurt, if desired.

1. In a large non-stick skillet, melt butter over medium heat. Add onion, cook, stirring until soft, about 6 minutes. Add garlic and chiles and cook for 1 minute.

2. Stir in tomato, ginger, cumin and turmeric; cook for 2 minutes until most of the juice from tomatoes has evaporated.

3. In a medium bowl, beat eggs lightly; season with salt and pepper. Stir eggs into tomato mixture; add chives and half of the cilantro. Cook, stirring until soft, thick curds form.

4. Serve immediately, topped with remaining cilantro.

MAKES 4 SERVINGS

2 tbsp	butter
1 cup	finely chopped onion
1	clove garlic, minced
1 to 2	fresh green chile peppers, or to taste
1 cup	diced tomatoes
1 tsp	grated fresh ginger
3/4 tsp	ground cumin
1/2 tsp	ground turmeric
8	eggs
	Salt and pepper, to taste
1 tbsp	chopped fresh chives
2 tbsp	chopped fresh cilantro, or to taste

Scrambled Eggs
WITH HERBS

In mid-summer, when herbs are abundant in her garden, my friend Sonja likes to make these quick and easy eggs. Sometimes she adds cheese, or a little salsa and fresh cilantro, for a taste variation.

1. In a small bowl, beat together eggs and milk.

2. Stir in parsley, chives, tarragon and cheese, if using. Season with a little salt and pepper.

3. In a small skillet over medium-high heat, melt butter. Pour in egg mixture; cook, stirring often, until eggs begin to set. Serve immediately.

MAKES 1 SERVING

2	eggs
1 tbsp	milk
2 tsp	*each*: finely chopped fresh parsley and chives
1 tsp	chopped fresh tarragon
2 tbsp	shredded Gruyère or Cheddar cheese (optional)
	Salt and pepper
2 tsp	butter

VARIATIONS

- Use 2 tsp finely chopped fresh basil and 1 tsp *each*: chopped fresh chives, marjoram and parsley in place of other herbs.

- Use 2 tsp *each*: finely chopped fresh chives and dill in place of other herbs.

- Use 1 tsp *each*: finely chopped fresh thyme and parsley in place of other herbs.

- Add 1 tsp chopped fresh chervil.

Vegetable Strata

A strata is a layered egg dish made with dry bread cubes and savory ingredients. This one is full of tasty veggies and cheese – perfect for brunch, a weekend lunch or a casual dinner. It's also wholesome vegetarian fare.

1. In a large non-stick skillet, heat oil over medium heat. Add onion; cook for 5 minutes, stirring occasionally.

2. Stir in garlic, zucchini and mushrooms; cook for 5 minutes, stirring occasionally.

3. Stir in tomatoes, roasted pepper and basil. Cook for 1 minute or until thickened. Season with a little salt and pepper.

4. In a large bowl, whisk together eggs and milk; set aside.

5. Spoon one-third of the tomato sauce into lightly greased 9-inch square baking pan. Sprinkle with half of the bread cubes; top with another one-third of the sauce and half of the mozzarella, then repeat with remaining bread cubes, sauce and mozzarella.

6. Pour in egg mixture; cover and refrigerate for about 3 hours or overnight.

7. Sprinkle with Parmesan cheese. Bake in a 350°F oven for about 40 minutes or until puffed and golden brown. Let stand for 10 minutes before serving.

MAKES 6 SERVINGS

1 tbsp	olive oil
1	medium onion, diced
1	clove garlic, minced
1	small zucchini, diced
1/2 lb	mushrooms, sliced
1	can (28 oz) tomatoes, well drained and chopped
1/2 cup	diced roasted red pepper
2 tbsp	chopped fresh basil
	Salt and pepper
4	eggs
2 cups	milk
6 cups	firm bread cubes (1/2 inch thick)
1 cup	shredded mozzarella cheese (about 4 oz)
3 tbsp	grated Parmesan cheese

Smoked Salmon Strata
WITH CREAM CHEESE AND DILL

This elegant strata is the perfect make-ahead brunch dish.

1. Spread bread slices with about 1 tbsp of the softened butter and place them, buttered side down, in 13 × 9-inch baking pan (trim to fit if necessary).

2. Place salmon slices in a single layer over bread.

3. In a large skillet over medium heat, melt remaining 1 tbsp of the softened butter. Add onions; cook, stirring, until softened; distribute over salmon. Dot salmon with cream cheese cubes. Top with bread cubes.

4. In a large bowl, whisk together eggs, milk, dill and melted butter. Season with salt and a little pepper. Pour over strata, moistening all the bread cubes. Cover and refrigerate for 4 hours or overnight.

5. Bake in a 350°F oven for 35 to 40 minutes, or until puffy and golden. Serve immediately.

MAKES 6 TO 8 SERVINGS

6	slices Texas toast bread (or thickly sliced white bread)
2 tbsp	butter, softened
5 oz	smoked salmon
1 cup	chopped red onion
4 oz	cream cheese, cut into small cubes
4 cups	3/4-inch cubes of Texas toast bread (or cubes of thickly sliced white bread)
6	eggs
2 cups	milk
2 tbsp	chopped fresh dill
2 tbsp	butter, melted
1/4 tsp	salt
	Pepper

Huevos Rancheros Tostadas

These Mexican ranch-style eggs are served as a tostada, on a tortilla. Great for a special breakfast, or any time of the day, for an easy, nourishing meal. If desired, replace eggs with roasted chicken or grilled pork. Add diced jalapeño peppers or hot pepper sauce to elevate the heat. Huevos Rancheros are usually served with sunny-side up eggs and fried potatoes.

1. Heat the refried beans in the microwave in a medium bowl or in a pot on the stovetop; keep warm.

2. Heat flour tortillas in non-stick skillet over medium heat until warmed and a bit browned. Transfer to large plate; cover with foil.

3. In same skillet, melt butter. Cook eggs to desired doneness or if desired, scramble them. Season with salt and pepper.

4. Place tortilla on each plate, spread with half of the refried beans, sprinkle with cheese; place eggs on top. Sprinkle each with cilantro and chives.

5. Serve with salsa, sour cream and avocado.

VARIATION: If desired, cook diced red and green peppers in skillet first and set aside. Sprinkle on top of eggs or add to eggs when scrambling. Chives may be added to the scramble also.

NOTE: Queso fresco is a fresh, white, dry, crumbly cow's milk cheese with a sharp, slightly salty taste but milder and creamier than cotija. Cotija, a part-skim milk cheese is a bit more crumbly and has a stronger taste.

MAKES 2 SERVINGS	
2/3 cup	refried pinto beans
2	small (7-inch approx.) flour tortillas, or 4 (4-inch) corn tortillas
2 tsp	butter
4	eggs
	Salt and pepper
1/2 cup	shredded Monterey Jack, Cheddar cheese, queso fresco or cotija
2 tbsp	chopped fresh cilantro
1 tbsp	chopped fresh chives
2/3 cup	tomato salsa, your preference for heat (see page 167)
1/2 cup	sour cream
1/2 cup	diced avocado or Guacamole Dip (see page 50)

TIP

How to Buy Avocados
Avocados ripen after they are picked, turning from a dark green colour to a deep purplish, almost black. Avoid any with large indentations which is a sign of bruising. Gently squeeze with your hand, not applying pressure with finger tips to avoid bruising. When ripe, it should yield to gentle pressure. If firm, they will ripen in a few days. To speed up ripening, place in a paper bag with an apple or banana. For tip to remove pit, see page 50.

Wild Mushroom Frittata

A frittata is an Italian omelette in which the filling ingredients are mixed with the eggs before cooking. It is always served flat or cut into pieces, rather than folded. Try making one to use up leftovers or cooked vegetables such as asparagus, zucchini and sweet peppers. If you are a mushroom connoisseur (rhymes with sir not sewer), you will enjoy this rendition accented with fresh herbs.

MAKES 4 SERVINGS

2 tbsp	butter or olive oil (or half of each)
1/2 lb	fresh mixed wild mushrooms (shiitake, cremini, oyster, etc.), chopped
1/2 lb	button mushrooms, sliced
2 tbsp	*each*: finely chopped fresh parsley and thyme
6	eggs
1/4 cup	grated Parmesan cheese
1/2 cup	shredded Gruyère cheese

1. In a large non-stick skillet, heat butter over medium heat. Add wild and button mushrooms; cook for about 5 minutes or until soft and lightly browned. Stir in parsley and thyme; cook for 1 minute.

2. In a medium bowl, beat eggs; stir in Parmesan cheese. Pour over mushrooms in skillet. Lift around the cooked edges with a spatula during the first 2 minutes, to allow uncooked egg to flow underneath. Cover; cook for 3 or 4 more minutes, or until eggs are almost set. Sprinkle with Gruyère cheese.

3. If the skillet is not oven-proof, cover the handle with foil. Put skillet under broiler; broil for 1 or 2 minutes or until cheese melts. To serve, cut into wedges.

   NOTE: Stems of shiitake mushrooms are tough and need to be removed before slicing. Reserve for stock.

Veggie Burgers

This vegetarian option is great for anyone (including meat eaters) as it is full of vegetables and legumes, making it a high source of fibre.

1. In a large skillet, heat 1 tbsp of the oil over medium heat. Add onion, mushrooms, carrot, celery, red pepper, thyme and garlic. Cook until lightly softened, stirring occasionally.

2. In a large bowl, mash lentils and beans well with a fork or potato masher. Stir in vegetable mixture, parsley, chives, breadcrumbs and salt and pepper.

3. Shape into 4 patties, 1/2 inch thick; coat lightly with breadcrumbs. Cover and chill for at least an hour.

4. In the same skillet (don't need to wash), heat the remaining oil over medium heat. Add patties; cook for about 3 or 4 minutes per side, until golden brown.

5. Serve on burger buns with your choice of sauces: Tzatziki, Remoulade or Basil Mayonnaise, as well as your choice of burger fixings.

MAKES 4 BURGERS

2 tbsp	vegetable oil
1 cup	finely chopped onion
1 cup	finely chopped mushrooms
1/2 cup	coarsely grated carrot
1/2 cup	finely chopped celery
1/3 cup	finely chopped red pepper
1 tsp	finely chopped fresh thyme leaves
2	large cloves garlic, minced
1 cup	canned or cooked lentils
1 cup	canned or cooked cannellini beans (white kidney beans)
1/4 cup	finely chopped parsley or cilantro
2 tbsp	finely chopped fresh chives
2 tbsp	dry breadcrumbs or panko crumbs
1/4 tsp	salt
	Pepper, to taste
1/2 cup	dry breadcrumbs or panko crumbs for coating
4	burger buns (such as: whole wheat, multigrain or pretzel)
	Sauces: Tzatziki (see page 165), Remoulade (see page 143) or Basil Mayonnaise (see page 111)

TIP

To barbecue, cut 4 rectangles of foil (may be doubled in thickness) about twice the width of the burgers; grease well. Place each patty on one half of the foil; fold the other half over top. Chill as above. Place patties on grill (still on the foil); fold back foil (so one side is empty). Cook for 4 minutes. Flip patty onto the other half of the foil; cook for 4 minutes more or until golden brown. This cooking technique prevents the burgers from sticking to the grill and allows for easy removal. Serve as above.

PESTO, SAUCES AND SALSAS

Let the condiment be the star! Add an herbal touch to meats, fish and seafood, eggs, or veggie burgers! Serve creamy dill sauce with grilled salmon, serve rosemary applesauce with roast chicken or pork, add a pesto pizzazz to recipes throughout the book and serve cucumber raita as a cooling condiment to spicy Indian dishes, add salsa to fish or Mexican dishes.

ALL ABOUT PESTO

Traditional basil pesto originated in Genoa, Italy, and is now renowned the world over. Its name comes from the word "pestare," which means to pound or grind. It can be made in the food processor, but traditionalists still make it using a mortar and pestle.

Typically made using large-leaf basil, this delicious and versatile paste can be used with vegetables (especially tomatoes, eggplant and zucchini), with meats and seafood, in soups and cheese spreads, in breads, etc. Refer to the index for many uses of pesto throughout the book.

IDEAS FOR USING PESTO

- toss on hot cooked pasta; add to cheese filling for lasagna
- mix equal parts with sour cream or plain yogurt for a veggie dip
- spoon onto a baked potato and top with extra Parmesan cheese
- stir into mashed potatoes along with a bit of warmed milk
- spread on crackers or toasted bread
- spread on toasted bread and cover with sliced tomatoes
- *Bruschetta*: rub bread with garlic, brush with olive oil, top with pesto and fresh diced tomatoes
- halve beefsteak tomatoes, place 1 tbsp pesto on each and let marinate for an hour; sprinkle with Parmesan cheese; eat cold or broil
- halve an eggplant and bake until almost soft; make slices 1 inch apart and several inches deep but not all the way through; spread with pesto, sprinkle with thinly sliced Parmesan cheese and bake until cheese is melted and golden
- add to mayonnaise or sour cream and use as a sandwich spread, a dressing for seafood or pasta salads or potato salads, a dip or a topping for a baked potato
- spread on the bottom crust for a tomato tart, tomato quiche or pizza
- add a dollop to omelettes or frittata
- stir into a finished risotto
- stir a spoonful into a vinaigrette for salad, or into dressing for grilled vegetables, bean salads
- stir into a vegetable stew (onions, garlic, sweet green and red peppers, zucchini, tomatoes, potatoes)
- stir into soups such as minestrone, zucchini, lentil
- serve a dollop with grilled foods such as chicken or fish
- marinate chicken or lamb in 2 tbsp pesto, 1 tbsp lemon juice and pepper; for about 2 hours; brush on additional marinade when grilling or broiling
- brush on refrigerator crescent rolls, roll up and bake
- brush on puff pastry strips, twist and bake
- use to fill mushroom caps, top with breadcrumbs and bake

SUBSTITUTIONS

- In place of pine nuts, use pistachios (unsalted, roasted), cashews, walnuts, pecans, sunflower seeds, or blanched almonds. To enhance their flavor, toast in a 325°F oven for about 8 minutes; cool to room temperature before adding.
- For a lower-fat version, reduce the oil to 1/4 cup and add 2 tsp lemon juice and 1/2 cup chicken stock. Use right away.
- Replace some of the oil with the oil from sun-dried tomatoes.
- Use sunflower oil in place of olive oil.
- Use 1/4 cup grated Pecorino Romano cheese and 1/4 cup grated Parmigiano Reggiano cheese.
- Roast the garlic (see page 138).

VARIATIONS

You can also make other pesto-like sauces with soft herbs like cilantro and chives. See also Pistou (page 81), Chimichurri (page 163) and Chermoula Sauces (page 164).

Basil Pesto

There is nothing quite like this amazing herb sauce. Every second year, Genoa Italy hosts the World Pesto Championship in March or April. Traditionalists use only basil but I like to add a bit of parsley to bring the flavors together. An Italian lady in one of my classes said it was excellent.

2 cups	packed basil leaves
1/4 cup	Italian parsley leaves (or 1/2 cup curly parsley) (optional)
3	cloves garlic
1/2 cup	pine nuts
1/2 cup	grated Parmesan cheese (use Parmigiano Reggiano)
1/3 to 1/2 cup	olive oil

1. In food processor, combine basil, parsley (if using), garlic and pine nuts; pulse until finely minced.

2. Add cheese and process to blend.

3. Using the feed tube, slowly drizzle in oil, processing to a moist paste.

4. Remove to a small bowl and cover with plastic wrap pressed onto the surface. (This prevents oxidative browning.) Or cover surface with a thin film of oil, or place pesto in a medium zip-lock bag, remove air and seal. Pesto will keep, refrigerated, about a week.

TIP: If you purchase the Parmesan cheese already grated, use the small container it came in to freeze the Pesto in.

NOTE: To freeze pesto, prepare as above, omitting the cheese (if desired) and using the smaller amount of oil. Place in a small freezer container, smoothing the top; pour a thin layer of olive oil over top. Then press a piece of plastic wrap onto the surface, smoothing out any air. Place lid on container and mark with the date. Other options are to freeze small amounts in ice cube trays (keep ones just for herbs); when frozen transfer to freezer bags (label and date.) May be kept frozen up to 6 months. Stir in Parmesan after thawing.

TIPS FOR THAWING: Thaw in refrigerator. Do not microwave to thaw as it can cook the pesto. To perk up the color after thawing, stir in 2 tbsp finely chopped fresh parsley.

Chimichurri Verde

This delicious, garlicky, uncooked herb sauce rivals basil pesto. The name derives from the Basque region (an area between northern Spain and France). It translates to "a mixture of several things in no particular order" and is believed to have been brought to Argentina and Uruguay by Basque peoples who migrated there. It then spread to many countries in Central and South America giving birth to its many variations. It is a condiment to grilled meats, especially beef, and fish (or slathered on before cooking) but is also good on vegetables such as potatoes and sweet potatoes (tossed in before roasting), squash, beets and more. Stir into rice or spoon over hummus. You may like it with eggs or on pizza too!

MAKES 3/4 CUP

2 tbsp	minced garlic (2 to 3 large)
2 tbsp	minced shallot
2 cups	loosely packed curly parsley (flat leaf Italian may also be used)
2 tbsp	finely chopped fresh oregano (or 2 tsp dried)
2 tbsp	red wine vinegar
1/2 tsp	salt
1/4 tsp	pepper
1/2 tsp	crushed red chile pepper flakes (or 1 tbsp minced small red chiles)
1/3 cup	olive oil

1. Place garlic and shallots in food processor and chop more finely. Add parsley and oregano; pulse to chop finely.

2. Add vinegar, salt, pepper and chile flakes. Pulse to combine well.

3. Using feed tube, drizzle in the olive oil. Finished sauce should not run off a spoon but be the consistency of a loose pesto. Transfer to a jar. Let stand for about 2 hours before using. (Make the day before if you can.) Cover and refrigerate up to 2 weeks (let come to room temperature before using).

CHIMICHURRI MAYONNAISE: Mix equal parts chimichurri sauce and mayonnaise. Serve with grilled chicken or add to a chicken salad. Spread on bread for a meat sandwich.

CHIMICHURRI DIP: Mix with equal parts sour cream and mayonnaise.

VARIATIONS:
- Add 1 tbsp finely chopped fresh rosemary (for beef, chicken or lamb) or lemon thyme (for fish or chicken).
- Add 1 cup loosely packed fresh cilantro leaves if desired, replace the vinegar with lime or lemon juice and add more oil as needed to desired consistency.
- Add 1/2 tsp smoked paprika, or minced jalapeño peppers, to taste.
- Add 1/2 tsp ground cumin.

Chermoula Sauce

This green herb sauce hails from North Africa, and this version is from Morocco. Serve with meats, chicken, seafood and vegetables. Use it to finish foods at the end of cooking, or for roasting vegetables.

1. Place garlic in food processor and chop finely. Add cilantro and parsley; pulse to chop finely.

2. Add lemon rind and juice, coriander, cumin, paprika and salt. Pulse to combine well.

3. Using feed tube, drizzle in olive oil; pulse until smooth.

MAKES 2 CUPS

3	large cloves garlic
2-1/2 cups	loosely packed fresh cilantro
1-1/2 cups	loosely packed fresh parsley
1 tsp	finely grated lemon rind
1 tbsp	lemon juice
2 tsp	*each*: ground coriander, ground cumin and paprika
1/2 tsp	salt
1/2 cup	olive oil

Chicken Chermoula

1. In a large skillet, heat oil over medium heat. Brown chicken thighs for about 5 minutes per side.

2. Place in baking pan; brush all over with about 1/2 cup of the Chermoula Sauce. Bake in 350°F oven for about 15 minutes more (depending on thickness) until internal temperature reaches 165°F. Or grill chicken on barbecue.

3. Serve with additional sauce or chermoula stirred into mayonnaise or plain Greek yogurt.

MAKES 4 SERVINGS

8	boneless chicken thighs (about 2 lbs)
1 tbsp	olive oil
1/2 to 3/4 cup	Chermoula Sauce (see above)

Raita
CUCUMBER-YOGURT SAUCE

This condiment is a great complement to the heat of spicy Indian dishes.

1. In a medium bowl, mix together all ingredients. Refrigerate up to 2 days. If making ahead, sprinkle chopped cucumber with salt; let stand for 5 minutes. Rinse and drain; then add to yogurt.

   VARIATION: Replace cucumber with grated carrot and add 1/4 cup golden raisins.

MAKES ABOUT 1-1/2 CUPS

1 cup	plain yogurt
1/2 cup	diced English cucumber (or peeled and seeded field cucumber)
1/4 cup	chopped green onions or sweet onion (or 2 tbsp chopped fresh chives)
2 tbsp	liquid honey (optional)
2 tbsp	finely chopped fresh cilantro (or 1 tbsp finely chopped fresh mint)
Pinch	*each*: salt and ground cumin and ground coriander, or to taste

Tzatziki
MINT-CUCUMBER DIP

This garlicky Greek sauce or dip can be served with warmed pita bread or raw vegetables. It may also be served over sliced tomatoes or to top burgers or alongside grilled chicken skewers.

1. Place yogurt in a coffee filter or wet paper towel set into a sieve over a bowl. Cover and refrigerate about 3 hours, until some of the liquid drains off and yogurt thickens slightly. If using Greek yogurt that is very thick, this step can be skipped.

2. Sprinkle cucumber with a little salt. Let stand for 5 minutes; pour through sieve and squeeze to remove liquid.

3. In a medium bowl, mix together thickened yogurt, cucumber, garlic, lemon juice, mint and dill, if using. Season with a little salt and pepper.

MAKES ABOUT 2-1/2 CUPS

2 cups	plain yogurt or Greek yogurt
3/4 cup	finely grated, peeled and seeded cucumber
2	cloves garlic, crushed
1 tsp	lemon juice
1 tbsp	finely chopped fresh mint
2 tbsp	finely chopped fresh dill (optional)
	Salt and pepper, to taste

Rosemary Applesauce

Serve this sweet sauce with pork roast or pork chops. Use apples that soften when they cook, such as McIntosh, Empire, Cortland, Golden Delicious or Russet. If the apples are sweet enough, eliminate the sweetener.

MAKES 1 CUP

2	large, tart apples, peeled, cored and sliced (about 3 cups)
3	3-inch sprigs fresh rosemary
2 tbsp	pure maple syrup or brown sugar (optional)

1. In a 4-cup glass measuring cup, gently mix together apples and rosemary sprigs. Cover with plastic wrap; microwave on high for 3 to 6 minutes, stirring occasionally, until apples are very soft. Let stand until cool.

2. Remove rosemary; discard. Stir until apples are smooth. Stir in maple syrup, if using.

About Salsas

Tomato salsa currently outsells ketchup in North America as the hottest appetizer/condiment going, no doubt because it's low in fat and has spice-appeal. Today salsa can mean anything from fruity concoctions nestled alongside grilled foods to fresh or cooked tortilla dips, but all have one thing in common – the addition of chile peppers.

Choose your hot peppers wisely; most available are jalapeños and red finger hots, but if you think the hotter, the better, then go for the fiery blaze of Jamaican, habaneros or Scotch bonnets.

> **CAUTION**
>
> Use plastic gloves when working with hot chile peppers and avoid touching eyes.

> **NOTE**
>
> The hotness of chile peppers is measured in Scoville heat units (SHU). A sweet or bell pepper is a 0; poblano 1,000 – 2,000; jalapeno 2,500 to 8,000; serrano 8,000 to 22,000; Thai 50,000 to 100,000; orange Habanero 150,000 to 325,000 and so on up to over 1,000,000.

Black Bean and Corn Salsa

Feel free to turn up the heat by using some of the scorching varieties of chili peppers out there. This makes a great little side salad to chicken or ribs, a delicious topping for tacos or great dip for nachos.

1. In a large bowl combine all ingredients, stirring gently to mix well. May be made ahead and refrigerated up to 3 days.

MAKES ABOUT
3-1/2 CUPS

1 cup	cooked black beans, drained
1 cup	cooked kernel corn
1 cup	chopped, seeded tomatoes
1/3 cup	diced sweet onion or green onion
1/4 cup	diced roasted red peppers
1 tbsp	minced jalapeño pepper
1 tbsp	chopped fresh cilantro or parsley
1	large clove garlic, minced
	Salt and pepper, to taste

Mango Pineapple Salsa

Serve this salsa with grilled chicken, or fish such as swordfish, shark and tuna. It also makes a tasty appetizer when spooned on top of small crab, shrimp or salmon cakes (see page 62), or add to chicken "Buddha bowls."

1. In a medium bowl, combine all ingredients. Let stand for 30 minutes to allow flavors to develop.

MAKES ABOUT 2 CUPS

3/4 cup	diced mango, peach or papaya
3/4 cup	diced pineapple
1/2 cup	diced red pepper
1/4 cup	chopped green onion
2 tbsp	minced jalapeño pepper, or to taste
2 tbsp	chopped fresh cilantro
2 tsp	lime juice
1/4 tsp	ground cumin

Fresh Tomato Salsa

Make this fresh salsa when tomatoes are at their sweet best. Cilantro gives it the authentic Mexican taste. It's a tasty combination that's a great substitute for bruschetta topping.

1. In a medium bowl, combine all ingredients, stirring gently to mix well. For best flavor, do not refrigerate, and use salsa within a few hours of making.

MAKES 2 CUPS

2 cups	diced, seeded tomatoes
2	green onions, chopped
1	clove garlic, minced
1 tbsp	minced jalapeño pepper
1 tbsp	finely chopped fresh cilantro
1 tbsp	*each*: lime juice and olive oil
1/4 tsp	ground cumin
	Salt and pepper, to taste

PASTA, RICE AND GRAINS

From delicate homemade basil Fettuccine, or pasta with lemon and herbs to piquant pesto, polenta, rich risotto and hearty grains, herbs add flavors that take these starches to new heights.

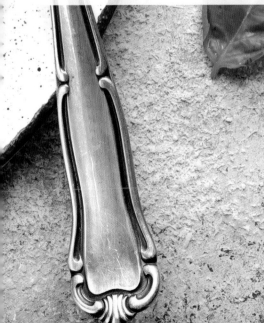

Chicken Fettuccine
IN PESTO-CREAM SAUCE

Pesto lovers will enjoy this creamy pasta sauce. Substitute shrimp for the chicken, if you like.

1. In a large pot of boiling salted water, cook fettuccine until tender but firm.

2. Meanwhile, in a very large skillet, heat oil over medium heat. Add chicken; cook on both sides until lightly browned and no longer pink inside.

3. Stir in pesto and sun-dried tomatoes; cook until heated through. Add cooked pasta to skillet.

4. Pour in cream; stir gently to coat pasta and heat through. Garnish with parsley and serve immediately with cheese.

MAKES 2 SERVINGS

8 oz	fettuccine (or linguine or penne)
1 tbsp	oil
2	boneless, skinless chicken breasts, sliced
1/2 cup	Basil Pesto (see page 162)
1/3 cup	soft sun-dried tomatoes, sliced or chopped
1 cup	table cream (18%)
	Parsley sprigs, for garnish
	Freshly grated Parmesan cheese

Herbed Orzo

This speedy dish is excellent served with grilled chicken or lamb, or as a summer pasta salad with sliced cooked chicken or fish stirred in.

1. In a medium saucepan of boiling salted water, cook orzo for 6 to 8 minutes or just until tender. Drain well.

2. In a large skillet, heat oil over medium-low heat. Stir in garlic, parsley, oregano and lemon rind. Cook, stirring, for about 1 minute.

3. Stir in orzo and feta; heat through.

   NOTE: Orzo is a tiny rice-shaped pasta. Look for it in supermarkets and bulk food stores.

MAKES 4 SERVINGS

2 cups	orzo pasta
2 tbsp	olive oil
1	large clove garlic, minced (or 2 tsp minced garlic chives)
1/3 cup	finely chopped fresh parsley
2 tbsp	finely chopped fresh oregano
1 tsp	finely grated lemon rind
1/2 cup	crumbled feta cheese

Pad Thai

It is the variety of interesting ingredients that makes this trendy stir-fried rice noodle dish so popular. Fresh cilantro gives this dish its final signature.

1. In a small bowl, mix together soy sauce, lemon juice, ketchup, brown sugar, sesame oil and hot red pepper flakes; set aside.

2. Cook noodles in boiling salted water for 2 to 3 minutes or until tender. Drain noodles, cover and set aside.

3. In a large wok or non-stick skillet, heat oil over medium heat. Cook chicken just until it changes color; remove with a slotted spoon.

4. Add tofu, garlic and ginger to pan; cook for 1 minute. Stir in peppers; cook for 2 minutes.

5. Stir in shrimp (if using), bean sprouts and cooked noodles. Pour in soy sauce mixture. Toss well and heat through.

6. Serve immediately, sprinkled with peanuts, chives and cilantro.

   VARIATION: For a meatless version, omit the chicken and replace with 2 eggs. Beat eggs in a small bowl, and cook in the centre of wok or pan, after the peppers are cooked. Stir eggs into the mixture.

MAKES 4 SERVINGS

2 tbsp	*each*: soy sauce, lemon juice
1 tbsp	*each*: ketchup, packed brown sugar
2 tsp	dark sesame oil
1/4 tsp	hot red pepper flakes
5 oz	wide rice stick noodles
1 tbsp	oil
1	boneless chicken breast, thinly sliced
6 oz	extra-firm tofu, cut into 1/2-inch cubes
2	cloves garlic, minced
1 tbsp	minced fresh ginger
3/4 cup	*each*: sweet red and yellow peppers, thinly sliced
12	peeled and deveined, cooked jumbo shrimp (optional)
1 cup	bean sprouts
1/4 cup	*each*: chopped roasted peanuts, sliced chives or green onions, chopped fresh cilantro

Pasta
WITH LEMON AND HERB CREAM SAUCE

This is a great side dish to serve with grilled shrimp or chicken.

1. In a large pot of boiling salted water, cook pasta until tender but firm; drain.

2. In a large skillet, heat oil over medium heat. Add shallots; cook, stirring often, for 2 or 3 minutes or until softened.

3. Stir in cream and stock. Simmer, uncovered, until sauce reduces and is slightly thickened, for about 5 minutes.

4. Add pasta, lemon rind, parsley and chives; toss to coat well. Serve immediately.

MAKES 2 SERVINGS

8 oz	spaghetti or linguine
1 tbsp	olive oil
1/2 cup	finely chopped shallots
3/4 cup	table cream (18%)
1/2 cup	chicken or vegetable stock (or half stock and half white wine)
2 tsp	grated lemon rind
4 tbsp	finely chopped fresh parsley
2 tbsp	snipped fresh chives

VARIATIONS

- If serving with fish, add 2 tbsp chopped fresh dill; add 2 tbsp chopped toasted walnuts just before serving.

- Use 2 tbsp finely chopped fresh sage in place of chives. Add 1/2 cup fresh or frozen cooked peas, 3 oz diced prosciutto or smoked ham; cook 1 minute longer. Sprinkle with 1/4 cup Parmesan cheese.

Pesto Pasta

The rich herbal aroma of this dish promises a treat for the taste buds! Savor the crunch of toasted pine nuts, the chewiness and tang of sun-dried tomatoes and the robustness of fresh curls of Parmesan in this speedy pasta. Serve it as the main course with a salad, or as the perfect side dish to roasted chicken. This dish was a big hit at my herb cooking classes.

MAKES 4 TO 6 SERVINGS

1 lb	penne rigate (ridged)
1 cup	Basil Pesto (see page 162)
12	cherry tomatoes, halved
1/3 cup	chopped soft sun-dried tomatoes
1/4 cup	toasted pine nuts
	Pepper, to taste
1/4 cup	shaved Parmesan cheese
	Fresh basil leaves, for garnish

1. In a large pot of boiling salted water, cook penne until tender but firm; drain well. Save a bit of the pasta cooking water. Transfer to a heated serving dish.

2. Add pesto to penne and toss. If pesto is too thick to blend in, add 1 tbsp pasta water or hot water.

3. Stir in cherry tomatoes, sun-dried tomatoes and pine nuts; season with pepper.

4. Use a cheese plane or vegetable peeler to make cheese shavings; sprinkle on top of pasta. Garnish top with fresh basil leaves. Serve hot or at room temperature.

Fresh Tomato and Basil Sauce

Enjoy this delicious fresh sauce with pasta or as a bruschetta (bru-sketta) topping.

1. In a large skillet, heat oil over medium heat. Add onion; cook for 5 minutes or until softened. Stir in garlic; cook for 1 minute.

2. Stir in fresh and sun-dried tomatoes. Reduce heat to medium-low; cook for 3 minutes or until fresh tomatoes begin to break down.

3. Stir in basil, parsley and hot red pepper flakes, if using. Cook for 1 minute; season with salt and pepper. Serve over hot rotini or fusilli with freshly grated Parmesan cheese.

   BRUSCHETTA: Spread sauce on prepared toasts; top with grated Parmesan and broil for 2 minutes or until cheese is golden.

MAKES 2 LARGE
SERVINGS OR 4
APPETIZER SERVINGS

1/4 cup	olive oil
1	small onion, chopped
2	cloves garlic, minced
1-1/2 lb	fresh tomatoes, seeded and chopped
1/3 cup	drained and chopped sun-dried tomatoes (oil-packed)
1/2 cup	coarsely chopped fresh basil
1/4 cup	coarsely chopped fresh parsley
1/4 tsp	hot red pepper flakes (optional)
	Salt and pepper, to taste

Basil Fettuccine

HOMEMADE

This easy dough can be made in a large bowl if you do not have a food processor and rolled thin and cut by hand if you do not have a pasta machine. A stand mixer fitted with a dough hook can be used for larger batches. Semolina flour is made from hard, durum wheat that is high in protein. It has a slight yellow colour and is perfect for pasta. You will find it in most supermarkets.

1. Blanch basil in medium pot of boiling water for 1 minute. Drain well and place on paper towel. Blot leaves and set aside.

2. Combine flours in food processor fitted with the metal blade; pulse to mix. Pulse in basil until well combined. Add eggs; process until it forms a breadcrumb-like texture. It should press together between fingers into a slightly sticky dough. If too dry, drizzle in a very little amount of warm water through the feed tube and continue processing until the dough comes together. (By hand, make well in center of flour; add eggs and scramble. Blend into flour. For stand mixer, mix 3 to 4 minutes.)

3. Scrape dough onto a lightly floured surface. Knead dough for about 2 minutes, until it becomes a smooth ball. Wrap with plastic wrap; let rest for 30 minutes to an hour.

MAKES 1 LB (3 TO 4 SERVINGS)

1 cup	packed fresh basil leaves (finely chop if making by hand)
1-2/3 cups	Double Zero "00" flour or unbleached all-purpose flour
1/3 cup	semolina flour (or more all-purpose flour)
3	eggs

4. Divide dough into 4 pieces. Cover 3 portions with a clean cloth. Set the pasta machine roller on the widest setting. Lightly flour the first piece; pass once through rollers. Fold dough over in thirds; press down to force out any air. Feed dough back through rollers from the narrow side. Repeat folding and rolling 5 times, adding flour if needed.

5. Reset rollers for the next thinner setting. Lightly flour the dough but do not fold it this time. Pass through pasta machine again. Repeat, lower the setting until it is on the thinnest setting. Lay dough on lightly floured surface; cover. Repeat with remaining pieces. (By hand, roll to 1/16-inch thickness and cut with pizza cutter or knife.)

6. Choose Fettuccine cutting attachment. Pass dough through machine. Separate strands with a little flour to keep them from sticking. Lay flat after drying for 5 minutes, wrap around into "nests" and place on baking sheet; cover with clean cloth. If you plan to cook them the same day, dry the noodles for 30 minutes. Repeat with remaining dough.

7. To cook: Bring a large pot of water to a boil over high heat. Salt water generously (should taste salty). Add Fettuccine and return to a boil; cook for 3 minutes; test doneness. If still too firm, cook for another 1 to 3 minutes. Drain well. Reserve about 1/2 cup pasta water (ladle into a glass measure). Use to make Basil Fettuccine Alfredo (see page 180) or Basil Fettuccine with Zucchini and Eggplant (see page 181).

TIPS

- Dried noodles can be stored for 2 days if wrapped well and put in airtight container in the refrigerator.

- Dough may be well wrapped and frozen up to 4 weeks. When ready to make pasta, thaw in refrigerator overnight.

- Freezing cut pasta: Toss pasta in flour; shake to remove excess. Lay out on a baking sheet and freeze until solid (this prevents sticking). Package in freezer bags in individual serving amounts. Mark with the" use by" date. Keeps up to 4 weeks.

Basil Fettuccine Alfredo

Use Basil Fettuccine to make this dish. Alfredo is a rich, creamy sauce created and served by restauranteur Alfredo di Lelio in Rome in the 1920's. The story is that he made it to nourish his wife after childbirth, then added to his restaurant menu later on. It was made with 3 simple ingredients; pasta, butter and cheese. Here garlic and cream are added (and less butter), which makes it more North American.

1. In a large non-stick skillet, over medium heat, melt butter. Add garlic; cook for 1 minute.

2. Immediately stir in 1 lb cooked and drained fettuccine. Toss to coat.

3. Stir in cream; heat and stir until it bubbles. Stir in 1/2 cup of the cheese; stir to coat fettuccine. Cook until cream evaporates and sauce thickens.

4. Transfer to platter or large bowls. Sprinkle with parsley. Serve with remaining cheese.

   NOTE: May also be made with 1 lb cooked dry fettuccine or plain fresh pasta. Add 1/4 cup chopped fresh basil to sauce at end of cooking time.

   VARIATION: Add chopped cooked chicken or turkey or serve alongside grilled chicken.

MAKES 4 SERVINGS

3 tbsp	butter
1	clove garlic, minced
1 lb	cooked Basil Fettuccine (see page 178)
1 cup	whipping cream (35%) or table cream (18%)
1 cup	freshly grated Parmesan cheese, divided
2 tbsp	finely chopped fresh Italian parsley

Basil Fettuccine
WITH ZUCCHINI AND EGGPLANT

Use Basil Fettuccine to make this dish. Serve topped with good quality grated Parmigiano Reggiano (Parmesan) or Grana Padano cheese and garlic bread on the side.

1. In a large non-stick skillet, heat 2 tbsp of the oil over medium heat. Add eggplant; cook and stir for 5 minutes or until tender. Remove to a plate.

2. Add remaining 1 tbsp oil to pan. Add zucchini and tomatoes; cook until zucchini is tender.

3. Return eggplant to pan. Add garlic and oregano. Season with salt and pepper. Cook for 2 to 3 minutes until heated through.

4. Stir in 1 lb cooked and drained fettuccine. Toss to coat. Add a little of the reserved pasta water if needed. Transfer to platter or large bowls.

   NOTE: May also be made with 1 lb cooked dry Fettuccine or plain fresh pasta. Add 1/4 cup chopped fresh basil to sauce at end of cooking time.

   VARIATION: If desired, add cooked shrimp.

MAKES 4 SERVINGS

3 tbsp	olive oil
2 cups	diced Italian eggplant
2 cups	diced zucchini
2 cups	diced Roma tomatoes
2	cloves garlic, minced
1 tbsp	chopped fresh oregano (1 tsp dried)
	Salt and pepper, to taste
1 lb	cooked Basil Fettuccine (see page 178)

Shrimp, Salmon and Asparagus Pasta Salad

This is a nice, light summer salad that is attractive served on lettuce leaves and garnished with fresh dill sprigs and lemon wedges.

Salad

1. In a large pot of boiling salted water, cook pasta shells until tender but firm. Drain and rinse under cold running water; drain well.

2. Trim asparagus and cut into small pieces. Cook in microwave or in a saucepan of boiling water just until tender-crisp. Immediately drain and cover with cold water until cool; drain well.

3. In a large bowl combine pasta, asparagus, shrimp, salmon and onion.

Dressing

1. In a small bowl, mix together yogurt, mayonnaise, lemon juice and garlic. Stir in chives and dill; add a little salt and pepper. Pour over salad and mix gently. Taste and adjust seasoning.

2. Cover and chill for 1 to 2 hours to blend flavors. Serve on lettuce leaves on individual salad plates; garnish with dill sprigs and lemon wedges.

SALAD

3 cups	small pasta shells
1/2 lb	asparagus (or 6 oz snow peas, halved diagonally)
1 cup	*each*: cooked peeled shrimp and chunks of poached or grilled salmon
1/4 cup	chopped red onion

DRESSING

1/4 cup	low-fat plain yogurt or sour cream
2 tbsp	low-fat mayonnaise
1 tbsp	lemon juice
1	clove garlic, crushed
1/4 cup	chopped fresh chives
2 tbsp	finely chopped fresh dill
	Salt and pepper
	Leaf lettuce
	Dill sprigs and lemon wedges, for garnish

Summer Vegetable Pasta

Enjoy the sweet taste of summer's tomatoes with zucchini or summer squash, garlic and a bounty of fresh herbs. Parsley has the ability to soften the taste of other herbs as well as to blend the flavors of mixed herbs with each other and with other ingredients. When using Italian parsley in place of curly parsley, less is needed, as it has a stronger flavor.

1. In a large pot of boiling salted water, cook pasta until tender but firm; drain.

2. Meanwhile, in a large skillet, heat oil over medium heat. Add zucchini and garlic and cook for 5 minutes, stirring frequently.

3. Add tomatoes and wine; cook for 5 minutes, stirring frequently, until sauce thickens. Stir in basil, chives, parsley and marjoram; cook for 2 minutes. Season with salt and pepper.

4. Toss sauce with pasta; serve immediately with cheese.

MAKES 4 SERVINGS

1 lb	fusilli or rotini
2 tbsp	olive oil
4 cups	diced or chopped zucchini
1	clove garlic, minced
4 cups	chopped tomatoes
1/4 cup	white wine or dry sherry
1/3 cup	chopped fresh basil
1/4 cup	chopped fresh chives
1/4 cup	chopped fresh Italian parsley
2 tbsp	chopped fresh marjoram
	Salt and pepper, to taste
	Grated Parmesan cheese

Asparagus and Mushroom Risotto
WITH ROASTED GARLIC

Risotto is a classic, creamy rice dish from Italy, typically made with Arborio rice. The rice will be slightly firm in the center when done. Serve with roast pork or chops.

1. In a large skillet, heat 2 tbsp of the oil over medium-high heat. Add sliced mushrooms; cook, stirring frequently, until tender.

2. Drain porcini mushrooms, reserving soaking liquid. Stir porcini mushrooms, onion, yellow pepper and thyme into cooked mushrooms. Cook for about 2 minutes, stirring occasionally; set aside.

3. Cut asparagus tips about 1-1/2 inches long; set aside. Chop stems into 3/4-inch pieces. Cook stems in boiling water for 2 minutes; add tips and cook for 1 minute longer; drain and set aside.

4. In a large skillet or wok, heat remaining 1 tbsp of the oil over high heat. Add rice; cook, stirring, for 1 minute. Add wine and reserved liquid from dried mushrooms. Cook, stirring constantly, until liquid is almost completely absorbed. Stir in stock 3/4 cup at a time, stirring constantly, adding more when it is almost completely absorbed. This should take about 20 minutes.

5. Stir in roasted garlic, mushroom mixture, asparagus, 1/2 cup of the Parmesan cheese and parsley. Season with salt and pepper. Sprinkle each serving with remaining 1/4 cup of the Parmesan cheese.

   NOTES: Arborio rice is a short-grained rice from Arborio, Italy (Piedmont region) and is used when a creamy texture is desired in a dish.

MAKES 4 SERVINGS

3 tbsp	olive oil
1/2 lb	mushrooms, sliced
1/2 oz	dried porcini mushrooms (re-hydrated in very hot water for 30 minutes)
3/4 cup	*each*: diced red onion and diced sweet yellow pepper
1 tbsp	finely chopped fresh thyme or lemon thyme
1/2 lb	fresh asparagus
1-1/2 cups	Arborio rice
1/2 cup	dry white wine
6 cups	hot chicken stock
1	whole head roasted garlic or Herb Roasted Garlic (see page 203)
3/4 cup	grated Parmesan cheese
1/4 cup	chopped fresh Italian parsley
	Salt and pepper, to taste

RISOTTO VARIATIONS

PESTO RISOTTO
Serve with chicken or veal.

1. In a large skillet, heat oil over medium heat. Add 1/2 cup chopped onion; cook until softened, about 7 minutes. Reduce heat to low and cover to speed softening without burning. Stir occasionally.

2. Skip to Step 4 (omit mushrooms, red onion, yellow pepper, thyme, asparagus and roasted garlic).

3. When rice is creamy and tender, stir in 1/3 cup Basil Pesto (see page 162) and 1/2 cup of the Parmesan cheese. Season with salt and pepper. Sprinkle each serving with the remaining cheese.

ROSEMARY AND ASIAGO RISOTTO

1. In a large skillet, heat oil over medium heat. Add 1/2 cup chopped onion; cook, until softened, about 7 minutes. Reduce heat to low and cover to speed softening without burning. Stir occasionally. Stir in 2 minced garlic cloves and 1 tbsp finely chopped fresh rosemary; cook 1 minute longer.

2. Skip to Step 4 (omit mushrooms, red onion, yellow pepper, thyme, asparagus and roasted garlic).

3. When rice is creamy and tender, stir in 1/2 cup grated Asiago cheese and 1/4 cup grated Parmesan cheese. Season with salt and pepper. Sprinkle each serving with 2 tbsp chopped fresh Italian parsley.

SALMON AND TARRAGON RISOTTO

1. In a large skillet, heat oil over medium heat. Add 1/2 cup chopped shallots; cook, stirring often, until softened, about 7 minutes. Reduce heat to low and cover to speed softening without burning. Stir occasionally.

2. Skip to Step 4 (omit mushrooms, red onion, yellow pepper, thyme, asparagus and roasted garlic).

3. When rice is creamy and tender, stir in 2 tbsp *each*: finely chopped fresh parsley and tarragon (or 3 tbsp chopped fresh dill to replace both) and 3/4 cup cooked fresh or frozen peas. Stir in 1 lb chunks of grilled or poached Atlantic salmon (omit Parmesan cheese); heat through. Season with salt and pepper. Dry smoked salmon can be used also.

SHRIMP RISOTTO
Use 1 lb grilled, sautéed or poached shrimp in place of salmon in the above variation.

Barley, Wild & Brown Rice Pilaf

Barley combines with brown rice and wild rice to give an interesting crunch to this whole-grain pilaf.

1. In a large saucepan, heat 1 tbsp of the oil over medium heat. Add onions and cook for 7 minutes or until soft.

2. Stir in barley, brown and wild rice; cook, stirring, for 1 minute.

3. Add stock; increase heat to high and bring to a boil. Reduce heat; cover and simmer 50 to 60 minutes or until grains are tender.

4. In a Dutch oven, heat remaining 1 tbsp of the oil over medium heat. Stir in mushrooms, celery, carrot and thyme; cook for 5 minutes or until celery is tender. Stir in cooked grains and parsley. Season with salt and pepper.

MAKES 6 SERVINGS

2 tbsp	oil
1	medium onion, chopped
1/3 cup	pot barley
1/3 cup	long-grain brown rice
1/4 cup	wild rice
2 cups	beef, chicken or vegetable stock
1/2 lb	mushrooms, chopped
1	stalk celery, diced
1	large carrot, grated
2 tsp	chopped fresh thyme
1/4 cup	chopped fresh parsley
	Salt and pepper, to taste

Arroz Verde
GREEN RICE

Serve this tasty rice dish with grilled chicken, fish or baked bean or lentil casseroles. Texmati is a variety of rice grown in the southern United States and is related to Indian basmati rice.

1. In a large saucepan over high heat, mix together rice and chicken stock; bring to a boil. Reduce heat; cover and simmer for about 15 minutes or until rice is tender.

2. Remove from heat; stir in cilantro, chives, lime rind (if using) and lime juice. Season with salt and pepper.

3. Cover and let stand for 10 minutes before serving.

MAKES 6 SERVINGS

1 cup	Texmati rice
2 cups	chicken or vegetable stock
1/2 cup	finely chopped fresh cilantro
1/4 cup	snipped fresh chives
1 tsp	finely grated lime rind (optional)
1 tbsp	lime juice
	Salt and pepper, to taste

Stuffed Sweet Peppers

These tasty peppers are stuffed with a high-fiber mixture of brown rice, lentils and corn. Prepared salsa and canned legumes (beans, lentils and peas) provide extra convenience. Make these as hot or as mild as you like.

1. Cut the tops from the peppers; remove seeds and membranes. Trim bottoms flat so peppers stand up. In a large pot of boiling water, cook peppers for 2 minutes; drain, cut side down, on a paper towel.

2. In a large non-stick skillet, heat oil over medium heat. Add onions; cook for 5 minutes. Add garlic; cook for 1 minute.

3. In a large bowl, mix together onion mixture, rice, lentils, corn and cilantro. Stir in 1 cup of the cheese and salsa. Season with salt and pepper.

4. Fill prepared peppers with rice mixture. Place in an 8-inch square baking dish; add a little water to pan. Cover with foil; bake in a 400°F oven for about 25 minutes. Top each pepper with 2 tbsp of the remaining cheese. Return to oven, uncovered, for 5 minutes or until cheese melts.

MAKES 4 SERVINGS

4	large sweet peppers
1 tbsp	oil
1/2 cup	diced onions
1	clove garlic, minced
2 cups	cooked brown or white rice
3/4 cup	cooked green lentils or black beans
1/2 cup	frozen corn kernels
1/3 cup	chopped fresh cilantro
1 1/2 cups	coarsely shredded Monterey Jack cheese
1 cup	mild or medium salsa (or to taste)
	Salt and pepper, to taste

Polenta
WITH HERBS

Polenta is an Italian dish made with cornmeal. It can be eaten as a side dish, as a base for Osso Bucco (see page 137) to be spooned over, or topped with a cooked mushroom mixture. If left to cool, it will solidify and can be used for layers of vegetable lasagne, cut into pieces and fried as a base for appetizers or topped with eggs (see Eggs Benedetto, page 148).

1. Pour water into a large saucepan; add salt. Bring to a boil over high heat. Measure cornmeal into a bowl.

2. When water boils, reduce heat to low. Whisk or stir in cornmeal in a slow steady stream. Keep stirring for the first 5 minutes while it simmers. Cook for about 15 minutes, stirring often.

3. Remove from stove. Stir in cheese, butter and rosemary.

4. Serve warm sprinkled with chives.

MAKES 4 CUPS

4 cups	water or stock (or half water and milk)
3/4 tsp	salt
2 cup	fine cornmeal
1/3 cup	grated Parmesan cheese
1 tbsp	butter
1-1/2 tsp	finely chopped rosemary
1 tbsp	chopped chives

VARIATIONS

- Stir in roasted garlic (see page 203).

- A bit of cream or milk can be added for a softer texture.

- For squares, cook 5 minutes longer. Do not add butter. Pour into 13 × 9-inch pan (sprayed with cooking spray or lightly greased). Top with chives. Press plastic wrap onto surface. Refrigerate for 1 to 2 hours or until firm. Cut into squares and fry in a little olive oil until lightly browned. Top with Fried Sage Leaves (see page 139).

Quinoa and Squash Casserole

Quinoa (pronounced "keen-wah"), once the food of Incas, is still a staple in South America. In this recipe, the nutritious whole grain has been toasted to give it a nutty flavor to go with its slightly crunchy texture.

1. Rinse quinoa (to remove bitter tasting saponin from the exterior); drain well. In a large skillet over medium-high heat, cook and stir quinoa until water is gone; reduce heat to medium and continue to stir until toasted. Place toasted quinoa in 2-quart baking dish.

2. In a skillet, heat oil over medium heat. Add onion and cook, stirring occasionally, for about 7 minutes or until softened. Add garlic and squash; cook for 2 minutes.

3. Add onion mixture, juice, stock and salt to quinoa in baking dish; stir to combine. Cover and bake in a 375°F oven for 30 minutes; remove cover and continue to cook for about 10 minutes longer or until liquid is absorbed and grain and squash are tender.

4. Stir in parsley and marjoram; fluff with fork.

NOTE: There are many varieties of quinoa now widely available in large supermarkets and bulk stores. White, black and red are the most common, or mixed. Look for purple, orange, etc.

MAKES 4 SERVINGS

1 cup	quinoa
1 tbsp	oil
1/2 cup	diced onion
1	clove garlic, minced
1 cup	diced butternut squash or carrot
1 cup	orange or apple juice
1 cup	chicken or vegetable stock
1/2 tsp	salt
1/4 cup	chopped fresh parsley
2 tbsp	chopped fresh marjoram (or 1 tbsp chopped fresh savory)

VEGETABLES AND LEGUMES

Eat your veggies, in style. What wonders herbs do for vegetables! Use a touch of herb butter or herb vinegar to bring out the best in vegetables, beans and lentils. Drizzle with a touch of herbal oil or add fresh herbs to a sauce.

VEGETABLE/HERB CHART

THIS VEGETABLE GOES WITH...	...THESE HERBS
Artichokes	Bay leaves, parsley, sage, tarragon, thyme
Asparagus	Basil, bay leaves, chives, lemon balm, marjoram, parsley, sage, savory, tarragon, thyme
Avocados	Cilantro, dill, marjoram
Beans (green, wax)	Basil, chives, cilantro, dill, marjoram, mint, oregano, parsley, rosemary, sage, savory, tarragon, thyme
Beets	Bay leaves, dill, summer savory, tarragon
Broccoli	Basil, chives/garlic chives, dill, lemon balm, marjoram, oregano, savory, tarragon, thyme
Brussels sprouts	Marjoram, sage, savory
Cabbage	Dill, oregano, parsley, sage, savory, tarragon
Carrots	Basil, bay leaf, chervil, chives, cilantro, dill, lemon balm, marjoram, mint, oregano, parsley, sage, savory, tarragon, thyme
Cauliflower	Basil, chives/garlic chives, dill, marjoram, parsley, rosemary, savory, tarragon
Celery	Basil, chives, cilantro, marjoram, oregano, parsley, tarragon, thyme
Corn	Basil, chervil, chives, cilantro, lemon balm, marjoram, oregano, parsley, sage, savory, rosemary, thyme
Cucumbers	Chervil, chives, dill, mint, parsley
Eggplant	Basil, bay leaves, chervil, chives, cilantro, marjoram, oregano, parsley, rosemary, sage, savory, thyme
Greens (Kale, collards, Swiss chard, tarragon, dandelion, mustard, etc.)	Marjoram, rosemary, savory

THIS VEGETABLE GOES WITH...	...THESE HERBS
Leeks	Chives, oregano, parsley, thyme
Mushrooms	Basil, chives, cilantro, marjoram, oregano, parsley, tarragon, thyme
Okra	Dill, oregano, parsley, thyme
Onions	Basil, marjoram, oregano, parsley, sage, tarragon, thyme
Parsnips	Basil, chervil, chives, dill, marjoram, parsley, savory, tarragon, thyme
Peas	Basil, bay leaves, chervil, chives, dill, marjoram, mint, oregano, rosemary, savory, tarragon, thyme
Peppers, sweet	Basil, chives, marjoram, oregano, parsley, thyme
Potatoes	Basil, chives, cilantro, dill, marjoram, mint, oregano, parsley, sage, rosemary, tarragon, thyme
Potatoes, sweet	Parsley, sage, thyme
Spinach	Basil, chervil, chives, dill, marjoram, mint, oregano, rosemary, tarragon, thyme
Squash, summer	Basil, chives, dill, marjoram, oregano, parsley, sage, savory, thyme
Squash, winter	Parsley, rosemary, sage
Tomatoes	Basil, bay leaf, chives/garlic chives, cilantro, dill, marjoram, oregano, parsley, sage, savory, tarragon, thyme
Turnip	Basil, chives, dill, marjoram, parsley, rosemary, sage, savory
Zucchini	Basil, chives, dill, marjoram, parsley

Baby Carrots
IN DILL-CHIVE CREAM SAUCE

Not at all like the flavor of dill pickles, fresh dill leaves have a delicate, fresh taste. Save a few pretty dill sprigs for garnish. Chives are a convenient way to add a subtle onion essence. This dish will nicely complement chicken or fish.

1. Cook carrots whole in boiling water just until tender; drain well.

2. In a small saucepan over medium heat, melt butter. Whisk in flour; cook for 1 minute, stirring constantly.

3. Stir in stock; bring to a boil, stirring frequently until sauce thickens.

4. Stir in cream; cook for 1 minute.

5. Stir in dill and chives. Pour over hot carrots; toss to coat. Season with a little salt.

MAKES 4 SERVINGS

1 lb	baby carrots
2 tbsp	butter
1 tbsp	all-purpose flour
1/3 cup	*each*: chicken or vegetable stock and light cream (5%)
1 tbsp	finely chopped fresh dill
1 tbsp	snipped fresh chives
	Salt

Baked Acorn Squash
WITH ROSEMARY

I discovered this easy way of getting the flavor of herbs into the squash one fall day while making dinner. You can use the squash to make soup as well as serving it as a vegetable.

1. Cut squash in half lengthwise; with a spoon, scoop out the seeds.

2. Place half of the herbs into the hollow of each squash half. Carefully place the squash halves, cut side down, on a foil-lined baking sheet so the herbs stay enclosed under the squash.

3. Bake in a 400°F oven for 40 to 50 minutes, or until very tender when pierced with the tip of a sharp knife.

4. Turn squash halves over; remove and discard herbs. Add butter and brown sugar to hollow and return to oven, cut side up, for 3 to 5 minutes or until butter and sugar begin to bubble.

MAKES 2 TO 4 SERVINGS

1	acorn squash
4	3-inch sprigs fresh rosemary (or 6 large sage leaves)
4 tsp	butter
2 tbsp	brown sugar

Braised Greens

Hearty, leafy veggies are a storehouse of nutritional goodness. In this recipe, you can substitute spinach, or collard, beet, mustard, dandelion or turnip greens.

1. In a Dutch oven or large, heavy saucepan, heat oil over medium heat. Add onion and cook for 7 minutes or until softened.

2. Stir in garlic and greens. Cook, stirring frequently, for 5 minutes or until greens begin to wilt. Stir in cilantro.

3. Stir together vinegar, water and sugar; stir into greens and cook until greens are tender. Stir in pine nuts and season with salt and pepper.

1 tbsp	olive oil
1	large onion, chopped
1	clove garlic, minced
10 cups	chopped kale (discard stems)
8 cups	chopped red or green Swiss chard (including stems)
1/2 cup	chopped fresh cilantro or basil
4 tbsp	red wine vinegar
2 tbsp	water
2 tsp	granulated sugar
2 tbsp	toasted pine nuts
	Salt and pepper, to taste

Broad Beans

WITH SAVORY AND PROSCIUTTO

This is a hearty legume dish that can be eaten on its own as a meal. Sometimes I eat it for lunch.

1. In a large skillet, heat oil over medium heat. Stir in beans; cook for 3 minutes, stirring occasionally.

2. Stir in garlic, prosciutto and savory; cook for 3 minutes, stirring often.

3. Stir in sherry; cook for 1 minute.

4. Stir in parsley. Serve warm.

MAKES 2 TO 4 SERVINGS

1/3 cup	olive oil
1	can (15 oz or 19 oz) broad beans, drained and rinsed
2	cloves garlic, minced
2 oz	prosciutto, cut into 1/2-inch dice
1 tbsp	finely chopped fresh savory or sage
1 tbsp	dry sherry
1 tbsp	finely chopped parsley

Confetti Cauliflower Rice

In this wonderful vegetable medley, the sweetness of the peppers balances the stronger flavors of the cauliflower and cabbage. Make your own "cauliflower rice" by chopping or grating a head of cauliflower, or purchase ready-to-use from the salad section of your grocery store. It's a pretty and tasty side dish, or it can be eaten cold with a salad dressing, or to top salad greens.

1. In a large non-stick skillet, heat oil over medium heat. Add onion; cover and cook on medium-low for 6 minutes, stirring occasionally.

2. Add carrots and garlic; cook for 2 minutes.

3. Stir in cauliflower, cabbage and peppers; cover and cook for 5 minutes, stirring occasionally until vegetables are tender-crisp and heated through.

4. Stir in dill and parsley.

MAKES 4-1/2 CUPS (4 TO 6 SERVINGS)

1 tbsp	oil
1 cup	diced red or white onion
1/2 cup	diced carrots
1	large clove garlic, minced
1 pkg (12 oz)	cauliflower rice (3 cups)
3/4 cup	finely sliced and chopped red cabbage (small pieces)
1/2 cup	*each*: diced red and yellow (or orange) sweet peppers
2 tbsp	finely chopped fresh dill
2 tbsp	finely chopped fresh parsley

VARIATIONS

- Replace carrots with zucchini and replace dill with fresh basil.

- Replace dill with 1 tbsp finely chopped marjoram or 2 tsp finely chopped lemon thyme.

- Replace cauliflower with cooked quinoa.

- Omit carrots and cabbage, add 1/2 cup chopped dried apricots or dried cranberries and 1/3 cup chopped toasted walnuts or sliced almonds. Replace dill with chopped fresh mint and add 2 tbsp chopped fresh cilantro. Add oil and lemon vinaigrette.

Chickpeas and Tomatoes

If your impression of Indian food is some type of curry, you are in for a pleasant surprise. Chickpeas are a hearty legume, rich in flavor and fiber. Serve as a vegetarian entrée or with chicken, basmati rice and Raita (see page 165).

1. In a large skillet, heat oil over medium-high heat. Add onions, ginger, garlic, turmeric and hot red pepper flakes; cook for 7 minutes, or until onions are golden and softened.

2. Drain tomatoes, reserving 1 cup of the juice; chop tomatoes. Add tomatoes and reserved juice, ground coriander and chickpeas; cook, uncovered, for 20 minutes or until thickened.

3. Stir in garam masala and lemon juice; cook for 2 or 3 minutes. Stir in cilantro.

4. Garnish with additional cilantro leaves, if desired.

   NOTE: Ground coriander is ground from the seed of the fresh coriander (cilantro) plant. See Herb Seeds, page 40. Garam Masala ("hot mixture") can be purchased from Indian grocery stores and some supermarkets. It is a variable blend of cardamom, cinnamon, cloves, coriander, cumin, nutmeg, dried chilies and black pepper.

MAKES 4 TO 6 SERVINGS

3 tbsp	oil
2	onions, finely chopped
1 tsp	grated fresh ginger
1	clove garlic, crushed
1/2 tsp	ground turmeric
1/4 tsp	crushed hot red pepper flakes, or to taste
1	can (28 oz) tomatoes
1 tbsp	ground coriander (see note)
1	can (15 oz or 19 oz) chickpeas, drained and rinsed
2 tsp	garam masala (see note)
2 tbsp	lemon juice
3 tbsp	chopped fresh cilantro
	Cilantro leaves for garnish (optional)

Broiled Tomatoes
WITH BASIL PESTO

Serve these delicious tomatoes with eggs for breakfast.

1. Cut tomatoes in half horizontally. Place on baking sheet, cut side up.

2. Spread about 1 tbsp of the pesto over each tomato half. Sprinkle with Parmesan cheese.

3. Broil for 3 to 4 minutes or until bubbly and lightly browned.

MAKES 4 SERVINGS

4	large tomatoes
4 tbsp	Basil Pesto (see page 162)
1 tbsp	grated Parmesan cheese

Green Beans
WITH DILL MUSTARD SAUCE

Green beans are one of my favorite vegetables, enjoyed year round, but best when in season locally. Here are three great ways to enjoy them.

1. Cook or steam green beans until tender-crisp, about 5 to 7 minutes. Drain and keep warm.

2. In a large bowl, mix together mayonnaise, sour cream, vinegar, mustard, garlic, shallots and herbs. Season with salt and pepper.

3. Add hot green beans to bowl and toss to coat in sauce.

MAKES 4 TO 6 SERVINGS

1-1/2 lbs	green beans, stem ends trimmed

DILL MUSTARD SAUCE

1/3 cup	mayonnaise
1/4 cup	sour cream
4 tsp	apple cider vinegar (or lemon juice)
1 tbsp	Dijon or deli mustard
1/4 tsp	minced garlic
2 tbsp	minced shallots
2 tbsp	*each*: chopped fresh chives and dill
	Salt and pepper, to taste

VARIATIONS

- Replace green beans with sliced carrots. If desired, replace dill with chopped fresh cilantro or marjoram.

- Replace dill with 1 tbsp chopped fresh tarragon.

Green Beans
WITH GREMOLATA AND PINE NUTS

Another great recipe is to finish cooked green beans with Gremolata (see page 137), a mixture of fresh parsley, garlic and lemon peel.

1. Cook beans as above. Heat 1 tbsp olive oil in a large skillet.

2. Add beans and toss for a few minutes. Stir in Gremolata.

3. Top with 1/3 cup toasted pine nuts, if desired.

Green Beans
WITH PESTO

Toss cooked green beans with Basil Pesto (see page 162). Sprinkle with additional Parmesan. Add toasted pine nuts, if desired.

Grilled Vegetables
WITH PESTO-LEMON DRESSING

Try this tasty vegetable dish at your next outdoor cook-out.
Serve with grilled chicken.

1. Slice each eggplant into 4 lengthwise slices. Slice zucchini into
   1/2-inch rounds. Leave mushrooms whole or cut in half if very large.
   Slice peppers into 1-inch strips and cut onion into 6 wedges. Toss all
   vegetables with olive oil.

2. Grill or broil vegetables until tender-crisp and lightly browned.

3. In a large bowl, toss vegetables with dressing. Garnish with
   basil sprigs.

MAKES 4 SERVINGS

2	Japanese eggplants
2	medium zucchini
2	large portobello mushrooms
1	*each*: sweet red and yellow pepper
1	medium red onion
1 tbsp	olive oil
	Pesto-Lemon Dressing (see below)
	Fresh basil sprigs, for garnish

Pesto-Lemon Dressing

1. Mix together all ingredients. (Dressing may be made ahead and stored
   in the refrigerator.)

MAKES ABOUT 1/3 CUP

1/4 cup	olive oil
2 tbsp	Basil Pesto (see page 162)
1 tbsp	red wine vinegar or balsamic vinegar
2 tsp	lemon juice
1	clove garlic, minced
	Pepper, to taste

Herb and Roasted Garlic Mashed Potatoes

These fluffy mashed potatoes will jazz up a "meat and potatoes" meal! Serve with roast chicken, pork chops, grilled steaks, lamb, etc.

1. Peel potatoes; boil in salted water until very soft. Drain well.

2. Mash potatoes; keep hot.

3. In microwave or in a small saucepan, heat milk over medium heat until hot but not boiling. Stir into potatoes. Squeeze roasted garlic from cloves and stir into potatoes.

4. Stir in parsley, basil, chives, tarragon and butter, if using.

*ROASTED GARLIC: Trim about 1/4 inch from the top of a whole head of garlic. Place garlic head on a piece of foil; drizzle with a little olive oil and close foil. Bake in a 325°F oven for 50 to 60 minutes or until very soft. Let cool; squeeze softened garlic from papery skins.

3 lbs	russet or Yukon Gold potatoes (about 6)
1/2 cup	milk or or table cream (18%)
1	whole head roasted garlic*
3 tbsp	chopped fresh parsley
2 tbsp	*each*: finely chopped fresh basil and chives
2 tsp	finely chopped fresh tarragon
2 tbsp	butter (optional)

VARIATION

Replace all herbs and roasted garlic in recipe above with:

Herb Roasted Garlic
Follow as above for roasted garlic but add 1 tbsp finely chopped fresh rosemary and 2 tsp chopped fresh thyme or lemon thyme.

Minted Peas and Pearl Onions

This classic combination has been updated with the addition of pearl onions and a touch of orange. If you grow your own herbs, grow some orange mint to use in this recipe (omit orange rind). This dish is wonderful with almost any meat but especially lamb, grilled steaks and poultry.

1. Cut a small × in the root end of each unpeeled onion. In a small saucepan, boil onions for 8 minutes or until tender; drain and rinse under cold water. Skins will slip off easily; drain onions on paper towel.

2. Cook peas just until tender; drain well.

3. In a large skillet over medium-high heat, melt butter. Add onions and cook, stirring, until golden brown.

4. Stir in peas and orange rind. Cook, stirring, just until peas are heated through.

5. Remove from heat; stir in mint leaves and serve. Garnish with sprig of mint.

MAKES 4 SERVINGS

24	pearl onions (approx.)
2 cups	fresh shelled peas
1 tbsp	butter
1 tsp	grated orange rind
2 tbsp	thinly sliced fresh mint leaves
	Mint sprig, for garnish

Pesto Potatoes

Add some pizzazz to potatoes! This scalloped potato dish uses basil pesto between the layers with a golden cheese crust on top.

MAKES 6 SERVINGS

6	large potatoes, peeled and thinly sliced
3/4 cup	Basil Pesto (see page 162)
2/3 cup	grated Parmesan cheese

1. Cook potato slices in boiling salted water for 3 to 4 minutes until tender but firm; drain well. Let cool slightly. Dry with paper towel to remove excess water.

2. Spread about one-third of the Basil Pesto into the bottom of a 12-cup baking dish. Make the next layer using about one-third of the potatoes; spread with another one-third of the remaining pesto and sprinkle with about one-third of the cheese. Repeat layers, reserving last one-third of cheese.

3. Cover and bake in a 350°F oven for 35 minutes. Remove cover; sprinkle with reserved cheese. Cook, uncovered, for 5 minutes more, or until potatoes are tender and cheese is golden.

Baby Potatoes
WITH ROSEMARY AND THYME

The skin of new potatoes is tender and delicious, even more so when cooked with robust Mediterranean herbs and garlic. They are a delightful accompaniment to lamb, poultry or pork.

1. In a large skillet, heat oil over medium-high heat. Add potatoes and onions; cook, stirring frequently, until potatoes are almost soft.

2. Stir in garlic, rosemary and thyme; season with a little salt and pepper. Cook until potatoes are tender and onions are golden.

2 tbsp	olive oil
1-1/2 lb	small new potatoes unpeeled, halved
1	medium onion, chopped
2	cloves garlic, minced
1 tbsp	chopped fresh rosemary
1 tbsp	chopped fresh thyme
	Salt and pepper

Puréed Parsnips and Carrots

Herbs with a mild anise (licorice) flavor, like chervil and tarragon, work well with parsnips. This is a vegetable dish to serve with roast turkey, chicken or pork.

1. In a large saucepan, mix together carrots and parsnips. Add water to cover; bring to a boil over high heat. Reduce heat, partially cover and cook for 10 to 12 minutes or until tender.

2. Drain; mash until smooth. Stir in butter, chervil and chives.

MAKES 4 SERVINGS

3 cups	*each*: chopped carrots and parsnips
2 tbsp	butter
1 tbsp	finely chopped fresh chervil or tarragon
1 tbsp	finely chopped fresh chives

Ratatouille

This dish originates in Provence, France, and is a kind of vegetable stew. It tastes best served the day after you make it. The dish was made famous more recently, by a little rat in a movie by the same name. It's a tasty vegetarian dish on its own, or served as a side to veal chop or scaloppine, schnitzel or chicken, with an omelette or over rice or quinoa.

1. Cut zucchini, peppers and eggplant into 1-inch chunks; set aside.

2. In a Dutch oven, heat oil over medium heat. Add onions and garlic; cook, stirring, for 5 minutes.

3. Add zucchini, peppers and eggplant; cook, stirring, for about 5 minutes or until almost tender.

4. Stir in tomatoes and juice, tomato paste, thyme and bay leaf. Cook, uncovered, stirring often, for 20 to 30 minutes or until vegetables are tender and sauce is thickened.

5. Stir in basil and parsley; season with salt and pepper.

MAKES 4 TO 6 SERVINGS

2	7-inch zucchinis
1	*each*: medium sweet green and sweet red pepper
1	medium eggplant (about 3/4 lb), peeled if desired
1/4 cup	olive oil
2	medium onions, coarsely chopped
3	large cloves garlic, minced
1	can (28 oz) diced tomatoes, with juice (or 4 large tomatoes, seeded and chopped)
1/4 cup	tomato paste
2 tsp	chopped fresh thyme
1	fresh or dried bay leaf
1/2 cup	chopped fresh basil
1/4 cup	chopped fresh parsley
	Salt and pepper, to taste

VARIATIONS

Potato Ratatouille
Replace eggplant with 3 medium potatoes, peeled and chopped.

Au Gratin
Spoon prepared, hot ratatouille into large shallow baking dish. Sprinkle with 1/3 cup shredded Parmesan cheese. Bake in 375°F oven 8 to 10 minutes, until cheese is golden.

Roasted Sweet Potatoes

Sweet potatoes are rich in beta carotene, the precursor of Vitamin A. Roasting enhances their natural sweetness. If desired, drizzle with balsamic vinegar as a finishing touch. Great as a side dish, as a topping to Buddha bowls, or room temperature on a salad. If making as fries, omit onion; cooking time will be less, depending on how thick they are cut.

1. In a large bowl, combine sweet potatoes, onions, oil, garlic and thyme; toss to coat well.

2. Spread mixture on a baking sheet. Roast in a 400°F oven for 40 to 45 minutes; stir twice during baking. Roast until softened and slightly browned.

3. Remove to serving bowl; season with a little salt and pepper. Drizzle with balsamic vinegar, if using.

MAKES 4 SERVINGS

2 lb	sweet potatoes, peeled and cut into 1-1/2-inch chunks, or fries (thin sticks)
2	medium red onions, cut into wedges
3 tbsp	olive oil
1 tbsp	minced garlic
1 tbsp	finely chopped fresh thyme, rosemary or sage
	Salt and pepper, to taste
1 tbsp	balsamic vinegar (optional)

Tandoori Roasted Sweet Potatoes

Omit onion, herbs and balsamic vinegar from recipe above.

1. In a small bowl, mix together spice mix ingredients.

2. In a large bowl, toss sweet potato cubes in sunflower oil and garlic. Stir in spice mixture. (Works well in a large zipper-lock plastic bag.)

3. Spread mixture on a baking sheet. Roast in a 400°F oven for 25 to 30 minutes, stirring twice during baking. Roast until softened and slightly browned. Sprinkle with chopped fresh cilantro.

MAKES 6 SERVINGS

SPICE MIX

1 tbsp	*each*: ground coriander, cumin and granulated sugar
1/2 tsp	*each*: ground ginger, paprika and turmeric
1/4 tsp	*each*: black pepper and ground cloves
pinch	cayenne pepper or crushed red chili flakes
8 cups	sweet potato cubes (3/4-inch)
3 tbsp	sunflower oil
1	large clove garlic, crushed
3 tbsp	chopped fresh cilantro

Sautéed Portobellos
WITH ROSEMARY AND THYME

These meaty mushrooms go great with grilled steaks, use to top a burger or to accompany scrambled eggs.

1. In a large non-stick skillet, heat oil and butter over medium-high heat until butter foams.

2. Stir in mushrooms, garlic, rosemary, thyme and parsley. Cook, stirring often, for 3 to 5 minutes, or until mushrooms are lightly browned and tender.

3. Stir in sherry, if using.

MAKES 4 SERVINGS

2 tbsp	olive oil
1 tbsp	butter
1/2 lb	portobello mushrooms, sliced or chopped (about 3 large)
1	clove garlic, minced
2 tsp	*each*: finely chopped fresh rosemary, thyme (or lemon thyme) and parsley
1 tbsp	dry sherry or balsamic vinegar (optional)

Roasted Whole Rainbow Carrots
WITH HAYDARI SAUCE

Haydari (hay-dar-ee) is a Turkish yogurt sauce or dip, delicious as meze (appetizer), with meat kebabs, meatballs called kofte and pita bread. Prepare sauce a couple of hours ahead of time for best flavor.

1. Peel carrots; trim, leaving a small piece of stem.

2. In a small bowl, mix together oil, garlic, rosemary and thyme. Season with salt and pepper.

3. Place carrots on a foil-lined baking sheet. Brush all over with herb-garlic oil. Roast in a 400°F oven for 28 to 30 minutes; stir twice during baking. Roast until softened and slightly browned.

4. Serve with Haydari Sauce.

MAKES 4 SERVINGS

2 lb	whole "rainbow" carrots (about 2 bunches, approx. 12 carrots)
1 tbsp	sunflower oil
2 tsp	minced garlic
1 tsp	*each*: finely chopped fresh rosemary and lemon thyme
	Salt and pepper, to taste
	Haydari Sauce (see page 211)

Haydari Sauce

MAKES 1 CUP
(WITHOUT
THE FETA)

In Turkey, this sauce is made with thickened yogurt called *suzme*. Thick Greek yogurt is more widely available. Or you can make your own by draining yogurt in layers of cheesecloth over a bowl. It's a bit like tzatziki but without cucumbers. Also serve with grilled eggplant or sweet peppers. If desired, add finely chopped walnuts.

1 cup	plain Greek yogurt
2 tsp	minced garlic
3 tbsp	finely chopped fresh dill
1 tbsp	finely chopped fresh mint
2 to 3 tbsp	finely crumbled feta cheese (optional)
	Olive oil
	Dill or mint sprig, to garnish

1. In a medium bowl, mix together yogurt, garlic, dill and mint.

2. Stir in feta, if using. Cover and refrigerate for 2 hours or up to 2 days. Before serving, drizzle a little olive oil over the top. Garnish with herb sprig.

Cacik (caw-seek) Sauce

This sauce, similar to Tzatziki is popular in Southeast Europe and the Middle East.

1. Prepare as for Haydari (without the feta), adding 1 cup finely diced English cucumbers (unpeeled). Regular yogurt may be used as it is a bit thinner sauce.

2. Add 1 tsp lemon juice. Season with salt and pepper. Use up within a day or so as the cucumber will weep a bit and make the sauce watery.

SPICE GARNISHES: If desired, sprinkle top of either sauce with sweet paprika, smoked paprika or ground sumac.

NOTE: Sumac is ground from the dried, deep red berries of the sumac bush grown in the Middle East. It has a tangy, lemony, bit fruity flavor. Buy at major grocery or from most bulk stores. Use on grilled meats or fish or to top hummus. It is a component of the spice mixture Za'atar (see page 4).

Vegetable Tempura

This recipe was contributed by my mom, Beti, who made it for many years. She tried it using fresh herbs and was delighted with the results. The herbs become crispy and the flavor mellows.

1. In a large bowl, whisk together egg yolk, stock and oil.

2. In a small bowl, mix together flour, cornstarch, Parmesan, salt and garlic powder. Whisk into egg mixture until smooth.

3. In a small bowl, using electric mixer, beat egg white until stiff; fold into batter. Fold in parsley.

4. Pour oil into a deep fryer or deep skillet to 1 inch deep. Heat to 360°F setting.

5. Pat vegetables and herbs dry with paper towel, if necessary. Dip in batter one at a time, allowing batter to drip off. Using tongs, place in hot oil 6 pieces at a time. (If oil is hot enough, they will begin to sizzle immediately.) Deep fry until golden, for 2 or 3 minutes.

6. Drain on paper towels; keep hot in a 200°F oven if desired, until all are cooked.

MAKES 4 SERVINGS

1	egg, separated
1 cup	chicken or vegetable stock
2 tsp	oil
1 cup	all-purpose flour
1 tbsp	cornstarch
1 tbsp	grated Parmesan cheese
1/2 tsp	salt
Pinch	garlic powder
2 tbsp	finely chopped fresh parsley or cilantro
	oil for deep frying
4 cups	vegetables, cut into 1/4-inch thick pieces or slices: sweet peppers, mushrooms, onion rings, broccoli, cauliflower, thin green beans; fresh herbs, such as curly parsley sprigs, Italian parsley, cilantro and large sage leaves

Zucchini with Tomatoes
AND MARJORAM

Harvest some of your zucchini while they are still small and pair them with tomatoes and garlic. The crowning touch is the addition of marjoram, sweet cousin to the more earthy oregano. This is a perfect side dish for hot Italian sausages, poultry, lamb, pork or fish.

1. In a large skillet, heat oil over medium-high heat. Add zucchini and cook, stirring frequently, until almost tender.

2. Stir in tomatoes and garlic; cook until zucchini is tender and most of the liquid from the tomatoes has evaporated.

3. Stir in marjoram; season with salt and pepper. Serve with cheese sprinkled over top.

MAKES 4 SERVINGS

1 tbsp	olive oil
2 lb	small zucchini (about 4)
2	medium tomatoes, chopped
1	large clove garlic, minced
1 tbsp	chopped fresh marjoram or oregano
	Salt and pepper, to taste
2 tbsp	grated Parmesan cheese

CRACKERS, BISCUITS AND BREADS

Fill your home with the tantalizing aroma of herbs in your baking. Serve hot Cheddar chive biscuits or scones, rosemary buns, focaccia or breadsticks, or sage cornbread with soups, chili and stews. Serve easy-to-make herb crackers with hummus, dips and paté.

Basil and Parmesan Butter Crackers

Homemade crackers are very easy to make. These may also be cut into shapes with cutters. For crisp crackers, roll as thin as possible.

1. In a large bowl, mix together flour, salt, garlic powder and pepper. Cut in butter using a pastry blender or 2 knives, one in each hand.

2. Stir in cheese, basil and chives.

3. Stir water into flour mixture; adding more until dough comes together (neither dry nor sticky). Knead about 10 times to get a cohesive ball on floured surface.

4. Roll dough evenly, as thin as possible (about 1/8 inch) into a rectangle (about 16 × 10 inches). Place whole on parchment-lined large baking sheet. Prick every half inch or so with a fork. If desired, score surface (3 × 1-inch rectangles or wedges) with a knife. If using cutters, dip cutting edge in flour occasionally to prevent sticking.

5. Bake in a 400°F oven for 8 to 10 minutes, until edges are lightly browned. Let cool on baking rack. Break into pieces along score lines. Store in covered container.

MAKES ABOUT
48 CRACKERS
(3 × 1-INCH)

1 cup	all-purpose flour
1 tsp	salt
1/8 tsp	garlic powder
	Pinch pepper
3 tbsp	butter
1/4 cup	grated Parmesan cheese
2 tbsp	finely chopped fresh basil
1 tbsp	finely chopped fresh chives
4 to 5 tbsp	water

VARIATIONS

*   Replace basil with dill, savory or marjoram.
*   Use grated Pecorino Romano cheese in place of Parmesan.

Rosemary Asiago Crackers

These crispy crackers are easy to make and will keep for a week. Serve with cheese, hummus and pâté, or alongside soup.

1. In a large bowl, mix together flour, cheese, salt and pepper. Stir in rosemary.

2. In a small glass measuring cup, stir together water and oil; immediately stir into flour mixture. Stir until it forms a ball. Cover and let dough rest for 30 minutes.

3. Divide dough in half; cover the rest. On a lightly floured surface, roll dough evenly, as thin as possible (about 1/8 inch) into a rectangle. The thinner it is, the crispier the crackers will be. Cut into 3 × 1-inch strips. Place on parchment-lined baking sheet. Prick every half inch or so with a fork.

4. Brush tops with a little water then sprinkle with coarse salt, if using, and seeds (water helps them to stick). Repeat with remaining dough.

5. Bake in a 450°F oven for 10 to 12 minutes, until edges are lightly browned. Let cool on baking rack. Store in covered container.

MAKES ABOUT 60 CRACKERS (3 × 1-INCH)

1-1/2 cups	all-purpose flour
1/2 cup	finely shredded Asiago cheese
1 tsp	salt
	Pinch black pepper
4 tsp	finely chopped fresh rosemary
1/2 cup	water
2 tbsp	olive oil
	Coarse salt (optional)
1 tbsp	mixed seeds (or ancient grain and super seeds mixture, sesame seeds, poppy seeds, chia seeds, etc.)

VARIATIONS

- Replace 1 tsp of the rosemary with chopped fresh thyme or lemon thyme.

- Replace rosemary with 1 tbsp finely chopped sage.

Citrus and Sage Scones

These are drop scones, so no rolling or cutting is needed. They are slightly sweet, but the sugar may be omitted for a savory scone to serve with soups. The citrus rind accents the sage nicely. I used to make these for a day-long Saturday class I taught on cooking with fresh herbs. Everyone loved them.

1. In a medium bowl, mix together flour, sugar, baking powder and salt. Cut in butter until mixture resembles coarse crumbs.

2. Using a fork, stir in sage, lemon rind and orange rind.

3. In a small bowl, whisk together milk and eggs; using a fork, quickly stir liquid ingredients into flour mixture just until blended.

4. Using two large spoons, drop dough onto a lightly greased baking sheet, about 2 inches apart. Press lightly to smooth top and slightly flatten.

5. Bake in a 425°F oven for 10 to 12 minutes or until golden brown. Serve warm or at room temperature.

MAKES 8 TO 10

2 cups	all-purpose flour
2 tbsp	granulated sugar
2 tsp	baking powder
1/2 tsp	salt
1/4 cup	butter, slightly softened
2 tbsp	finely chopped fresh sage
	Finely grated rind of 1 large lemon
	Finely grated rind of 1 large orange
1/2 cup	milk
2	eggs

VARIATIONS

Lemon Thyme Scones
Omit sugar, lemon and orange rinds and sage. Add 1 tbsp finely chopped fresh lemon thyme.

Orange-Rosemary Scones
Omit lemon rind and sage. Add 1 tbsp finely chopped fresh rosemary.

Savory Scones
Omit sugar; use 1 tbsp finely chopped savory in place of sage.

Cheddar Chive Biscuits

These fluffy biscuits are excellent served hot with soup – try the dill variation with chicken soup. If desired, freeze the formed raw biscuits or already baked biscuits.

1. In a medium bowl, mix together flour, baking powder, salt and cayenne, if using. Cut in butter until mixture resembles coarse crumbs.

2. Stir in cheese and chives. Using a fork, quickly stir in milk until mixture forms a soft dough. If dry, add another tablespoon of milk.

3. In small bowl, mix together melted butter, parsley and garlic powder.

4. Turn dough out onto a lightly floured surface; knead 8 to 10 times. Flatten dough to 1/2-inch thickness; cut out with a 2-1/2-inch biscuit cutter or roll out to 9 × 12-inches and cut into squares. Place on an ungreased cookie sheet; brush tops with melted butter mixture.

5. Bake in a 425°F oven for 15 to 18 minutes or until golden brown.

MAKES ABOUT 1 DOZEN

2 cups	all-purpose flour
1 tbsp	baking powder
1/2 tsp	salt
1/8 tsp	cayenne pepper (optional)
1/2 cup	butter, slightly softened
3/4 cup	finely shredded medium or old Cheddar cheese
1/4 cup	chopped fresh chives
3/4 cup	milk
2 tbsp	melted butter
2 tsp	finely chopped fresh parsley
1/8 tsp	garlic powder (optional)

VARIATIONS

Dill and Cheddar Biscuits
Use 2 tbsp chopped fresh dill in place of chives.

Savory or Rosemary Biscuits
Omit cheese, use 1 tbsp finely chopped fresh savory or rosemary in place of chives.

Cheddar Sage Cornbread

This colorful "confetti" cornbread made with sweet corn and sweet and hot peppers, is moist and delicious. Serve with soups or roasted chicken.

1. In a large bowl, combine cornmeal, flour, sugar, baking powder, salt and baking soda.

2. Stir in corn, 1-1/4 cups of the cheese, red peppers and jalapeño peppers, if using. Stir in chives and sage.

3. In a small bowl, beat eggs with buttermilk and oil; stir into corn mixture just until combined.

4. Spread batter in a greased 9-inch square baking pan or 12 greased muffin cups. Sprinkle top with the remaining 1/4 cup cheese. Bake in a 375°F oven for about 30 minutes (for muffins, bake for 16 to 18 minutes), or until light golden brown and a tester inserted in the center comes out clean.

VARIATION

Sun-dried Tomato Basil or Marjoram Cornbread
Replace sweet red pepper with sun-dried tomatoes, use fresh basil or marjoram in place of sage; omit chives.

MAKES ABOUT 12 SERVINGS OR 12 MUFFINS

1 cup	cornmeal
1 cup	all-purpose flour
1 tbsp	granulated sugar
1 tbsp	baking powder
3/4 tsp	salt
1/2 tsp	baking soda
1-1/2	cups fresh or frozen corn kernels (or 12 or 15.2 oz can, drained)
1-1/2 cups	shredded old Cheddar cheese
1/3 cup	finely chopped sweet red pepper
2 tbsp	minced jalapeño pepper (optional)
3 tbsp	chopped fresh chives
2 tbsp	finely chopped fresh sage
2	eggs
1 cup	buttermilk (or half plain yogurt and half milk)
1/4 cup	vegetable oil

Cilantro Cornbread

This cornbread has a slightly sweeter taste than the Cheddar Sage Cornbread, less cornmeal and no corn or peppers added. Feel free to add some hot peppers.

1. In a large bowl, combine flour, cornmeal, sugar, baking powder and salt.

2. In a small bowl, beat eggs with milk and oil; stir into dry ingredients just until combined. Stir in butter until mixed in.

3. Stir in cheese, cilantro and chives just until combined.

4. Spread batter in a greased or parchment-lined 9-inch square baking pan, or 12 greased muffin cups. Bake in a 350°F oven for 40 to 45 minutes (for muffins, bake at 375°F for 16 to 18 minutes), or until light golden brown and a tester inserted in the center comes out clean.

VARIATION

Asiago Rosemary
Replace Cheddar with Asiago cheese, replace sage with 1 tbsp finely chopped fresh rosemary.

MAKES ABOUT 12 SERVINGS OR 12 MUFFINS

2 cups	all-purpose flour
1 cup	fine cornmeal
1/2 cup	granulated sugar
1 tbsp	baking powder
1 tsp	salt
2	eggs
1-1/2 cups	2% milk
2 tbsp	vegetable oil
1/4 cup	melted butter
1/2 cup	shredded Tex-Mex, Monterey Jack or Cheddar cheese
4 tbsp	finely chopped fresh cilantro or fresh dill
3 tbsp	chopped fresh chives

Buttery Rosemary Buns

My friend Pat is a bread-making pro who also teaches bread-making courses. I asked her to create this bun recipe for me. (Yes, you may eat one right away!)

1. In a small bowl, dissolve granulated sugar in warm water. Sprinkle in yeast; let stand 10 minutes or until frothy.

2. In a medium microwave–safe bowl, whisk milk and egg until combined. Microwave on high for 20 to 30 seconds or until warm.

3. In a stand mixer with paddle attachment mix together flour, yeast mixture, brown sugar, salt, 1/4 cup of the butter and 2 tbsp of the rosemary until combined. Add milk/egg mixture; mix to combine. Remove paddle attachment and attach dough hook; knead dough until smooth and elastic, about 5 minutes. Remove hook.

4. Cover bowl with damp kitchen towel. Let rise at room temperature until doubled in size, about 1-1/2 hours.

5. Spray a 13 × 9-inch baking pan with cooking spray. Transfer dough to a lightly floured counter and knead for 1 minute. Divide into 12 portions. Shape each into ball, stretching and pinching dough underneath to make tops smooth. Place 2 inches apart in prepared pan. Cover and let rise for 30 to 45 minutes or until doubled in bulk.

6. Combine remaining 1/4 cup butter and 1 tbsp rosemary. Brush rolls with mixture and sprinkle tops with salt. Bake in a 375°F oven, on center rack, for 20 to 25 minutes or until deep golden brown. Remove from pan; let cool on racks. Serve warm or reheat in 325°F oven for 5 minutes.

MAKES 12 BUNS

1/4 cup	warm water
1 tbsp	granulated sugar
1 packet (2-1/4 tsp)	active dry yeast
1 cup	milk
1	egg
3-1/2 cups	all-purpose flour
1/4 cup	packed brown sugar
1-1/4 tsp	salt
1/2 cup	butter, melted, divided
3 tbsp	finely chopped fresh rosemary leaves, divided
	Coarse flaky sea salt, for garnish

TIP

If you can find yeast with dough-enhancers, the buns will rise higher and in a shorter time.

Herbed Bread Sticks

Here a bread machine is a real time-saver. This recipe can also be made using any traditional white bread dough recipe. These aromatic bread sticks are great any time but perfect with soups or pasta.

1. In a bread machine, place water, flour, 2 tbsp each of the rosemary, sage and thyme, the yeast, sugar and 3/4 tsp salt, in the order suggested by the manufacturer. Process on the dough/manual cycle. When cycle is complete, remove dough to a lightly floured surface. Cover; let rest for 5 to 10 minutes.

2. Divide dough into 10 equal pieces. Roll each piece on lightly floured surface into a 10-inch rope.

3. Place on a greased baking sheet; brush with oil. Sprinkle with coarse salt and remaining 1 tbsp of the rosemary, sage and thyme. Cover with greased waxed paper; let rise in a warm place for 20 to 30 minutes or until doubled in bulk.

4. Bake in a 425°F oven for about 15 minutes or until golden. Remove from baking sheet; let cool on a wire rack.

NOTE: To make without a bread machine, use instant yeast instead of bread machine yeast. In an electric stand mixer, fitted with a dough hook, combine yeast, 1 cup of the flour, sugar, salt and herbs. Use warm water; stir into flour mixture. Add the remaining 1 cup flour until dough comes away from the sides. Knead dough for 2 to 3 minutes, until dough is soft but not sticky. Let rest in bowl for about 10 minutes. Continue to Step 2. May also be combined by hand.

VARIATION: If desired, add fresh herbs to any white or whole wheat bread recipe.

MAKES 10 BREAD STICKS

2/3 cup	water
2 cups	all-purpose or bread flour
3 tbsp	*each*: finely chopped fresh rosemary, sage and thyme
1-1/2 tsp	bread machine yeast
1 tsp	granulated sugar
3/4 tsp	salt
1 tbsp	olive or vegetable oil
1 tbsp	coarse salt

Sage and Red Onion Focaccia

Sage and onions are ideal partners for this savory bread. Serve cut into wedges with soups or stews, or to liven up a meat-and-potatoes dinner. Sweet white onions can be used in place of red onions. If you do not have a bread machine, use 1 lb pizza dough.

MAKES 4 TO 6 SERVINGS

3 tbsp	olive or vegetable oil
3 cups	halved and thinly sliced red onions
12	fresh sage leaves
1 cup	water
3 cups	all-purpose flour
3 tbsp	butter
2 tbsp	skim milk powder
1 tbsp	granulated sugar
2 tsp	bread machine yeast
1 tsp	salt
1 tbsp	cornmeal

1. In a large skillet, heat oil over medium heat. Add onions; reduce heat to medium-low. Cook for 20 to 30 minutes, stirring occasionally, until onions are softened and golden. Stir in sage leaves; cook for 1 minute. Let cool.

2. In bread machine, place water, flour, butter, milk powder, sugar, yeast and salt, in the order suggested by manufacturer. Process on the dough/manual cycle. When the cycle is complete, remove dough to a lightly floured surface. Cover; let rest for 5 to 10 minutes.

3. Roll out dough into a 10 × 14-inch rectangle. Sprinkle cornmeal onto a baking sheet; place dough on top. Cover; let rise in warm place for 20 to 30 minutes or until doubled in bulk.

4. With your fingertips, make indentations all over the dough. Spread onion and sage mixture over dough.

5. Bake in a 400°F oven for 20 to 25 minutes or until golden. Remove from the pan and let cool slightly on a wire rack. Cut into squares or wedges; serve warm.

Rosemary and Thyme Focaccia

1. Roll out dough following steps 3 and 4 above.

2. In place of onion mixture, brush dough with mixture of 1/3 cup olive oil and 1 clove garlic, crushed. Sprinkle dough with 1 tbsp *each* chopped fresh rosemary and thyme, and 1/2 tsp coarse salt.

3. Bake following step 5 above.

DESSERTS

Make the grande finale to your meal a dessert kissed with fresh herbs and decorated with edible flowers. Infuse the cream or milk you use to make cakes or puddings with fresh herbs. Use herb butters to make crusts for tarts or pies; use herb syrups to glaze a loaf or muffins. Herb sugars add sparkle to the top of cookies or over fruit. The herbs most commonly used with desserts are cinnamon basil, lavender, lemon herbs (lemon balm, lemon basil, lemon thyme, lemon verbena, etc.), mints, rosemary and thyme.

Chocolate Mint Fondue

Serve with slices of fresh pineapple, small strawberries, cubes of angel food cake, etc. Recipe may be doubled.

1. In a small saucepan, combine cream, mint and chocolate. Heat just to boiling point; remove from heat. Let stand for 20 minutes.

2. Strain through a sieve; discard mint. When ready to serve, transfer to a fondue pot and warm slowly.

MAKES 4 TO 6 SERVINGS

1/2 cup	whipping cream (35%)
1/2 cup	chopped fresh mint (spearmint, orange mint or chocolate mint)
6 oz	bittersweet chocolate

Chocolate Mint Sauce

This is a great sauce to pour over ice cream or pears.

1. In a medium saucepan, mix together chocolate, mint, sugar and water. Over medium heat, bring to a boil; boil gently for 3 minutes, stirring constantly.

2. Remove from heat; whisk in butter. Let stand for 20 minutes. Strain through a sieve; discard mint.

3. May be served warm or cold. Store in a covered jar in the refrigerator; reheat in a saucepan over low heat or microwave, stirring occasionally.

MAKES ABOUT 1 CUP

8 oz	semi-sweet chocolate
3/4 cup	chopped fresh mint
1/2 cup	granulated sugar
1/2 cup	water
2 tbsp	butter

VARIATION

Lavender Chocolate Sauce
Use 2 tbsp fresh lavender flowers in place of mint.

Cream Puffs
WITH CHOCOLATE-MINT CREAM

These small cream puffs are just the thing for an elegant dessert. If you like, serve them with raspberries or sliced strawberries. The Chocolate-Mint Cream can also be used for a chocolate cake or a jelly roll.

1. In a medium saucepan over high heat, bring water and butter to a boil.

2. Stir in flour all at once; beat until mixture forms a ball that comes away from the sides of the pan. Remove from heat; let cool for 5 minutes.

3. Using an electric mixer, beat in eggs one at a time, beating until smooth after each addition. Transfer to a bowl; refrigerate for 10 minutes.

4. Drop dough by the spoonful onto a lightly greased or parchment-lined baking sheet, to make 10 cream puffs, mounding puffs high in center.

5. Bake in a 450°F oven for 10 minutes. Reduce temperature to 300°F; bake for 15 to 20 minutes, or until they are golden brown and appear dry. Remove from the oven; cut a small slit in each puff to release steam. Turn the oven off; return puffs to the oven for 30 minutes, leaving oven door ajar.

6. Cut a small piece off the top of each puff; remove dough filaments from inside. Replace tops. Let cool completely.

7. Spoon about 1/4 cup Chocolate-Mint Cream into each cream puff; replace tops. Dust with icing sugar. Garnish plate with mint leaves.

MAKES 10 PUFFS

1/2 cup	water
1/4 cup	butter
1/2 cup	all-purpose flour
2	eggs
	Chocolate-Mint Cream (recipe follows)
	Icing sugar and mint leaves, for garnish

Chocolate-Mint Cream

1. In a small saucepan over medium-low heat, mix together cream, mint and chocolate. Heat, stirring often, until chocolate melts. Stir until smooth.

2. Refrigerate until well chilled. Strain through a sieve; discard mint.

3. Using an electric mixer, beat chocolate mixture until peaks form.

MAKES 1-1/2 CUPS

1 cup	whipping cream (35%)
1/4 cup	chopped mint leaves (spearmint or peppermint)
2 oz	semi-sweet chocolate

Lavender Dark Chocolate Truffles

I asked my friend Wendi to develop this recipe as she loves chocolate. They are delicious!

Use a fine quality chocolate, one you enjoy eating, to make these decadent truffles. The lavender adds a subtle floral flavour while the honey contributes a delicate sweetness. These truffles pair beautifully with a glass of Muscat wine (flavours of peach, wine, apricot, floral) or a cup of black or Earl Grey tea.

1. In a small saucepan, stir together whipping cream and lavender. Bring to a simmer over medium heat. Remove from heat, cover and let stand for 15 minutes to infuse cream with lavender.

2. Meanwhile, chop chocolate into fine shards (see Tip, page 231). Place chocolate in a small bowl.

3. Stir honey into infused whipping cream and lavender mixture. Bring to simmer again over medium heat.

4. Remove from heat. Pour hot cream, through a fine mesh strainer or a piece of cheesecloth, over chocolate. Press down on lavender in strainer to remove as much cream as possible. If necessary, stir chocolate gently just to be sure all the pieces are covered with hot cream.

5. Let stand for one minute, then whisk until chocolate melts and cream and chocolate blend together to form a smooth, silky mixture. Scrape down the side of the bowl with a spatula. Cover and refrigerate for 1 to 1-1/2 hours until firm but not hard.

MAKES 16 TO 18 TRUFFLES

1/3 cup	whipping cream (35%)
2 tbsp	dried culinary lavender florets, lightly crushed between your fingers
1 tbsp	liquid honey
3.5 oz	dark chocolate (65 to 70%)
2 to 3 tsp	cocoa powder

6. With a fork, stir the mixture to break it up. Using a melon baller, mini scoop or a spoon, portion about 1-1/2 teaspoons per truffle onto a plate. Form each truffle by pinching it into a round shape, then rolling between your palms to smooth it into a ball. If balls are very soft and difficult to roll, chill them in the fridge for 20 minutes before rolling. Or cool your hands by occasionally rinsing them under cold water, drying them, then rolling the truffles quickly and lightly. The heat of your hands will make rolling the balls a messy endeavour if you spend too much time trying to get perfectly round shapes. It's okay for truffles to be slightly irregular!

7. Place cocoa powder in a small bowl and roll truffles around, a few at a time, to coat lightly. Place truffles on a clean plate or in a container, then cover and refrigerate.

8. The truffles will keep for about a week in the fridge. Ideally, before serving, warm them to room temperature for about 20 minutes.

TIPS

- Chop the chocolate into fine pieces, almost shavings. The small size will help the chocolate melt readily when the hot cream is poured over top. If a few pieces of chocolate still remain after stirring in the hot cream, warm the mixture carefully for 10 seconds at Medium-high power in the microwave, stirring well after heating. Add another 10 seconds if necessary.

- Instead of cocoa powder, the truffles can be dipped in melted tempered chocolate, or rolled in finely chopped nuts (try almonds, hazelnuts, walnuts or pistachios); desiccated coconut; chocolate or coloured sprinkles; Lavender Sugar (see page 40) or coloured sugar (often available at bulk food stores or you can tint sugar as desired using food colouring (purple will echo the lavender flavour!).

Lavender White Chocolate Bark
WITH DRIED CHERRIES AND PISTACHIOS

Chocolate bark makes a deliciously, decadent yet easily assembled treat or edible gift. Often dried fruit and nuts are simply sprinkled over the top of the melted chocolate when making bark. With this version, the flavorings are mixed into the chocolate as well as scattered over the surface of the bark so every bite tastes of lavender, cherries and pistachios. Thanks to my friend Wendi for this amazing bark which we very much enjoyed taste-testing!

1. Line the bottom of a baking sheet with foil or parchment paper. Set aside.

2. In a small bowl, heat chocolate in the microwave on Medium-high for 1 minute. Stir well, then heat in 10 second intervals, stirring well after each heating, until chocolate is completely melted. (Alternately, heat chocolate gently in a double boiler or in a heatproof bowl set over a small saucepan filled with simmering water. The bottom of the bowl should not touch the water. Stir chocolate when it begins to melt. Before chocolate melts completely, remove it from the heat; stir until completely melted.)

3. Crush 1 tsp of the lavender gently between your fingers; add it to the chocolate along with 2 tbsp of the pistachios and 2 tbsp of the cherries. Stir to combine.

4. Pour mixture onto the prepared baking sheet. Using a regular or offset spatula, or the back of a spoon, quickly and evenly spread mixture to about 3/8 inch thickness. Sprinkle remaining pistachios, cherries, and lavender over top. Press toppings gently into the chocolate with the back of a clean spoon or the palm of your hand to help ingredients adhere.

5. Refrigerate until firm, 1 to 1-1/2 hours. Break or cut into pieces.

6. Store in a covered container in a cool place. Bark will keep for about a week.

MAKES ABOUT 24 PIECES

7 oz	white chocolate, chopped
3 tbsp	coarsely chopped pistachios, divided
3 tbsp	coarsely chopped dried cherries, divided
1-1/2 tsp	dried culinary lavender florets, divided

TIPS

- Vary the type of chocolate and the mix-ins/toppings to suit your tastes and what you have on hand. Experiment with other dried fruits (cranberries, blueberries, mango, raisins, coconut), nuts (almonds, walnuts, hazelnuts), and types of chocolate (milk and dark).

- Bark can also be made in an 8 or 9-inch square baking pan. Use foil to line the bottom and sides of the pan. (Foil will take on the shape of the pan more readily than parchment paper.) Once the bark is set, grab the foil sides to lift it out of the pan, peel off the foil, and break the bark into pieces.

Lavender Ice Cream

Several years ago while visiting my brother Richard in London, England, we thought we would try making lavender ice cream in his new ice cream maker. So we set off to find some lavender. Unfortunately it was the end of the summer and most of the lavender was past blooming. Luckily we were able to obtain a few last flower heads from a neighbour's garden; we made this delicious ice cream, which we enjoyed with fresh sliced peaches. It would also be very good with raspberries, sliced strawberries or nectarines.

MAKES 4 SERVINGS

4	egg yolks
3/4 cup	granulated sugar
3/4 cup	half-and-half cream (10%)
2 tbsp	dried culinary lavender)
3/4 cup	whipping cream (35%)
	Red and blue food coloring (optional)
	Lavender flower heads, for garnish

1. In a medium bowl, whisk together egg yolks and sugar until light in color and foamy.

2. In a medium saucepan, combine half-and-half cream and lavender florets. Over medium heat, bring to a boil; simmer for 1 minute. Remove from heat and strain through a sieve; discard lavender.

3. Slowly whisk infused cream into egg yolk mixture. Return to saucepan and cook over low heat, stirring constantly, until the mixture thickens slightly and coats the back of a spoon. Do not allow to boil. Pour back into bowl and refrigerate until very cold.

4. In a medium bowl, with an electric mixer, beat whipping cream until stiff peaks form. Fold into cold lavender custard. Tint with food coloring, if desired, to light shade of purple. Pour into ice cream maker and process, or pour into a freezer container and freeze. Spoon into bowls, add fruit and garnish with lavender, if desired.

VARIATION

Chocolate-Mint Ice Cream
Use 1/3 cup finely chopped fresh spearmint in place of lavender. Add 3 oz semi-sweet chocolate to the cream; stir until chocolate melts. Follow from Step 2 but skip tinting with food coloring.

Lavender Lemon Cream
IN PHYLLO CUPS

This dessert starts with an easy microwave lemon curd, then herb-infused whipped cream is folded into it. This light filling is spooned into crispy paper-thin phyllo cups and topped with assorted fresh berries.

MAKES 9 SERVINGS

2	whole eggs
1	egg yolk
2/3 cup	granulated sugar
1 tbsp	grated lemon rind
4 tbsp	lemon juice
1 tbsp	butter
1/2 cup	whipping cream (35%)
1 tsp	dried culinary lavender florets (or 2 tsp fresh)
9	Phyllo Cups (recipe follows)
1 cup	fresh berries (such as raspberries, blueberries, sliced strawberries)
	Small mint sprigs, for garnish

1. In a large microwavable bowl, whisk together eggs, egg yolk, sugar, lemon rind and juice. Microwave on high for 2 minutes; whisk and microwave for 2 minutes longer. Whisk in butter, about 1 teaspoon at a time. Set aside.

2. In a small saucepan, heat cream and lavender over medium-heat just to a boil. Remove from heat; let cool. Strain and discard lavender; refrigerate cream for 20 minutes or until very cold. Using an electric mixer, whip cream.

3. Reserve 1/2 cup of the whipped cream; fold remaining whipped cream into the egg mixture.

4. Divide the lemon cream among phyllo cups; top with dollop of the reserved whipped cream, berries and a mint sprig.

   VARIATION: Minted Lemon Cream – use 2 tbsp finely chopped fresh mint in place of lavender.

Phyllo Cups

4	sheets phyllo pastry (thawed, frozen sheets)
3 tbsp	melted butter

1. Stack 2 sheets of phyllo pastry; brush top lightly with melted butter. Cut in half lengthwise, then in 3 crosswise. Place squares into 6 greased large muffin cups.

2. Repeat with 2 more sheets, placing a second square crosswise over each of the first squares. Repeat with 2 more sheets, this time using the 6 squares to make 3 additional cups.

3. Bake on lower rack of a 375°F oven for about 6 minutes, or until golden brown. Remove from pan to baking rack; let cool. Fill just before serving.

Lavender Panna Cotta

Panna cotta originated in northern Italy and the name means "cooked cream." It's a cool, non-baked dessert that is great to make in summer. Serve in glass dishes, glass stemware or unmold onto plates and surround with a berry coulis or compote. Or simply top with fresh berries or other fruit such as peaches and blueberries, or kiwi and raspberries. Lavender goes well with all of these. Try the non-milk version.

MAKES 6 TO 8 SERVINGS

4 cups	2% or whole milk, or coconut beverage
2 cups	half-and-half cream (10%) or whipping cream (35%), or 1 can (13.5 oz) coconut cream
3/4 cup	granulated sugar
2 tsp	dried culinary lavender (or 4 tsp fresh lavender florets)
3	envelopes unflavored gelatin
20 drops	*each*: blue and red food colouring (optional)
	Lavender spring or herb leaves for garnish
	Raspberry Coulis (see page 237)

1. In a large saucepan, combine 3-1/4 cups of the milk, cream, sugar and lavender. Bring to a boil over medium heat; reduce heat and simmer for 5 minutes, stirring often.

2. In a small bowl or glass measuring cup, stir gelatin into the remaining 3/4 cup milk. Let stand for 2 minutes. Add gelatin mixture to hot milk mixture; stir until dissolved. Do not allow to boil. Remove from heat and pour through fine sieve; discard lavender. Stir in food coloring to desired purple color.

3. Pour into four to six 1/2-cup ramekins sprayed with cooking spray or glass serving dishes. Place in a large cake pan for easy moving and stability in the refrigerator. Cover and refrigerate for 4 hours or overnight. If desired, unmold ramekins onto a small plate. Run knife around edge or dip briefly in hot water. Turn upside down and gently shake to loosen. If desired, spoon coulis to flow around panna cotta. Or, top with fresh mango, peaches, nectarines and/or berries. Garnish with lavender sprig or herb leaves such as mint.

Raspberry Coulis

Coulis (coo-lee) is a French word meaning to "pour or flow."

4 cups	fresh raspberries
1/3 cup	granulated sugar (or to taste)

1. Combine berries and sugar in medium saucepan. Heat and stir over medium heat until berries break down completely and release juices.

2. Pour through a fine strainer into a medium bowl. Press berries with back of a spatula to release all of the pulp and juices. Scrape outside bottom of strainer. Discard seeds. Cover and refrigerate coulis; keep up to 2 days.

Berry Compote

Follow coulis recipe above using your choice of berries. Stir 2 tsp cornstarch into the sugar (to prevent clumping) and stir into the berries, once some of the juices have been released. For a thinner sauce, add a bit of water. Will thicken as it cools.

VARIATIONS

(omit food coloring)

Lemon Verbena Panna Cotta
Replace lavender with 1 cup torn lemon verbena leaves (loosely packed). Lovely with blueberries or blackberries.

Lemon Basil Strawberry Panna Cotta
Replace 1 cup of the milk with puréed strawberries. Steep milk/cream with 1/2 cup loosely packed lemon basil (or 1/4 cup regular basil and add a 1 × 3-inch strip of lemon rind). Pour through strainer and press with back of spatula. Top with sliced strawberries.

Minted Mango or Peach
Replace 1 cup of the milk with puréed mango or peaches. Steep milk/cream with 1/3 cup loosely packed mint. Pour through strainer and press with back of spatula. Top with blueberries, raspberries or strawberries.

Lavender Shortbread

This lovely shortbread has a subtle hint of lavender and a texture that is crisp but still a bit soft.

1. In a large bowl, using an electric mixer, cream butter until very smooth. Beat in 1/2 cup Lavender Sugar a little at a time, until light and fluffy.

2. In a small bowl, mix together flour, cornstarch and lavender; stir into butter mixture just until blended.

3. Press into a 9-inch square cake pan or a 9-inch fluted round tart pan with removable base. Score the top surface with a knife, or use a fork poking down to the bottom, to create 18 bars (in a square pan: mark 6 across then into 3) or 12 wedges (in a fluted pan). Prick all over with a fork. Sprinkle top with granulated sugar. Sprinkle with lavender florets; press lightly onto top.

4. Bake on the lower rack of a 300°F oven for 25 to 35 minutes or until firm to the touch and golden. Let cool slightly; slice into wedges or bars along scored lines.

MAKES 18 BARS OR 12 WEDGES

1 cup	butter, softened
1/2 cup	Lavender Sugar, see page 40
1-1/2 cups	all-purpose flour
1/2 cup	cornstarch
1 tsp	fresh or dried culinary lavender florets, crushed
1 tsp	granulated sugar or Lavender Sugar
	Lavender florets to decorate top

Lavender Sugar Cookies
WITH LEMON GLAZE

Lavender and lemon partner beautifully in these dainty cookies perfect for afternoon tea!

1. In large bowl, using an electric mixer, cream butter and sugar (or Lavender Sugar below) until fluffy.

2. Beat in egg, lavender, lemon rind and vanilla.

3. In medium bowl, mix together flour, baking powder and salt. Stir into butter mixture until well combined. Place dough on plastic wrap and flatten into a 7-inch circle; seal well. Refrigerate for 1 hour.

4. Let dough rest at room temperature for 15 minutes. Remove plastic wrap and place on lightly floured surface. Roll with rolling pin to a bit less than 1/4-inch thickness. Cut using cookie cutters (2-inch floral). Place cookies on parchment-lined baking sheet. Double the baking sheet to create a layer of air underneath. Gather and re-roll trimmings.

5. Bake in 350°F oven for 10 to 12 minutes, until just starting to lightly brown at edges. Let rest on baking sheet a few minutes, then remove and cool cookies on a wire rack. Apply glaze when cool.

LEMON GLAZE: In a small bowl, mix together icing sugar and lemon juice. It should be a bit runny; add more lemon juice if necessary. Place cookies on a rack over a baking sheet or piece of waxed paper. Spread 1/2 tsp icing over surface of each cookie, allowing it to run a bit down the sides. Immediately sprinkle cookies with lavender flowers. (The icing has to be wet for lavender to stick.) Let set for 20 minutes to dry. Store in plastic container with waxed paper between layers.

LAVENDER SUGAR: For a finer texture of the lavender, process with sugar in food processor before creaming it with the butter. (See Lavender Sugar, page 40.)

VARIATION: If desired, make "sandwich" cookies by spreading with jam such as apricot, blackberry, strawberry, raspberry jam, etc. Glaze only half of the cookies and use the plain ones on the bottom (top side down).

MAKES ABOUT 5 DOZEN COOKIES

1 cup	butter, softened
3/4 cup	granulated sugar
1	egg
4 tsp	dried culinary lavender florets
1-1/2 tsp	finely grated lemon rind
1/2 tsp	vanilla
2 cups	all-purpose flour
1 tsp	baking powder
1/4 tsp	salt

GLAZE

1-1/3 cups	icing sugar
2 tbsp	lemon juice
2 tsp	dried culinary lavender florets

TIP

Store cookies in a plastic container. Cookies will soften. Keep up to 5 days.

Lemon Thyme Sugar Cookies

The subtle lemony flavor of lemon thyme elevates the simple sugar cookie to new heights.

1. In a large bowl, using an electric mixer, cream together butter and sugar. Beat in egg and vanilla.

2. In a small bowl, mix together flour, baking powder, baking soda and salt. Stir into creamed mixture.

3. Stir in lemon thyme. Divide dough in half; shape into two 7-inch logs. Wrap each in plastic wrap; refrigerate for 1 hour.

4. Cut logs into slices 1/4 inch thick. Place on greased baking sheets; bake in a 350°F oven for 10 to 12 minutes or until slightly browned. Let cool on racks; store in a covered container.

MAKES 36 TO 40 COOKIES

1/2 cup	butter, softened
3/4 cup	granulated sugar
1	egg
1/2 tsp	vanilla
1-1/2 cups	all-purpose flour
1/2 tsp	baking powder
1/4 tsp	baking soda
1/4 tsp	salt
4 tsp	very finely chopped fresh lemon thyme (or 2 tbsp cinnamon basil)

Lemon and Rosemary Cookies
WITH CORNMEAL

These cookies are made with a bit of cornmeal, which gives them a pleasing crunch.

1. In a large bowl, using an electric mixer, cream butter and sugar until fluffy; beat in egg. Beat in lemon rind, juice and vanilla.

2. In a separate bowl, mix together flour, cornmeal, baking powder, baking soda, salt and rosemary; stir into creamed mixture. Shape dough into a ball; cover with plastic wrap and refrigerate for 1 hour.

3. Roll dough into small balls, using about 1 tbsp of dough per cookie. Place on a lightly greased baking sheet, leaving about 2 inches between each cookie; flatten with fork.

4. Bake in a 350°F oven for 15 to 17 minutes or until light golden brown.

MAKES ABOUT 40 COOKIES

3/4 cup	butter, softened
1 cup	sifted icing sugar
1	egg
2 tbsp	grated lemon rind
1 tbsp	lemon juice
3/4 tsp	vanilla
1-1/2 cups	all-purpose flour
1/4 cup	cornmeal
3/4 tsp	baking powder
1/4 tsp	*each*: baking soda and salt
2 tsp	finely chopped fresh rosemary

Lavender Peach Galette

This is an easy-to-make free-form pie that looks very rustic. The lavender adds an interesting flavor that enhances the peaches. Serve it with vanilla ice cream or raspberry frozen yogurt. If desired, replace peaches with nectarines, apples or plums.

MAKES 8 SERVINGS

8	large peaches (about 2 lbs), peeled and pitted, cut into 1/4-inch slices
2 tbsp	lemon juice
1 tbsp	fresh or dried lavender florets, crushed
1/2 cup	granulated sugar
2 tbsp	cornstarch
1	pastry for double pie crust
1/2 cup	ground almonds
1	egg yolk
1 tsp	water
2 tbsp	granulated sugar

1. In a large bowl, toss peaches with lemon juice, lavender and 1/4 cup of the sugar. Let stand for about 1 hour; drain peaches, reserving juice. Mix together remaining 1/4 cup of the sugar and cornstarch; stir into peaches.

2. On a lightly floured surface, roll out pastry to 14-inch round. Place on a large baking sheet. Sprinkle ground almonds over pastry to within 2 inches of edge. Drain peaches and arrange on top of almonds. Fold the edges of the pastry in toward the center, overlapping slightly to form a 2-inch border. Combine egg yolk and water; brush over border and sprinkle with sugar. (Put into oven right away to prevent crust from becoming soggy.)

3. Bake in a 425°F oven for 15 minutes. Reduce temperature to 375°F and bake for 30 to 40 minutes longer, or until peaches are tender and crust is golden brown. (If crust browns too quickly, cover with foil.) Use reserved juice to brush over peaches several times during cooking.

Orange and Basil Biscotti

Biscotti (meaning "twice baked") are easier to make than you might think. I'm sure you'll enjoy this version with basil and orange. Give them as a gift from your kitchen in small cello bags tied with a decorative ribbon.

1. In a large bowl, cream together butter and sugar until fluffy; beat in egg. Beat in orange juice and rind.

2. In a separate bowl, mix together flour, cornmeal, baking powder and salt; add to creamed mixture all at once, stirring just until combined. Stir in pistachios and basil.

3. Divide dough in half. With floured hands, shape each half into a log about 12 inches long by 2 inches wide, leaving top slightly rounded. Place on a lightly greased baking sheet about 4 inches apart.

4. Bake in a 325°F oven for 30 minutes or until just beginning to brown. Let cool on the baking sheet for 10 minutes.

5. Using a sharp knife, cut logs into 1/2-inch slices on a slight diagonal. Arrange slices upright on the baking sheet, about 1 inch apart.

6. Reduce oven temperature to 300°F; bake for 20 to 25 minutes more, or until firm and dry. Let cool.

7. Store in an airtight container up to 1 week.

MAKES ABOUT 40 BISCOTTI

1/2 cup	butter
1 cup	granulated sugar
1	egg
1/4 cup	orange juice
	Grated rind from 1 medium orange
2-1/4 cups	all-purpose flour
2 tbsp	cornmeal
1 tsp	baking powder
1/2 tsp	salt
3/4 cup	coarsely chopped pistachios
2 tbsp	finely chopped fresh basil or cinnamon basil

VARIATIONS

Lavender Orange
Replace basil with 1 tbsp crushed dried lavender. Use almond slices in place of pistachios.

Cheddar Parmesan
Reduce butter to 1/3 cup, add 2 tbsp olive oil, reduce sugar to 1 tbsp, add 1/3 cup grated Parmesan cheese, add 2 tbsp toasted pine nuts to the batter and omit orange rind. If desired, replace basil with finely chopped fresh rosemary.

Mint and Lime Sorbet

Sorbets can be served between courses to cleanse the palate or as a light, refreshing dessert.

1. In a small saucepan, combine water, sugar and mint. Bring to a boil over high heat, stirring to dissolve sugar. Remove from heat. Let stand for 30 minutes; strain through a sieve and discard mint, squeezing to extract all of the syrup.

2. Return mint syrup to saucepan. Stir in corn syrup, lime rind and juice. Pour into a 9-inch square metal baking pan (or freezer trays). Freeze until firm.

3. Remove lime ice in chunks to a large bowl. Beat, using an electric mixer, until smooth and thick. (Or pulse in a food processor; transfer to a large bowl.)

4. In a medium bowl, beat egg whites with an electric mixer until stiff peaks form. Fold egg whites into lime mixture; return to pan and freeze again until firm. Let stand at room temperature until softened enough to scoop. Serve garnished with mint sprigs.

VARIATION: For Lemon-Lavender Sorbet, use lemon juice and rind in place of lime. Replace the mint syrup with lavender syrup, to taste (see page 40).

MAKES 4 TO 6 SERVINGS

2 cups	water
2/3 cup	granulated sugar
1/3 cup	chopped fresh mint
1/2 cup	clear or light corn syrup
1 tbsp	finely grated lime rind
1/3 cup	lime juice
2	egg whites
	Mint sprigs, for garnish

Minted Mango Mousse

This is a refreshing, light dessert. It is especially good to end a spicy, hot meal, such as those of Indian or Thai cuisines.

1. In a large bowl, using an electric mixer, beat cream cheese and sugar until smooth.

2. Purée mango in a food processor until smooth. Beat mango into cream cheese mixture until well combined.

3. Prepare gelatin according to package directions. Stir into mango mixture.

4. Fold in mint. Pour into a serving bowl or stemmed glasses; cover with plastic wrap and refrigerate for about 2 hours or until set. Garnish each serving with a dollop of whipped cream and a small mint sprig.

NOTE: I like to make this recipe with Atulfo mangoes which have a smooth, non-fibrous velvety texture. When in season, you can buy them by the case.

MAKES 4 TO 6 SERVINGS

1	pkg (8 oz) cream cheese, softened
1/3 cup	granulated sugar
2 cups	chopped ripe mango
1	envelope unflavored gelatin
1 tbsp	finely chopped fresh mint
	Whipped cream and mint leaves, for garnish

TIP

The best garnishes are usually at the top of the sprig. For the mint, choose the top-most small leaf formation.

Orange Mint Baked Custards

Orange mint has a lovely, subtle flavor that you will have to taste to believe. I have also infused the milk when making tapioca with orange mint.

1. In a medium saucepan, heat milk and mint over medium-high heat, stirring occasionally, just until it comes to a boil. Remove from heat; let stand for 20 minutes. Strain; discard mint.

2. In a large bowl, beat together eggs, sugar and salt. Slowly whisk warm milk mixture into eggs. Whisk in vanilla.

3. Place four 3/4-cup ramekins or custard cups in a baking dish; pour egg mixture into ramekins. Pour hot water into baking dish until it comes halfway up the sides of the ramekins.

4. Bake in a 350°F oven for 20 to 25 minutes, or until a knife inserted in the center comes out clean. Remove ramekins from water; let cool to room temperature. Cover with plastic wrap; refrigerate until chilled and firm, about 3 hours or overnight. If desired, garnish with edible flowers or mint sprigs.

NOTE: Cooking the custard in a pan of hot water is called a bain-marie, or hot water bath. It keeps the temperature even so the custard can cook slowly and avoid a tough edge around it.

MAKES 4 SERVINGS

2 cups	homogenized milk or light cream (5%)
1/2 cup	finely chopped orange mint, lemon balm or cinnamon basil (or 1 tbsp dried culinary lavender florets)
4	eggs
1/3 cup	granulated sugar
Pinch	salt
1/2 tsp	vanilla
	Violas or Johnny-jump-ups (see Edible Flowers, page 38), or sprigs of orange mint or lemon balm, for garnish

Poached Pears with Rosemary

Here's an interesting twist to poached pears, using cranberry juice, rosemary and orange. I like to cook the pears already halved and cored. They can be poached whole; double the recipe and place in a saucepan just large enough to fit the peeled whole pears standing upright.

MAKES 4 SERVINGS

2 cups	cranberry, cherry or pomegranate juice
1/2 cup	granulated sugar
1 tbsp	coarsely grated orange rind
1 tbsp	minced fresh rosemary
2	large firm, ripe Bartlett or Packham pears (or 4 small)
1 tbsp	orange liqueur or brandy (optional)
	Whipped cream or vanilla ice cream and small rosemary or mint sprigs, for garnish

1. In a large saucepan, mix together cranberry juice, sugar, orange rind and rosemary.

2. Peel and halve pears; remove cores, stems and blossom ends. Place pears in the saucepan with juice mixture.

3. Over high heat, bring to a boil. Reduce heat; simmer, uncovered, for 15 to 20 minutes or until pears are tender.

4. Using a slotted spoon, remove pears; cover and refrigerate. Increase heat to high; boil juice mixture until reduced to about 1 cup. Strain, discarding solids. Stir in liqueur, if using; refrigerate.

5. To serve, place pear halves on 4 individual serving plates; drizzle each with one-quarter of the syrup. Spoon a dollop of whipped cream into the center of each pear half. (Or slice pear halves lengthwise, not slicing all the way through at the stem end; fan out and place on plates with a scoop of ice cream.) Garnish with rosemary or mint sprigs.

VARIATIONS

Lemon-Lavender Poached Pears
Replace cranberry juice with half white grape juice and half Muscat wine. Replace orange rind with 2 tsp lemon rind. Replace rosemary with dried lavender and garnish with lavender flowers. Delete liqueur. If desired, replace whipped cream with a dollop of low-fat vanilla Greek yogurt or mascarpone cheese.

Lavender Poached Peaches
Prepare as for Lemon-Lavender Pears, using large peeled peaches. Use amaretto liqueur in place of orange liqueur as per original recipe. Garnish with toasted sliced almonds.

Rosemary and Lemon Custard Cakes

This is a simple but impressive dessert. As it bakes, it separates into a bottom layer of lemon custard with a top layer of soft sponge cake. Rosemary, with its piney essence, combines well with lemon.

1. In a large bowl, cream together butter and sugar. Stir in flour, salt, lemon rind, lemon juice and rosemary.

2. In a medium bowl, using an electric mixer, beat egg yolks until thick; beat in milk. Stir into creamed mixture.

3. In a medium bowl, beat egg whites with 1/4 cup icing sugar until soft peaks form. Fold into creamed mixture.

4. Divide mixture among 6 lightly greased 1-cup ramekins; place ramekins in a large baking pan. Pour enough hot water into pan to come halfway up the sides of the ramekins.

5. Bake in a 350°F oven for 30 to 35 minutes or until tops are puffed and golden brown. (Cake will rise to top and custard will form on bottom.)

6. Dust with icing sugar; garnish with rosemary sprigs and/or candied violets or violas. Serve warm, at room temperature or chilled.

MAKES 6 SERVINGS

2 tbsp	butter
3/4 cup	granulated sugar
1/4 cup	all-purpose flour
Pinch	salt
2 tsp	grated lemon rind
1/4 cup	lemon juice
1/2 tsp	finely chopped fresh rosemary
3	eggs, separated
1 cup	milk
1/4 cup	sifted icing sugar
	Icing sugar
	Rosemary sprigs, candied violets or violas, for garnish

Sweet Herb Crêpes

Serve these crêpes filled with fruit for brunch, or filled with ice cream to end a meal with a touch of flair. Crêpes can be made ahead, wrapped well and refrigerated up to two days, or frozen with waxed paper between the layers and placed in a freezer bag. Thaw completely before unwrapping and separating.

1. In a large bowl, using an electric mixer, beat eggs, sugar and salt.

2. Gradually beat in flour alternately with milk; beat until smooth.

3. Beat in butter, mint and vanilla until smooth. Let stand at room temperature for at least 1 hour. (May be refrigerated overnight.)

4. Heat a non-stick skillet (7-1/2 inches measured across base) over medium-high heat. Grease lightly with butter.

5. Stir crêpe batter a few times. For each crêpe, pour about 1/4 cup of the batter into the skillet. Immediately rotate pan to spread batter thinly and evenly. Cook until the underside is golden brown, about 1 minute. (Adjust heat if cooking too quickly or slowly.) Cook until the top feels dry to touch; flip over, and cook for about 20 seconds. Repeat with remaining batter. Stack crêpes on top of one another.

6. Fold crêpes into quarters; open up one fold to make a "cone" shape and fill with fruit or ice cream. If filling with fruit, stir a little vanilla yogurt or soft cheese product into fruit, if desired. Garnish with drizzled chocolate or a dusting of icing sugar and a small herb sprig.

MAKES 20 CRÊPES

4	eggs
1/4 cup	granulated sugar
Pinch	salt
2 cups	all-purpose flour
2 cups	milk
1/4 cup	melted butter or oil
2 tbsp	finely chopped fresh mint, orange mint or lemon balm
1 tsp	vanilla or 2 tsp finely grated lemon or orange rind, or 2 tbsp orange liqueur
	Melted semi-sweet chocolate, or icing sugar, for garnish
	Mint or lemon balm sprigs, for garnish

CRÊPE VARIATIONS

Chocolate-Mint

Add 1 tbsp finely chopped fresh spearmint or orange mint and 2 squares melted semi-sweet chocolate to the crêpe batter. Use for strawberry, banana or mixed berry (strawberries, raspberries and blackberries) crêpes.

Peach Melba

Fill crêpes with vanilla ice cream, sliced peaches and raspberries. Dust crêpe tops with icing sugar. Serve with whipped cream or Lavender Whipped Cream (see page 235).

Tropical Delight

Use cinnamon basil (2 tbsp) in crêpes in place of mint. Fill crepes with a mixture of pineapple, banana and papaya or mango); sprinkle with toasted coconut or toasted sliced almonds.

Strawberry-Kiwi

Fill crêpes with equal amounts of strawberries or raspberries and chopped peeled kiwi. Serve with whipped cream or low-fat vanilla Greek yogurt.

HERBAL TEAS AND BEVERAGES

Sip a hot lemony tea or a refreshing minty cold beverage to soothe and assuage body and soul. Drink in the sunshine that the herbs basked in while they grew, and enjoy a bit of aromatherapy, too. Herbs add a special touch of interest to popular beverages, whether it is an ice-cold lemonade, a refreshing white wine spritzer, or a soothing cup of hot tea.

HERBAL TEAS/TISANES

erbal teas are really *tisanes*, not true "tea," and are infusions of herbs in water. The following herbs are great for making teas: any lemony herb (such as lemon balm, lemon basil, lemon thyme and lemon verbena), lavender (flowers or leaves), any of the mints, oregano, rosemary and sage. Feel free to combine leaves, like lemon balm and lavender, rosemary and orange mint, mints and any lemon herbs. Or try sage tea with a spoonful of Lemon Verbena Honey (See Herb Honeys, page 36.)

Any of these herbs (fresh or dried) can be added to a pot of your favorite store-bought black tea or other herb teas as well. Use any of them you wish to make iced tea; chill and sweeten to taste. Add fresh herb leaves to ice in a tall glass to serve. Make a wine spritzer with fresh lemon balm leaves or lavender sprigs in a glass of ice; add wine and top with soda or fruit-flavored sparkling water.

All of these herbs retain their flavor well when dried. Store in glass jars with lids, away from heat and light. (See Drying Herbs, page 20.)

BASIC RECIPE FOR HERBAL TEA

Use about 2 cups hot or boiling water and 1 to 2 tbsp fresh herbs (1 to 2 tsp dried), or to taste.

TIPS ON MAKING HERBAL TEAS

- Use only the flowers or leaves; do not use stems.
- Use a pot for making hot tea so you do not lose too much aromatic oil.
- Use hot (boiled) water for fresh herbs and boiling water for dried herbs.
- Allow herbs to infuse/steep for about 5 minutes. Taste to determine if tea is to your liking; you can leave to infuse/steep longer, add more herbs or use less water the next time.
- It is not necessary to remove the leaves. If desired, pour through a small strainer into cups or mugs.
- Use juices to infuse/steep leaves: apple juice or cider, cranberry juice.

Fruit Smoothie

Here's a great breakfast or snack drink that whips up in no time in the blender.

1. In a blender, combine all ingredients except mint sprigs. Purée until smooth.

2. Pour into tall glasses; garnish with mint sprigs.

VARIATIONS

- Use 3 tbsp Chocolate Mint Sauce (see page 228) in place of honey; add 1 ripe medium banana.

- Try these fruit combinations – raspberry or strawberry and mango; raspberry or strawberry and kiwi or banana; raspberry and blueberry; blueberry and cantaloupe; orange, papaya and mango or passion fruit; pineapple, papaya and banana.

MAKES 2 SERVINGS

1-1/2 cups	plain yogurt
3/4 cup	chopped fresh fruit (or whole raspberries or blueberries)
2 tbsp	honey or sugar, or to taste
1 tbsp	finely chopped fresh mint (orange, chocolate or spearmint), lemon balm or lavender flowers
	Mint sprigs, for garnish

Lavender Lemonade

Lavender provides a lovely aroma to enjoy as you sip. Make lemonade with fresh lemon juice and sugar syrup, if desired, and use the steeped lavender as part of the water you would use. Or sweeten with Lavender Syrup or Honey (see page 40).

MAKES ABOUT 6 SERVINGS

1/4 cup	fresh culinary lavender florets (or 2 tbsp dried)
1 cup	boiling water
1	container (12 oz) frozen lemonade concentrate (or lemonade iced tea), thawed
	Long stems of lavender, for garnish

1. In a small bowl, place lavender; pour boiling water over top. Stir to submerge all the florets. Cover with plastic wrap and let stand for about 20 minutes. Strain through a sieve into a small bowl; discard lavender.

2. In a large pitcher, prepare lemonade according to directions, using lavender water as part of the water needed to reconstitute.

3. Pour over ice into tall glasses; garnish each with a long lavender stem. If desired, place several lavender flower heads in the pitcher.

   TIP: Use a bit of red and blue food coloring to tint the Lavender Lemonade to a purple color.

VARIATIONS

Sparkling Lavender Lemonade
Use only half of the water called for in the lemonade directions; fill glasses and top with carbonated or sparkling water.

Lavender Cranberry Cocktail
Use about 6 cups of cranberry juice cocktail or pink cranberry juice cocktail in place of lemonade.

Lavender Peach Iced Tea
Use frozen peach iced tea in place of lemonade.

Purple Basil Lemonade
Add chopped purple basil leaves to lemonade. Stir and let sit until color changes to pink; strain through sieve. Works well with cinnamon basil or lemon basil also. Add blackberries to glass.

Minted Lemonade
Use 1/2 cup chopped fresh spearmint or lemon balm in place of lavender, but add directly to the pitcher. Refrigerate for about 4 hours then strain through a sieve. Add a few fresh mint leaves to the glasses with ice and pour in drink.

Lavender Blueberry Margarita

Lavender goes so well with fruit flavors. Here it is beautifully matched with blueberries in these frozen Margaritas, but try also with peaches, raspberries and strawberries. This drink uses Lavender Syrup which can be made ahead (see page 40).

1. In a blender, combine blueberries, lime juice, tequila and orange liqueur. Sweeten with about 3 tbsp of the Lavender Syrup. Add ice; purée until smooth. Adjust to taste with more syrup or more lime juice.

2. Go around outside of the rim of glasses with lime wedge, then a dip in salt (or sugar). Pour Margarita into glasses; top with lavender and fresh blueberries. If desired, add a slice of lime to the rim also.

MAKES 2 DRINKS

	Lavender Syrup (see page 40)
1/4 cup	blueberries (wild ones, if you can get them)
2 tbsp	lime juice
3 oz	tequila
1 oz	orange liqueur (such as Triple Sec)
3 cups	ice cubes
	Lime wedges
	Short stems of lavender and blueberries, for garnish

Mint Julep

This is a refreshing summer drink originating in the southern United States, and was popular in Virginia in the early 1800s and made with rum, brandy or aged gin (genever). It traveled west and became the official drink of the Kentucky Derby in 1938, made with local bourbon (corn whiskey). The vanilla and caramel taste of the bourbon or the flavor of a spiced rum enhance this drink nicely.

MAKES 1 SERVING

10	large fresh spearmint leaves
1 tsp	granulated sugar
2 tbsp	boiling water
	Crushed ice
2 oz	bourbon
	Fresh mint sprigs, for garnish

1. In a small glass measuring cup, place mint leaves. Sprinkle leaves with sugar; use a spoon to bruise leaves against sugar. (Great if you have a muddler or use the handle of a wooden spoon.) Pour in boiling water; stir to dissolve sugar.

2. Pour mint mixture into a tall glass. Fill glass three-quarters full with crushed ice. Pour in bourbon; garnish with fresh mint sprigs.

   LAVENDER MINT JULEP: Use lavender syrup or honey to sweeten in place of the sugar and water (see page 40).

Mint Mimosa

A mimosa is named after a tropical flower and is a champagne and orange juice beverage served at brunch. Serve it well chilled (but without ice) in tall, chilled champagne glasses.

1. In a blender, purée orange juice concentrate and mint. Strain through a sieve into a liquid measuring cup, pressing to extract juice; discard mint.

2. Pour about 2 tbsp mint-orange concentrate into a chilled champagne glass. Fill with chilled champagne. Garnish with begonias or mint sprigs. Serve immediately.

MAKES 6 TO 8 SERVINGS

1 cup	frozen orange juice concentrate
1/3 cup	chopped fresh mint (such as peppermint, spearmint or orange mint)
2	bottles (750 mL each) well-chilled champagne or sparkling wine (such as Prosecco)
	Begonia flowers or mint sprigs, for garnish

Mint Mojito

The mojito is another mint-based drink originating in Havana, Cuba that was made popular in 1930 likely by writer Ernest Hemingway and other movie stars who visited there.

1. Place mint leaves in a large, tall glass. Add sugar; use a muddler or the handle of a wooden spoon to bruise leaves against sugar.

2. Pour in lime juice and rum. Fill with crushed ice and top with soda water. Garnish with mint sprig.

MAKES 1 SERVING

1	large sprig fresh spearmint
2 tsp	granulated or brown sugar
2 oz	white rum, or any rum
1 tbsp	fresh lime juice
	Soda water
	Mint sprig, for garnish

VARIATIONS

Frozen Mojito
Use frozen lime juice concentrate, add to blender with ice, mint, rum and fresh lime juice, to taste; blend well. If desired, add fresh berries.

Mint Mocktail
Fill a tall glass one-third full with thawed frozen juice concentrate such as lime, orange, pineapple or peach, or black currant syrup. Add mint or lemon balm leaves; crush with spoon. Add crushed ice and top with soda water or flavored sparkling water.

Herbed Wine

Herbs and wines go well together. Drink herbed wine straight, or use to make spritzers by adding soda water or fruit-flavoured sparkling water and a slice of lemon or lime, or fresh berries or fruit slices.

1   bottle (750 mL) wine (see below)

1 cup   chopped fresh herbs (see below)

1. Pour wine into a large pitcher.

2. Stir in chopped herbs. Stir with wooden spoon to bruise leaves.

3. Cover and refrigerate for about 8 hours. Strain through a sieve; discard leaves. Taste. The herbs should be recognizable but not overpowering; dilute with more wine if too strong.

   TIP: Add mint leaves, lemon balm or lemon verbena to a white wine spritzer. As the glass moves, it bruises the leaves on the ice and glass and creates a nice scent and taste.

VARIATIONS

Dry White Wine, White Zinfandel or Fruit Wines
Use lemon balm, lemon verbena, basil leaves or any of the mints. If desired, add frozen seedless grapes, or add berries to fruit wines. When using basil, add orange juice and orange slices. Garnish with herb used.

Red Wine
Use lemon balm, or 1/4 cup coarsely chopped rosemary.

Sangria
Use orange mint, or 1/4 cup coarsely chopped rosemary.

Herbed Bloody Mary or Caesar

Herbs add an interesting variation to these tomato-based drinks. They make a tasty beverage to serve at brunch. Serve with a bottle of hot pepper sauce to allow guests to turn up the heat! The Bloody Caesar is quite popular in Canada though the tomato-clam juice is made in the USA. The juice is less thick than tomato and has a pleasant hint of clam. Both drinks may be spiked or virgin.

1. In blender, combine tomato juice, basil, Worcestershire sauce, lemon juice and bitters, if using. Purée until well combined.

2. Pour vodka (if using) into a tumbler over ice. Pour tomato-herb mixture into glass; season with hot pepper sauce, salt and pepper.

3. Garnish glass with a celery stick or cherry tomatoes on a wooden skewer; hook a shrimp or a cherry tomato sliced partway over the rim of the glass. Pickled green beans, dill pickle spears, pickled hot peppers, or olives are also a popular garnish as well as slices of lemon or limes on the edge of the glass.

MAKES ABOUT 4 SERVINGS

3 cups	tomato or tomato-clam juice
2 tbsp	finely chopped fresh basil or dill, or 1 tbsp fresh marjoram (or to taste)
1 tbsp	Worcestershire sauce
2 tsp	lemon juice
2	dashes Angostura bitters (optional)
1 oz	vodka (optional)
	Hot pepper sauce, to taste
	Salt and pepper, to taste
	Celery sticks, cherry tomatoes, cooked jumbo shrimp (tails on), for garnish

TIP

For a Caesar, the glass is usually rimmed by first going around outside of the rim with lemon or lime wedge, then a dip in celery salt or Caesar rim mix. My preference is for seasoning salt.

PRESERVES

Fresh herb jellies, such as mint or rosemary, are wonderful condiments for meats. Lavender enhances fruity flavors in peach or strawberry jams. Savory herbs complement onion jam and tangy chutney. Canned peaches are taken to a new taste level with lavender or lemon verbena.

GENERAL CANNING INFORMATION

INTRODUCTION

I also like to add herbs to my preserves. These recipes are included, with permission, from my book *250 Home Preserving Favorites – Jams, Jellies, Marmalades and More* (c. 2010 Robert Rose). Carol's Cream Tea Scones, from my original jam and jelly book *Prizewinning Preserves*, are the perfect base for delicious jams! When canning peaches, I love the added flavor of lavender or lemon verbena.

FOOD SAFETY

When you are making preserves, it is most important to keep things sanitary. Microbes, usually molds, are responsible for spoilage which can ruin the flavor and consistency. Most important though, some of the toxins produced by microbes can be lethal (clostridium botulinum). It is never worth the risk to consume suspect food; discard food that has been kept too long, in which you can see bubbles moving, or if the seal is not intact or in which there is obvious mold growth.

NOTE: It is not safe to simply remove the mold from the preserves in a jar as mold spores can penetrated deeper into it. Discard the entire contents.

The high concentration of sugar found in jams and jellies and other preserves is responsible for deterring the growth of molds. Molds will grow on the surface as well as in the presence of air. That is why boiling water canning is recommended, to provide an airtight seal and to kill microorganisms that might get into the jar from utensils or during filling. Processing is even more important for low-sugar preserves.

EQUIPMENT

All you need for boiling water canning is a very large deep pot such as an aluminum stock pot. It must be deep enough to hold the jars as well as water that will cover the jars by one to two inches and not overflow when boiling.

Canning jars are made from special heat-resistant glass for boiling water canning. In the United States, jars are pint (16 oz), half pint (8 oz), etc. while in Canada they are metric: 500 mL, 250 mL, etc. The lids consist of metal rings (known as screw bands) and one-time-use metal lids with a sealing compound that needs to be softened to be effective. To prepare lids, boil a small pot of water. Add lids, turn off heat and cover. Do this a few minutes before you start to fill jars. (Do not boil lids.) *Always use new lids.*

A ladle is used to transfer preserves into jars. A canning funnel makes it easier as it is wider than jar mouths and helps to keep the rim clean.

A head space gauge is another handy tool. It is plastic and has notched measurements every 1/4 inch. The long end can also be used to remove bubbles, especially for canned fruit, by running it along the inside of the jar. *Do not use a metal knife as it can cause scratching to the inside of the jar.*

Wipe the rim with hot water (I dip a clean paper towel into the hot lid water). It is important that there is no stickiness remaining there as it will prevent sealing and could cause mold to growth underneath. Use a handy magnetic wand to remove lids from the hot water. Place lid on rim of jar. You can use your finger on the top of the lid to detach it from the wand. Take a clean screw band and apply to secure the lids but only "finger-tip tight." This means to make it snug but not overtighten. If it is too tight, then water cannot escape during processing to create the vacuum seal.

A jar lifter is handy for gripping hot jars to lift out of the water.

TIP: I always prepare one more jar, lid and ring than called for in the recipe, in case something goes wrong in filling jars. I have had a jar tip over.

USING A BOILING WATER CANNER

Processing jars after filling and applying lids is important for the safe, long-term room temperature storage of your preserves. Processing ensures that any microbes that may have gotten into your product while you were filling the jars are killed and that you achieve a strong vacuum seal that will be maintained for the duration of the jars' storage. A good seal is not possible from just letting jars cool. The lid may indent but the amount of pressure may be low and not last.

Ensure that the water in the large pot is boiling before adding jars. Lower jars carefully (one at a time, or on a rack), ensuring that they do not tilt. Make sure to leave some room between jars to allow the water to circulate and also so the jars do not bump while boiling and there is sufficient room to be able to lift them out. Measure how much water is above the jar lids (you can do this by dipping in the handle of a wooden spoon then measuring the water mark. Add boiling water if necessary. Remove water if you need to with a heatproof glass measuring cup. Make sure you have left a couple of inches of space above the surface of the water to prevent a boil over.

Cover the pot and return to a boil over high heat. Start timing the processing once the water has returned to a boil. Process for the time specified in the recipe (see High Altitude Processing for time adjustments).

Remove jars with jar lifter, lifting straight up and keeping them vertical *(do not tilt)*. Place them one at a time onto a clean tea towel placed on a tray or right on the counter. (A tray makes it easy to move them later if you wish). *Do not place jars on a cold surface.* As the jars begin to cool, you will hear the tell-tale popping sound and see that the lids have been sucked downward to create the vacuum seal. After cooling completely, check seals by pressing down in the center of the lid; they should not move.

Let jars rest until the jam or jelly has set. Once jars have cooled, check for set by tilting the jar slightly. Jellies will not move when set. Some jams and other preserves have a softer set and may move a bit.

Once set, remove the screw bands. Using a clean hot cloth, wipe the entire jar and under the bands to remove any sugary residue which could grow mold. You may replace the rings if you like for storage but do not overtighten or you will break or weaken the seal.

Refrigerate any unsealed jars and use within 3 weeks.

CURRENT PROCESSING TIMES

Home preserving experts recommend longer processing times (i.e. 10 minutes vs 5 minutes for jams and jellies, etc.) as this ensures improved food safety (in case people have not been 100% careful to keep everything sterilized). Although in theory these increased processing times mean there is no longer the need to sterilize canning jars (they just need to be hot), I still sterilize them anyway; it never hurts to be on the safe side.

HIGH ALTITUDE PROCESSING

If you live at an altitude more than 1,000 feet (306 m) above sea level, you will need to adjust the processing time in the recipes as follows:

- 1,000 to 3,000 feet (306 to 915 m) – increase time by 5 minutes
- 3,001 to 6,000 feet (916 to 1,830 m) – increase time by 10 minutes
- 6,001 to 8,000 feet (1.831 to 2,400 m) – increase time by 15 minutes
- 8,001 to 10,000 feet (2,441 to 3,050 m) – increase time by 20 minutes

LABELING AND STORING

Label jars with the name of the contents and the date. If you plan to store them in the box they came in, place the labels on the lids rather than on the side of the jars. This way you can see them from the top. The other benefit is that you throw away the lids after and there's no need to pick the label off the jars.

Store sealed, labeled jars in a cool, dry, dark place. Warmth, temperature fluctuations, dampness or light will deteriorate the flavor and color of your preserves. The ideal storage temperature is 40°F to 50°F (4°C to 10°C). Properly stored, your preserves will keep for more than a year but I recommend to use them up within a year. Once jams are opened, refrigerate and use up within 3 weeks.

TIP: Use the hook of a can opener to pop open the sealed lids.

TERMS

FULL ROLLING BOIL: A boil that cannot be stirred down, that bubbles constantly and vigorously.

SIMMER: A constant light bubbling over lower heat that slowly cooks the food.

FINGER-TIP TIGHT: To tighten the jar ring, with only your fingertips gripping it, just until the ring is snug, not as tight as it will go. If the ring is overtightened before processing, air will not be able to escape during processing and a good seal will not form. Tightening rings too tight after processing is likely to disturb and weaken the seal. (If sealed it does not really even need the ring; it is only there to close the lid after opening the jar.)

HEADSPACE: The space left between the top of the preserve and the top rim of the jar. It is important to leave the amount of space specified in the recipe to create the vacuum seal. Contents from overfilled jars may seep out.

Mint Jelly

This is a classic mint jelly, typically served with lamb. I usually make it with spearmint which is the type of mint found in most grocery stores. You can make this recipe with any kind of mint – peppermint, lemon mint, orange mint, pineapple mint.

1. In a large, deep, heavy-bottomed pot, combine water and the whole mint leaves. Bring to a boil over high heat. Reduce heat and simmer, covered, for 15 minutes. Strain through a sieve, over a bowl, squeezing leaves; reserve liquid and discard leaves.

2. Measure exactly 2 cups of the mint infusion, adding water if there is not enough; pour into a clean pot.

3. Stir in vinegar. Stir in pectin until dissolved. Bring to a full boil over high heat, stirring constantly.

4. Add sugar in a steady stream, stirring constantly. Return to a full boil, stirring constantly to dissolve the sugar. Boil hard for 1 minute.

5. Remove from heat and skim off any foam using a large metal spoon. Stir in finely chopped mint leaves and food coloring, if using. Slowly stir for 5 to 8 minutes, to prevent leaves from floating.

6. Ladle quickly into sterilized jars to within 1/4 inch of the rim; wipe rims. Apply prepared new lids and rings; tighten just until fingertip-tight (snug but not too tight).

7. Process jars in a boiling water canner for 10 minutes. Transfer jars to a towel-lined surface or tray. Let rest at room temperature until set. Check seals; refrigerate any unsealed jars up to 3 weeks.

   TIP: To check for floating *before* ladling into jars, pour into a 4-cup glass measure; stir and let sit for a minute or two. If mints stays suspended, then pour into jars. If floating re-appears after processing, once jars are completely sealed and cooled slightly, you may gently rotate jars to re-suspend the mint.

MAKES ABOUT 4 HALF PINT (250 ML) JARS

2-1/2 cups	water
2 cups	loosely packed whole mint leaves
3/4 cup	apple cider vinegar
2 pkgs	(1.75 oz/49 g or 57 g) powdered pectin
4 cups	granulated sugar
1/2 cup	finely chopped fresh mint (such as spearmint, peppermint or orange mint)
	Green food coloring (optional)

Refer to General Canning Information at the beginning of the chapter.

Rosemary Apple Cider Jelly

This amazing jelly is the very first preserve that I won a First Prize ribbon for at the Royal Agricultural Winter Fair in Toronto. It is a delicious condiment to serve with chicken, turkey and pork. My dad once took it out of the refrigerator at my parent's home to have it on toast for breakfast!

MAKES ABOUT 5 HALF PINT (250 ML) JARS

4 cups	unsweetened apple cider or all-natural apple juice
1/2 cup	loosely packed, coarsely chopped fresh rosemary
1 pkg	(1.75 oz/49 g or 57 g) powdered pectin
4-1/2 cups	granulated sugar

1. In a large, deep, heavy-bottomed pot, combine apple cider and rosemary. Bring to a boil over high heat. Reduce heat and simmer, covered, for 20 minutes. Strain through a sieve, over a bowl, squeezing leaves; reserve liquid and discard leaves.

2. Measure exactly 3-1/2 cups of the rosemary infusion, adding cider if there is not enough; pour into a clean pot.

3. Stir in pectin until dissolved. Bring to a full boil over high heat, stirring constantly.

4. Add sugar in a steady stream, stirring constantly. Return to a full boil, stirring constantly to dissolve the sugar. Boil hard for 1 minute.

5. Remove from heat and skim off any foam using a large metal spoon.

6. Ladle quickly into sterilized jars to within 1/4 inch of the rim; wipe rims. Apply prepared new lids and rings; tighten just until fingertip-tight (snug but not too tight).

7. Process jars in a boiling water canner for 10 minutes. Transfer jars to a towel-lined surface or tray. Let rest at room temperature until set. Check seals; refrigerate any unsealed jars up to 3 weeks.

> Refer to General Canning Information at the beginning of the chapter.

VARIATION

Cranberry Rosemary Jelly
Substitute cranberry cocktail or cranberry cocktail blend (e.g. cranberry-pomegranate) for the apple cider.

Peach Lavender Jam

Lavender adds a sweet aroma to luscious peaches. Use only the purple flowers, not the leaves of the lavender. This jam won first prize at the Royal Winter Fair in Toronto, Canada.

MAKES ABOUT 7 HALF PINT (250 ML) JARS

3 tbsp	dried culinary lavender florets
1/3 cup	boiling water
4 cups	finely chopped peeled peaches or nectarines (unpeeled)
1/4 cup	lemon juice
7-1/4 cups	granulated sugar
2 pouches	(each: 3 oz/85 mL) liquid pectin

1. Place lavender in a small heatproof bowl. Pour boiling water over the lavender; let steep for 20 minutes. Strain through a sieve, over a bowl, squeezing florets; reserve liquid and discard lavender.

2. In a large, deep, heavy-bottomed pot, combine lavender infusion, peaches and lemon juice. Bring to a boil over high heat, stirring constantly.

3. Add sugar in a steady stream, stirring constantly. Return to a full boil, stirring constantly to dissolve the sugar.

4. Immediately stir in pectin; return to a full boil. Boil hard for 1 minute; stirring constantly.

5. Remove from heat and skim off any foam using a large metal spoon. Stir for 5 to 8 minutes to prevent floating fruit.

6. Ladle quickly into sterilized jars to within 1/4 inch of the rim; wipe rims. Apply prepared new lids and rings; tighten just until fingertip-tight (snug but not too tight).

7. Process jars in a boiling water canner for 10 minutes. Transfer jars to a towel-lined surface or tray. Let rest at room temperature until set. Check seals; refrigerate any unsealed jars up to 3 weeks.

TIP FOR PEELING PEACHES: Bring a medium pot of water to a boil over high heat. Place peaches in water two at a time; boil for 30 seconds. Remove peaches with a slotted spoon and immediately immerse in a bowl of very cold or ice water. Repeat with remaining peaches. When peaches are cooled enough to handle, slit down the side of the peel with a paring knife; slip off the peel. Cut peaches in half and remove pits.

Refer to General Canning Information at the beginning of the chapter.

Strawberry Lavender Jam

Lavender adds a touch of sweetness and aroma to strawberries. Serve on fresh baked scones for a special "tea." This jam won first prize at the Royal Winter Fair in Toronto, Canada.

1. Place lavender in a small heatproof bowl. Pour boiling water over the lavender; let steep for 20 minutes. Strain through a sieve, over a bowl, squeezing florets; reserve liquid and discard lavender.

2. In a large, deep, heavy-bottomed pot, combine lavender infusion, crushed strawberries and lemon juice. Bring to a boil over high heat, stirring constantly.

3. Add sugar in a steady stream, stirring constantly. Return to a full boil, stirring constantly to dissolve the sugar.

4. Immediately stir in pectin; return to a full boil. Boil hard for 1 minute; stirring constantly.

5. Remove from heat and skim off any foam using a large metal spoon. Stir for 5 to 8 minutes to prevent floating fruit.

6. Ladle quickly into sterilized jars to within 1/4 inch of the rim; wipe rims. Apply prepared new lids and rings; tighten just until fingertip-tight (snug but not too tight).

7. Process jars in a boiling water canner for 10 minutes. Transfer jars to a towel-lined surface or tray. Let rest at room temperature until set. Check seals; refrigerate any unsealed jars up to 3 weeks.

MAKES ABOUT 7 HALF PINT (250 ML) JARS

3 tbsp	dried culinary lavender florets
1/3 cup	boiling water
3-3/4 cups	well crushed strawberries
1/4 cup	lemon juice
7 cups	granulated sugar
1	pouch (3 oz/85 mL) liquid pectin

Refer to General Canning Information at the beginning of the chapter.

Carol's Cream Tea Scones

These fresh baked scones are my favorite way to enjoy homemade jam. Here is the authentic Scottish family recipe shared with me by my dear (late) friend and former colleague Carol Ferguson (see acknowledgments).

1. In a large bowl, combine flour, sugar, baking powder and salt. Using a pastry blender, cut in butter until mixture resembles coarse crumbs.

2. In a small bowl, beat egg; set aside 1 tbsp to brush on top of scones. Stir milk into the remaining egg.

3. Using a fork, stir egg mixture into flour mixture to make a light, soft dough. If dough seems sticky, add a bit more flour.

4. Gather dough into a ball and knead lightly a few times on a lightly floured surface until smooth. Flatten with hands or a rolling pin to 3/4-inch thickness. Using a biscuit cutter (2-1/2-inch diameter), cut into rounds, re-rolling scraps or pressing them together to make scones about the same size.

5. Place on a baking sheet about 2 inches apart. Brush tops with reserved egg. Sprinkle with a little sugar, if desired. Bake in the center of a 425°F oven for 10 to 12 minutes, until golden brown. Reduce oven temperature if they begin to brown too quickly.

MAKES ABOUT 10 SCONES

2 cups	all-purpose flour (or replace 1 cup with cake and pastry flour)
2 tbsp	granulated sugar
1 tbsp	baking powder
1/2 tsp	salt
1/2 cup	butter, softened
1	egg, divided
2/3 cup	milk or light cream (5%)
	Granulated sugar for the top (optional)

VARIATIONS

Lavender Scones with Lemon Glaze
Add 2 tsp dried organic lavender flowers to the dry ingredients. Flatten dough into a circle about 3/4-inch thick; cut into 8 wedges. Bake as per Step 5. Do not sugar the tops. When cooled, drizzle with half batch of Lemon Glaze (see page 239) and sprinkle tops with additional lavender florets. For finer lavender in the scones, process sugar and lavender in food processor first.

White Chocolate Lavender
Add 4 oz chopped white chocolate to lavender version of recipe.

Orange Onion Jam
WITH SAGE AND THYME

This semi-soft jam has a marmalade-like golden color with a slight tang. If desired, add a bit of finely grated orange rind with the oranges. This jam is an excellent condiment to serve with pork, lamb or chicken.

1. In a Dutch oven or large, heavy-bottomed pot, combine onions and water. Bring to a boil over medium heat, stirring constantly. Reduce heat and simmer, covered, stirring occasionally, for about 10 minutes or until onions are very soft.

2. Stir in garlic, oranges, sage and thyme. Increase heat to high and bring to a boil. Reduce heat and simmer, covered, stirring occasionally, for 8 minutes or until oranges are softened.

3. Stir in vinegar, salt and pepper.

4. Stir in pectin until dissolved. Bring to a full boil over high heat.

5. Stir in granulated and brown sugars. Return to a full boil, stirring constantly to dissolve the sugar. Boil hard for 1 minute.

6. Remove from heat and skim off any foam using a large metal spoon. Stir for 5 to 8 minutes to prevent floating fruit.

7. Ladle into sterilized jars to within 1/2 inch of the rim; wipe rims. Apply prepared new lids and rings; tighten just until fingertip-tight (snug but not too tight).

8. Process jars in a boiling water canner for 15 minutes. Turn off water and allow water to stop boiling. Leave jars for a few minutes as this helps to prevent loss of syrup when removing jars.

9. Transfer jars to a towel-lined surface or tray. Let rest at room temperature until set. Check seals; refrigerate any unsealed jars up to 3 weeks.

NOTE: Onion jams are sweet, savory condiments to enjoy with cheeses, meats or cooked vegetables. Add them to make a sauce when deglazing the pan after cooking meat (this idea is from my older brother Gerard who is a chef), use as a finishing sauce on roasted meats (chicken, turkey, ham or pork roast), or toss with cooked vegetables.

MAKES ABOUT 5 HALF PINT (250 ML) JARS

5 cups	thinly sliced sweet onions (such as Vidalia or Walla Walla or red onions)
1/3 cup	water
1	clove garlic, minced
3 cups	chopped peeled oranges
2 tbsp	chopped fresh sage
1 tsp	finely chopped fresh thyme or lemon thyme
1/3 cup	white wine vinegar
1/2 tsp	salt
Pinch	freshly ground black pepper
1 pkg	(1.75 oz/49 or 57 g) powdered pectin
3-1/4 cups	granulated sugar
3/4 cup	packed brown sugar

Refer to General Canning Information at the beginning of the chapter.

Cran-Apple Sage and Thyme Chutney

This is a kind of chutney you'll want to eat with roasted turkey, chicken or pork, or add to your favorite stuffing. The flavour is a nice variation on traditional chutneys which are primarily seasoned with spices and hot peppers. Stir some into mayonnaise (see below) for a tasty spread for sandwiches, wraps or burgers, meat or veggie.

1. In a Dutch oven or large, heavy-bottomed pot, combine apples, cranberries, onions, garlic, sugar, water, vinegar and salt. Bring to a boil over high heat, stirring often.

2. Reduce heat and boil gently, stirring often. Reduce heat further as mixture thickens, for about 30 minutes; stir in sage and thyme. Continue to cook for another 5 to 10 minutes, until thickened.

   TEST FOR DONENESS: Place a spoonful of chutney on a plate. Draw a small spoon through the center. Chutney is done when no liquid seeps into the space.

3. Ladle into sterilized jars to within 1/2 inch of the rim; wipe rims. Apply prepared new lids and rings; tighten just until fingertip-tight (snug but not too tight).

4. Process jars in a boiling water canner for 15 minutes. Transfer jars to a towel-lined surface or tray. Let rest at room temperature until set. Check seals; refrigerate any unsealed jars up to 3 weeks.

   NOTE: Chutney will thicken as it cools and should not be overly thick. It should mound on a spoon but fall gently from it.

   TIP: The secret to great chutney is the long, slow cooking. The greater the diameter of the pot, the more evenly it will cook.

   CHUTNEY MAYONNAISE: Stir about 1/3 cup of the chutney into 1 cup of mayonnaise. If desired, stir in about 1 tsp curry powder, or to taste. Add some heat with minced chile peppers, if desired. Refrigerate until using or up to 5 days.

MAKES ABOUT 4 HALF PINT (250 ML) JARS

3 cups	chopped peeled apples that keep their shape (Golden Delicious, Jonagold, Crispin/Mutsu, Idared, Northern Spy, Spartan, etc.)
3 cups	chopped peeled apples that soften (McIntosh, Paula Red, Cortland, Empire, Russet, etc.)
3 cups	fresh or frozen cranberries
1-1/2 cups	chopped onions
2	cloves garlic, minced
2-1/2 cups	granulated sugar
2 cups	water
1 cup	apple cider vinegar
1 tsp	salt
1 tbsp	chopped fresh sage
2 tsp	chopped fresh thyme or lemon thyme

Refer to General Canning Information at the beginning of the chapter.

Peaches and Herbs

Flavoring the sugar syrup when canning adds a lovely taste to these peaches. They can be prepared for eating right away or for canning as a preserve. Delicious as a dessert with mascarpone cheese spooned into the center of halves, or sliced peaches spooned over ice cream or raspberry sorbet, or for breakfast with vanilla yogurt.

1. Prepare herbed sugar syrup: In a large saucepan, combine water and sugar. Add lavender. Bring to a boil over high heat; reduce heat and simmer for 2 to 3 minutes, stirring to dissolve sugar. Remove from heat and let steep for about 10 minutes. Strain through a sieve, over a bowl, squeezing florets; reserve liquid and discard lavender.

2. See Tip for Peeling Peaches, see page 267. Slip skins from peaches; discard. Halve or slice peaches. Place peaches in a large pot with herb-infused syrup. Bring to a boil over high heat; reduce heat and simmer, covered, for 10 minutes or until tender.

3. To preserve: Ladle peaches (not as much syrup) into sterilized canning jars. Top off with syrup to within 1/2-inch of the rims; wipe rims. Apply prepared new lids and rings; tighten just until fingertip-tight (snug but not too tight). If not preserving, cover and store in refrigerator.

4. Process jars in a boiling water canner for 15 minutes. Transfer jars to a towel-lined surface or tray. Let rest at room temperature until set. Check seals; refrigerate any unsealed jars up to 1 week.

   NOTE: You may adjust sugar to taste. Fruit canned with larger amounts of sugar keeps its texture better and for longer.

MAKES ABOUT 6 PINT (500 ML) JARS

6 cups	water
2-1/2 cups	granulated sugar
2 tbsp	dried culinary lavender florets (or 3 tbsp fresh)
16	large, ripe peaches

Refer to General Canning Information at the beginning of the chapter.

VARIATION

Lemon Verbena Peaches
Replace lavender with 1/2 cup loosely packed fresh lemon verbena leaves. Strain and discard leaves.

INDEX